King Arthur
The True Story

Praise for **King Arthur – The True Story**

'One of the most remarkable books of deductive history I have ever read' *Liverpool Daily Post*

'Vital new evidence relating to the Arthurian mystery' *Bath Evening Chronicle*

'Unfolds like a scholarly detective story' *Clwyd Evening Leader*

'Fascinating quest' *Wolverhampton Express & Star*

'A process of elimination of which Sherlock Holmes would have been proud' *Cardiff Western Mail*

'Convincingly argued' *Birmingham Post*

'A study which places legend firmly in history' *Burton Mail*

'A fascinating book' *Middlesbrough Evening Gazette*

'An extraordinarily absorbing and convincing study throwing a completely new historical light on the great Arthurian story' *County Warwickshire and Worcestershire*

'Sensational theory' *Sunday Mercury*

'The authors set out their claims clearly and convincingly' *The Brecon and Radnor Express*

KING ARTHUR
THE TRUE STORY

Graham Phillips and
Martin Keatman

ARROW

We would like to thank Mark Booth, Katrina Johnston, Dennis Barker, Andrea Henry, Tracey Jennings, Cathy Schofield, Gilly Smith, Roderick Brown, Jenny Johnson, Dan and Susanna Shadrake, Annette and Tim Burkitt, Andrew Lownie, Alison Patrick, Steven Griffin and Malcolm Ordever for all their invaluable help.

First published 1992

5 7 9 10 8 6 4 2

© Graham Phillips & Martin Keatman

Graham Phillips and Martin Keatman have asserted their rights under the Copyright, Designs and Patents Act, 1988 to be identified as the authors of this work

First published in the United Kingdom in 1992 by
Century Random House, 20 Vauxhall Bridge Road, London SW1V 2SA

Arrow Edition 1993

Random House Australia (Pty) Limited
20 Alfred Street, Milsons Point, Sydney
New South Wales 2061, Australia

Random House New Zealand Limited
18 Poland Road, Glenfield
Auckland 10, New Zealand

Random House South Africa (Pty) Limited
PO Box 337, Bergvlei, South Africa

Random House UK Limited Reg. No. 954009

A CIP catalogue record for this book is available from the British Library

ISBN 0 09 929681 0

Typeset by Deltatype Ltd, Ellesmere Port, Cheshire
Printed in Great Britain by
Cox & Wyman Ltd, Reading, Berkshire

#3506

Contents

List of Illustrations

Photographs

Maps and Tables

1
The Legend

Despite all the effort that has for centuries been expended in the search for King Arthur, he has continued to evade the pages of authentic history. Not only has there been a distinct lack of evidence to reveal who he really was; as yet, no one has been able to prove beyond doubt that he even existed at all. The clues exist, but in many different forms: in folklore, archaeology and recorded history. Solving the mystery of King Arthur is like trying to assemble a huge jigsaw puzzle. Many have tried to complete the picture, but very often the pieces were wrongly arranged, and until recently some were missing entirely.

We are about to embark upon an historical adventure – a search for the real King Arthur: his identity, his Camelot and his final resting place. By carefully disentangling the historical from the mythological, and piecing together the fascinating evidence that remains, we reveal for the first time a true story that is in every way as spellbinding as the romantic legend.

* * *

In a far-off time, when Britain was divided and without a king, barbarian hordes laid waste the once fertile countryside. The throne lay vacant for a just and righteous man, who could free the people from their servile yoke and drive the invaders from the land. But only he who drew from the stone a magnificent sword could prove himself the rightful heir. Years passed and many tried, but the mysterious sword stood firm and unyielding in the ancient, weathered rock. Then one day a young man emerged from the forest and, to the amazement of all, succeeded where even the strongest had failed. The people rejoiced; the king had come and his name was Arthur.

On accession to the highest office in the land, Arthur set about restoring the shattered country. After building the impregnable fortress of Camelot, and founding an order of valiant warriors, the Knights of the Round Table, the king rode forth to sweep aside the evil which had beset the land. The liberated peasants quickly took him to their hearts, and Arthur reigned justly over his newly prosperous kingdom, taking for his queen the beautiful Lady Guinevere.

Even a terrible plague which ravaged the country was overcome by the newfound resolve of Arthur's subjects, for they mounted a quest to discover the Holy Grail, a fabulous chalice that held the secret cure for all ills. But as happens so often during an age of plenty, there are those whom power corrupts. Soon a rebellion tore the kingdom apart, an armed uprising led by Modred, Arthur's traitorous nephew. Yet there was one, possessed by dark forces, who lay at the heart of the strife: the mysterious and satanic enchantress, Morganna. In a final battle, Modred was at last defeated and Morganna destroyed by Merlin the court magician. But all did not go well, for Arthur himself was mortally wounded.

As he lay dying on the field of battle, the last request by the mighty king was that Excalibur, the source of all his power, be cast into a sacred lake and lost forever to mortal man. When the magical sword fell to the water a sylphid arm rose from the surface, catching it by the hilt and taking it down into the crystal depths.

When the great king was close to death, he was spirited away on a barge to the mystical isle of Avalon, accompanied by three mysterious maidens, each dressed completely in white. Many say that he died and was buried upon the isle, yet there are those who believe that Arthur's soul is not to be found amongst the dead. It is said that he only sleeps and will one day return.

This, in essence, is the fabulous tale of King Arthur and the Knights of the Round Table as most people now know it. In one form or another it has been told the world over, translations being found in almost every language.

During the Gothic Revival of the last century, the haunting lines of Tennyson and the romantic paintings of the Pre-Raphaelites celebrated the Arthurian saga. Today we have the enchanting novels of Rosemary Sutcliffe, the plays of John Arden and the poems of John Heath-Stubbs. On stage we have seen the lavish musical 'Camelot', later filmed; on screen there has also been John Boorman's colourful epic, 'Excalibur', the marvellous animation of Walt Disney and even the zany humour of the Monty Python team. The world over, King Arthur is a bestseller.

But Arthur is more than simply an inspiration for book, stage and cinema. Travelling the length and breadth of the British Isles, we discover a wealth of Arthurian legend; in every part of the land the great king lives on in folklore. Tales tell how he was born here, or died there; that he fought a dragon in this valley, or killed a giant on that mountain. There are Arthur's Hills, Arthur's Stones and Arthur's Caves. King Arthur features in more legends attached to ancient sites in England and Wales than any other character.

King Arthur has come to personify the resolve of the nation; like Britannia or John Bull, he is the warrior spirit of Britain, ready to be awakened in time of need. His story contains every archetypal image: the innocent succeeding where the strong have failed, knights in shining armour and damsels in distress. But most compelling of all is the sense that something magical still awaits discovery; perhaps the Grail, the celestial answer to all our dreams.

King Arthur has always been many things to many people, but in recent years Arthurian myth-making has gone mad. Some of the more extreme notions are mind-boggling, from Arthur being an extra-terrestrial to his being the king of Atlantis. One recent theory, which actually gained a degree of acceptance, claimed that he was the first European to discover America. Obsessives have spent fortunes trying to track him down; indeed whole societies have been formed for this express purpose. Some even claim to have discovered his remains, while others have resorted to staging elaborate hoaxes as 'proof'. Since the 1960s, hippies have embarked on what the media dubbed 'The Grail Trail', descending in droves on the Somerset town of Glaston-bury, much to the annoyance of the locals. And in the 1980s, King Arthur was again sensationalised in the wake of the 'Dungeons and Dragons' craze.

There are guide books, lecture tours, coach trips, magazines and video tapes available for the enthusiast, even travel companies offering Arthurian Holidays. King Arthur is arguably the most popular character in British history and it is hardly surprising that the vast majority of the British population, and thousands of foreign tourists, are familiar with the stories about him. They may not believe all the fables, they may not accept all the legends, but many assume the tales to be based on truth. But is this a valid assumption? Are the stories founded on real historical events?

The story of King Arthur we know today was the work of Sir

Thomas Malory, printed in 1485 under the title *Le Morte Darthur* ('The Death of Arthur'). Malory did not invent the story, he simply collected together a wide variety of existing tales which were popular at the time and retold them. As one of the first books to be printed, Malory's established itself as the standard version. Yet from the Middle Ages, the era of jousting, chivalry and knights in armour in which the tales seem to be set, there are no records of such a king actually ruling, either in England or elsewhere in Christendom. Even if we go back to the Norman Conquest of 1066 we find no King Arthur. If we go back still further to the ninth century, when Athelstan became the first Saxon king of all England, again no such monarch exists. So who was Arthur? How did such an elusive and obscure character become so famous?

In addressing this question we must trace the development of the narrative itself, examining how the story evolved in the romantic literature of the Middle Ages. The earliest detailed account of Arthur's life was written around 1135 by the Welsh cleric Geoffrey of Monmouth, who later became Bishop of St Asaph. Geoffrey's work, the *Historia Regum Britanniae* ('History of the Kings of Britain') became the foundation upon which all the later stories of King Arthur were constructed. As its title suggests, his book was not intended to be read as fiction. On the contrary, it was presented as an accurate historical record of the British monarchy. But at a time when accurate historical records were almost non-existent, and history was not seen, as it is today, as a discipline dependent solely on the interpretation of proven facts, writers often felt free to embellish history as they saw fit. It is thus difficult to distinguish between fact and invention in the works of Geoffrey of Monmouth.

Written in Latin, Geoffrey's *Historia* traces the development of the isle of Britain, culminating in the golden age of King Arthur. According to Geoffrey, Arthur is born at Tintagel Castle in Cornwall, the son of the British king Uther Pendragon. Having become king while still in his teens, Arthur quickly asserts authority by defeating his barbarian enemies at the battle of Bath. Wielding a magical sword, Caliburn, said to have been forged on the mystical isle of Avalon, Arthur subsequently defeats the Scots in the North and unifies the nation. Having gone on to conquer Ireland and Iceland, Arthur reigns peacefully for twelve years, his queen Ganhumara at his side. He establishes an order of knights, accepting notorious warriors of all nations, before conceiving the ambitious notion of conquering Europe. When Norway, Denmark and Gaul (an area which once covered Northern Italy, France and Belgium, together with parts of Germany, the Netherlands and Switzerland) have fallen easily to his armies, Arthur returns home to a period of peace, holding court at the city of Caerleon in South-East Wales.

Eventually, Arthur is again drawn into war, setting off to fight in Burgundy. But all does not go well. He is soon forced to return to Britain to quell a revolt led by his nephew Modred, unwisely left to rule as regent in his absence. Although he succeeds in crushing the rebellion at the battle of Camlann, somewhere in Cornwall, Arthur is mortally wounded and taken to the isle of Avalon for his wounds to be tended. Geoffrey fails to tell us what then became of King Arthur.

Second only to Arthur in importance in Geoffrey's *Historia* is the magician Merlin, about whom he also wrote two poetic works. In the *Prophetiae Merlini* ('Prophecies of Merlin') and the *Vita Merlini* ('Life of Merlin') Geoffrey portrays Merlin as the guiding influence behind the throne.

Geoffrey's work quickly captured the popular imagination, and before long the adventures of King Arthur inspired writers from all over Europe. The first was the Jersey poet Wace, who in 1155 composed *Roman de Brut* (the 'Romance of Brutus'). Written in French, this poetic rendering of Geoffrey's account was the first of the Arthurian Romances and contains an important addition to the Arthurian story, namely the Round Table. Said to seat fifty of Arthur's knights, its purpose according to Wace was to promote a sense of equality amongst Arthur's noblemen.

Although Geoffrey of Monmouth popularised the Arthurian saga, and Wace then elaborated it in his poetry, it was the French writer Chrétien de Troyes who was chiefly responsible for establishing it as a fashionable subject of romantic literature. In his five Arthurian stories, written between 1160 and 1180, Chrétien imaginatively developed the narrative by introducing medieval notions of chivalry and courtly romance. Not only did Chrétien create many of the knights (including Sir Lancelot), he also used the more lyrical sounding Guinevere as the name for Arthur's queen, and introduced Camelot as the name for King Arthur's court.

In the coming decades King Arthur was all the rage, and in the late 1190s Robert de Boron, a Burgundian poet, composed a trilogy of Arthurian verses. Robert was responsible for interpolating perhaps the most popular theme into the story, the Holy Grail. The chalice used by Christ at the Last Supper, the Grail is said to possess miraculous healing properties, and is sought by Arthur's knights, who gain both worldly experience and spiritual insight during their epic quest.

With the addition of the Grail quest, the stories of King Arthur gained a Christian acceptability, and many clergymen began to write Arthurian stories of their own. The English priest Layamon, writing around 1200, was the first to relate the saga in native English. His work, *Brut*, was an adaptation of Wace's *Roman de Brut*. Paradoxically for a priest, Layamon elevates King Arthur into a messianic figure. In his version, Arthur survives as an immortal on the secret isle of Avalon, with the promise that he will one day return.

By the beginning of the thirteenth century, the remaining themes had been added to what became the accepted Arthurian story. Between 1215 and 1235, a large number of rambling Arthurian stories, known collectively as the *Vulgate Cycle*, were brought together. Anonymously composed, the *Vulgate Cycle* is responsible for many of the story's further embellishments, in particular the notion that Modred was the child of Arthur's incest with his sister Morgause.

Following the *Vulgate Cycle*, which marked the change in telling the story from verse to prose, successive writers added further themes, till the late fifteenth century produced the best known version of the Arthurian legend, *Le Morte Darthur*, by Sir Thomas Malory from Newbold Revel in Warwickshire. Completed in 1470, it was printed by William Caxton in 1485, and as such was one of the first published books with a wide circulation. It is in fact eight separate tales, which Malory originally entitled 'The Whole Book of King Arthur and his Noble Knights of the Round Table'. Although *Le Morte Darthur* was originally only the name of the last story, this shorter title for the entire work has survived to this day.

Le Morte Darthur opens with Arthur conceived as the illegitimate son of Uther Pendragon. After being brought up in secret, Arthur proves himself king by drawing the sword from the stone. He marries Guinevere, founds the Knights of the Round Table at Camelot (which Malory identifies as Winchester) and begets Modred in unknowing incest. Following a period of prosperity, Arthur's knights commence a quest to discover the Grail, during which time Lancelot has consummated an adulterous affair with Queen Guinevere. Ultimately, the couple are discovered and Arthur pursues Lancelot into France, leaving Modred behind as regent. At the end of the story, Arthur discovers an attempt by Modred to seize the throne and returns to quash the rebellion. In a final battle, Modred dies and Arthur receives a mortal wound, after which he is transported on a barge to the Vale of Avalon. Following the battle, Arthur's sword Excalibur is reluctantly cast to the Lady of the Lake by Sir Bedivere, while both Lancelot and Guinevere enter holy orders and live out their lives in peace.

This, then, is the evolution of the Arthurian story in literature. But is it merely a fictional tale, or does it have an historical basis? Although they may have used artistic licence in their Arthurian epics, the medieval Romancers (writers of medieval romantic literature) appear to accept the historical reality of King Arthur. Conversely, they seem uncertain when it comes to dating the events they describe. This is unfortunate, for if we are to unravel the truth, it is critical to discover when Arthur is supposed to have lived. At face value the tales appear to be set during the Middle Ages. The knights wear elaborate armour, fight with broadswords and observe the rules of chivalry. However, when medieval writers wrote their own versions of ancient stories, such as the legends of Greece or Rome, they invariably portrayed the characters in terms familiar to their readers, locating them in their own contemporary context.

If we are to identify the real Arthurian period we must start by returning to Geoffrey of Monmouth's account from the twelfth century. Unlike the later Romances, Geoffrey's version of events was presented as an accurate historical document, stating in its preface that it is translated from 'a certain very ancient book written in the British language', given to him by Archdeacon Walter of Oxford. Is Geoffrey reliable? Since no trace of this 'very ancient book' exists today, we are left with the content of Geoffrey's work to make its own case.

Although Geoffrey tells us that Arthur fought at the battle of Camlann in 542 A.D., he also presents a number of historical inconsistencies. We are told that Arthur fought a Gallic campaign during the reign of Leo I, who we know from other sources was emperor at Constantinople from 457 to 474. (In 364 the Roman Empire had split into two: the Western Empire, governed from Rome, and the Eastern Empire, ruled from Constantinople.) This suggests that Arthur was around a hundred years old at the time of the battle of Camlann. Such an inconsistency may have arisen as a result of confusion between two alternative systems of dating used at the time. The Victorius calendar, prepared for Pope Milarius by Victorius of Aquitaine around 465, began the first year at Christ's crucifixion, whereas the *Anno Domini* calendar, which Geoffrey used and which was devised by the Italian monk Dionysius Exiguus around 525, began its first year with Christ's birth. The latter system did not become popular till the late sixth century. If Geoffrey confused these two calendars, then Arthur may have died around 510, not 542, which would be only thirty-six years after the Gallic war.

Greater inconsistencies arise when we examine Arthur's contemporaries. Although history provides no record of Arthur's father, Uther Pendragon, Arthur's two uncles do seem to be based on historical characters; the problem is that they lived in different countries and at different times. Geoffrey tells us that Uther was the brother of Aurelius Ambrosius. This was most likely to have been Ambrosius Aurelianus, a genuine historical warlord who fought the Anglo-Saxons during the late fifth century, so Geoffrey's placing of Arthur during this period would seem consistent. However, this does not tally with what Geoffrey tells us about Uther's second brother, Constans. Geoffrey of Monmouth tells us that Constans was a monk and was the son of Constantine. According to Geoffrey, Constans was persuaded to leave his monastery and become king when Constantine died. Constans can be identified as the son of Emperor Constantine III, who was also a monk, and who was also persuaded to leave his monastery, to become joint emperor with his father. Unfortunately, this historical Constans lived over half a century *before* Ambrosius.

Even during Geoffrey's lifetime there was considerable speculation as to when King Arthur supposedly lived. Wace, for example, locates Arthur's death in the mid-seventh century, a hundred years later than Geoffrey. To find clues about the real Arthur, we are therefore left to search an historical epoch spanning a quarter of a millennium, possibly starting as early as 400 A.D., and ending perhaps as late as 650 A.D. By Malory's time Arthur was portrayed as a feudal king, but if he had lived in the fifth or sixth centuries he would have been a British warrior, more closely resembling what we know of a Viking chieftain than a monarch with a golden crown.

In battle, the British warrior would have been very different from the knights in shining armour that we now associate with the Knights of the Round Table. He would not have worn a steel helmet with a plume and visor, but a skull-cap made of iron plates, bronze strapping and panels to protect the nose and sides of the face. Body armour would have been little more than a short-sleeved mail shirt, while shields were made of thick wood covered with leather and reinforced with a metal rim. Swords would not have been long, heavy broadswords, but the Roman *spatha* type, about two and a half feet long with a stunted cross guard. Living conditions would have been far

-emoved from the splendour of the huge Gothic castles of the High Middle Ages. Even a chieftain would have lived in little more than a single roomed hall with wattle and daub walls and a thatched roof. And defences would not have been stone walls, battlements and draw-bridged moats, but timber stockades, earthen banks, and water filled ditches.

If Arthur really did live in the fifth or sixth century, the logical thing to do is to consult any reliable records from that period. But immediately, we hit a problem. The principal contemporary historical sources covering England and Wales at this time are the work of the sixth-century monk Gildas, the writings of a few visiting foreigners, and early monastic records. These are not primarily concerned with military affairs, but even so, with all the fame that Arthur was later to achieve, it is surprising that none of these sources, which would have been contemporary with his exploits, makes any reference to him. Was the story of Arthur, after all, nothing but a myth originating in the fertile imagination of Geoffrey of Monmouth despite his claim that his source was a 'very ancient book'?

Summary

The modern Arthurian story was popularised by Geoffrey of Monmouth in the twelfth century, when Arthur was believed to have been a British king who lived about six hundred years before. During the Middle Ages many tales of King Arthur were composed, which have been collectively termed the Arthurian Romances.

1. The oldest surviving Arthurian story, the *Historia Regum Britanniae* ('History of the Kings of Britain'), was written around 1135 by the Welsh cleric Geoffrey of Monmouth. According to Geoffrey, Arthur was born at Tintagel Castle in Cornwall, and after many great deeds was finally transported to the mysterious isle of Avalon after being wounded in the battle of Camlann, also in Cornwall.

2. During the second half of the twelfth century, the Arthurian story became a popular theme for romantic literature, with each successive writer adding to Geoffrey's original account. The first

was the Jersey poet, Wace, who in 1155 introduced the Round Table to the tale of King Arthur.

3. Around 1170, the French poet Chrétien de Troyes introduced the medieval notions of chivalry and courtly romance to the story. Not only is Chrétien responsible for creating many of the knights including Sir Lancelot, he is also the first writer to call King Arthur's court Camelot.

4. In the late 1190s the Burgundian poet, Robert de Boron, interpolated the most popular theme, the Holy Grail, the chalice used by Christ at the Last Supper.

5. About 1200, the English priest Layamon was the first to relate the saga in native English. His story elevates King Arthur into a messianic figure, for Arthur remains immortal on the secret isle of Avalon, with the promise that he will one day return.

6. By the early thirteenth century the Arthurian legend was firmly established, but it was not until 1470 that all these early stories were collected together by the English writer, Sir Thomas Malory. Malory's compilation, *Le Morte Darthur*, was the first telling of the legend to be printed, and therefore became the version of the King Arthur story so familiar today.

7. By Malory's time, the story of Arthur had been thoroughly medievalised. Arthur was a feudal king, living in a castle with knights in shining armour. In reality, if he had lived in the fifth or sixth century, he would have been a Celtic warrior with a different lifestyle.

2
The Setting

Although much of Geoffrey's Arthurian story cannot be supported by historical evidence, he did not invent King Arthur. Some ten years before the *Historia*, in 1125, William of Malmesbury, a monk from the abbey of Malmesbury in Wiltshire, wrote the *Gesta Regum Anglorum* ('Acts of the Kings of the English') in which Arthur is fleetingly mentioned. William tells us that Arthur aided Ambrosius Aurelianus in holding back the advancing Angles and led the British at the battle of Badon.

Additionally, in the British Library there are two manuscripts written in the early 1100s which also briefly include Arthur. In the *Annales Cambriae* ('Annals of Wales') it is stated that around 518 A.D. Arthur won the battle of Badon, and about 539 A.D. he was slain with Medraut at the battle of Camlann. The second work, the *Historia Brittonum* ('History of the Britons') includes a list of Arthur's battles, but tells us little more about him. Together with the information from William of Malmesbury (which we will analyse later), these two help us narrow down the Arthurian period to sometime between the late fifth and early sixth centuries. Unfortunately, since this was the Dark Ages, an era from which almost no written records survive, we are reliant on Geoffrey of Monmouth's account alone to provide us with any details of Arthur's life.

In the *Historia*, Geoffrey makes many historical claims known to be inaccurate from reliable contemporary sources. For instance, he begins by telling us that the British nation was founded by someone called Brutus, who established a colony of several thousand Trojans freed from slavery in Greece. He goes on to deny that Britain was ever conquered by the Romans, concluding with a description of how the Saxons eventually invaded England with the help of an army of Africans. Not only does Geoffrey fail to mention many of the great British leaders who did exist, but some of those he does name were kings of other countries entirely. Geoffrey is also given to more fanciful notions. For example, he explains how Britain was once inhabited by a race of giants and that Merlin was the son of a demon.

Still, as we have seen, Geoffrey does not appear to have invented King Arthur. It is obvious that Geoffrey drew upon the *Historia Brittonum*, (as we show later) – and likely that he used other, now unknown sources to construct a story which vaguely fitted the facts, echoing his approach when writing about better documented eras of British history. Perhaps the most intriguing question, however, is why did he devote so much attention to King Arthur at all. Moreover, why did so many others follow suit? Why should an obscure warrior of the Dark Ages rise to become such a popular figure of romance six centuries after his death?

The main reason seems to have been a political one; King Arthur became a crucial figure in a medieval propaganda exercise. The kings of England, of Norman blood following the battle of Hastings in 1066, desperately needed to prove their divine right to rule. At a time of poor communications, more than mere armies were required to maintain order; the monarchy needed the support of the Church; since, in the main, only churchmen were literate, they were essential to the administration of government. In addition, the Continental Capetian dynasty repeatedly laid claim to the English throne, further pressurising the Normans to legitimate their rule of England.

Many Saxon noblemen could rightfully claim descent from the pre-Conquest kings of England, such as Alfred the Great and King Edgar; to counter this, the Norman aristocrats required their own heroic, royal British ancestors. Having grounds to prove descent from Celtic warriors, who had fled to Normandy during the fifth and sixth centuries following Saxon invasions, it was to Celtic figures that the Normans looked in their search for appropriate forbears. Unfortunately, there was no evidence that any of these Celtic personages could really be titled 'king' in the medieval sense. The closest contender was the fabled warrior Arthur, and since the Arthurian saga met the needs of Norman dynastic pretensions, Geoffrey's *Historia* was well received, particularly by the king – of Norman descent – Henry I.

From the medieval historians cited above, we can assume an approximate dating for the Arthurian period – the fifth or sixth century. But what of location? Where was Arthur born? Where was his court? And where was he laid to rest? Whatever documentation may have been available to Geoffrey and others in their reconstructions of Arthur's life, little has survived for us to examine today. Much of the material relating to King Arthur exists only in the form of myth, legend and local folklore. So to investigate the locations that occur in Arthurian legends we turn to an examination of the places in Britain usually associated with King Arthur.

The Arthur of popular imagination was born at Tintagel Castle on the north coast of Cornwall. Anyone who visits the tiny village during the holiday season will find it teeming with sightseers of all nationalities. The ruins of the castle itself stand just outside Tintagel, on what is virtually an island surrounded by foaming sea, linked to the mainland by a narrow ridge of rock. The ridge crumbled long ago, so that any visitor to the ruins today must cross a footbridge and ascend a long flight of steps.

The earliest mention of Tintagel in association with King Arthur appears in Geoffrey of Monmouth's *Historia*, wherein Uther Pendragon has designs on Ygerna, the wife of Gorlois, Duke of Cornwall. Aided by a magic potion, prepared for him by Merlin the Magician, Uther is transformed for a time into the form of Gorlois, and as such he visits the duke's castle at Tintagel and makes love to the duchess. Thus Arthur is conceived. On the death of Gorlois, Uther makes Ygerna his queen and Arthur is born at Tintagel Castle.

Tintagel's tourist industry and its thousands of patrons seem unaffected by the simple historical fact that the present castle could not have been the birthplace of a warrior who lived centuries before the battle of Hastings (1066). It was only built in the early twelfth century for Reginald, Earl of Cornwall. The story was probably concocted by Geoffrey to please Reginald, who was the wealthy brother of his patron, Robert, Earl of Gloucester. Although in defence of Geoffrey it has been suggested that Arthur was born in a castle that previously occupied the site, modern excavations have shown that the promontory had previously been settled by an early monastic community, making it an unlikely place for the birth of anyone.

With a shadow of doubt cast across his traditional place of birth, we now investigate the legend of Arthur's magnificent castle, Camelot. Immediately, we find a problem: there is no evidence that a place with the name Camelot ever existed. Geoffrey makes no mention of it at all; neither does Wace. The earliest use of Camelot as the name for Arthur's court originates, as we have seen, with the twelfth-century poet Chrétien de Troyes. But it appears in only one of Chrétien's works, *Lancelot*, and is mentioned only once, and in passing.

During the thirteenth century, later Romancers began to make much more of Camelot, describing in graphic detail the splendid city and its impregnable castle. But although they differ considerably in their descriptions, they are united in their failure to specify its whereabouts. According to Malory however, it was sited at Winchester in Hampshire, and in the Great Hall of Winchester Castle the most famous of all Arthurian relics, 'The Round Table', still exists.

Eighteen feet in diameter, made of solid oak and weighing approximately one and a quarter tons, it is now a table top without legs, hanging on a wall. 'The Round Table' resembles an enormous dartboard, painted in green and white segments which are said to indicate the places where the king and his knights once sat. In Malory's day, many considered it to be the genuine article, and Winchester Castle was generally believed to be the site of Arthur's fortress. Unfortunately, as with Tintagel, the existing castle is not nearly old enough to be of the Arthurian period, having been built as late as the eleventh century by William the Conqueror.

But what of the table itself? Its painted design was added after Malory's time, during the reign of Henry VIII. The structure is much older, however. In 1976, scientific tests were conducted in an attempt to establish its true age. Examination of tree-ring patterns in the wood, analysis of its method of carpentry and radiocarbon dating were all employed. The results showed that the table was made during the reign of Edward III, probably in 1344 when the king conceived the notion of an order of chivalry based on the Knights of the Round Table as depicted in the popular Romances. (In 1348 he abandoned the idea, and instead founded the Order of the Garter.) There is no link with the real Arthur of the sixth century. However, the table does serve to demonstrate the considerable influence of the Arthurian legends during the Middle Ages.

Not only in England is there a town with pretensions to the title of Camelot. There are those who propose the small town of Caerleon, on the River Usk in South-East Wales. Geoffrey mentions Caerleon as the place where Arthur holds court for a time after his first campaign in Gaul. It is probably also the site of one of Arthur's battles, mentioned in the *Historia Brittonum* as the 'City of the Legion', this being the direct translation of the name Caerleon. In Roman times it was called Isca Silurum and was a military outpost with a large civilian population; indeed we know that as late as Geoffrey's time, impressive Roman ruins could still be seen, since Geoffrey makes reference to them in his writings. Modern excavations have uncovered a number of Roman remains, including an amphitheatre that was claimed by some to be the origin of the Round Table. However, although a case could be made for Caerleon having authentic Arthurian associations, it hardly fits the legends of Camelot. In Geoffrey's account, Arthur merely holds court there for a short time, while the *Historia Brittonum* mentions it simply as a battle site.

There are other candidates in England. Cadbury Castle, an Iron Age hill-fort in Somerset, was for many years proposed as the site of Camelot. The oldest such reference dates back to Henry VIII's chief antiquary, John Leland, in 1542. Although Leland says that local people believed that Cadbury had been the site of Camelot, he was unable to discover a specific Arthurian legend relating to the hill-fort. The tradition probably arose as a result of the word Camel being found in the names of two nearby villages: Queen Camel and West Camel. Although the hill-fort dates from well before the time when Arthur seems to have lived, there is no evidence to connect him with the place other than Leland's association of names. The word Camelot, almost certainly being the poetic invention of Chrétien de Troyes, does little to bolster the claim. Nonetheless, large scale excavations were conducted at Cadbury in the late 1960s, under the directorship of the archaeologist Leslie Alcock. Although they showed that the camp, like many other similar sites, had been re-used during the period in question, circa 500, no evidence was unearthed to associate it with the historical King Arthur.

If Camelot seems to be spurious, what can we make of modern associations with Avalon, Arthur's fabled resting place?

The first writer to mention Avalon was Geoffrey of Monmouth. In the *Historia*, he calls it *Insula Avallonis*, referring to it twice. He says that Arthur's sword, Caliburn, was forged on the island and that after his last battle he was carried there so that his wounds might be tended. In his poetic *Vita Merlini* he also calls the island *Insula Pomorum*, the Isle of Apples. According to Geoffrey, it lies somewhere over the western sea and is the home of Morgan (a kindly enchantress and not the witch of later stories) who heads a sisterhood of nine maidens. After the battle, Arthur is carried there and placed on a bed of gold, where Morgan offers to heal him in return for his promise to remain with her on the island.

The site that springs immediately to mind whenever Avalon is mentioned is the West Country market town of Glastonbury. Beside the main roads entering the district, signboards welcome the tourist to 'The Ancient Avalon'. The town's claim to be the mystical isle of Avalon, Arthur's final resting place, has long been the subject of controversy. Nestling amidst a small cluster of hills, Glastonbury was almost an island in early Christian times when much of the surrounding countryside was submerged. It is certainly an imposing location, for its highest hill, Glastonbury Tor, with a solitary stone tower at the summit, can be seen for miles around on the fertile Somerset plain.

How does Glastonbury come to be linked to this mystical isle? No evidence exists to suggest that anyone prior to 1190 associated Glastonbury with Avalon. On the contrary, early historians seem unaware of any such notion. William of Malmesbury, writing in the early twelfth century, compiled a history of Glastonbury. Not once does he link it with King Arthur, nor does he refer to Glastonbury in connection with Avalon. Even more damning is Caradoc of Llancarfan who, writing around 1140, scribed the earliest known text to mention the Arthurian story in association with Glastonbury. He does not regard it as Avalon, however, saying only that the Abbot of Glastonbury aided in the release of Guinevere from King Melwas of Somerset.

Glastonbury's link with King Arthur arose as a result of a discovery said to have been made in the late 1100s within the grounds of the abbey. The impressive ruins of Glastonbury Abbey that survive today date from the late twelfth century, replacing much older buildings destroyed by fire in 1184. In 1190, during reconstruction following the fire, the monks claimed to have discovered a grave containing the bones of a tall man, plus some smaller bones and a scrap of yellow hair. Along with these remains, a lead cross was said to have been found, bearing the following Latin inscription:

HIC IACET SEPULTUS INCLYTUS REX ARTHURIUS IN INSULA AVALLONIA CUM UXORE SUA SECUNDA WENNEVERIA.

'Here lies the renowned King Arthur in the isle of Avalon with his second wife Guinevere'.

Neither the bones nor the cross exist today, so unfortunately nothing can be proved one way or the other. But the discovery of the grave was, to say the least, timely. The abbey was in desperate need of funds for rebuilding, and the only sure way to raise money was to attract large numbers of pilgrims. Stories of King Arthur were so widely popular at the time that few other relics could be relied upon to bring in so many visitors. The inscription on the cross was also rather convenient, telling the world that not only was Arthur buried there, but that Glastonbury was also the island of Avalon.

The mention of Guinevere as Arthur's second wife was an additional stroke of luck, for at the time there were two separate and equally popular stories in circulation. One told that Arthur's queen was called Guinevere, the other that she was called Ganhumara. The reference to Guinevere being his second wife happened to satisfy everyone. A few years later, however, when it was generally accepted that Arthur only had one wife, it was claimed that the cross had simply said the following (in apparently slightly different Latin):

HIC IACET SEPULTUS INCLITUS REX ARTURIUS IN INSULA AVALONIA.

'Here lies the renowned King Arthur in the isle of Avalon'.

Conveniently, no mention at all of Guinevere.

In 1962, the archaeologist Dr Ralegh Radford excavated the site where the monks claimed to have dug, and did find indications of an ancient grave; perhaps, after all, the brothers had discovered some bones? Unfortunately without the cross to examine, there is no way to verify that it was the body of Arthur that had been exhumed. However, we do have the alleged inscription, which is itself controversial. It has been pointed out that the style of Latin betrays the cross as a twelfth-century fraud. According to the Oxford linguist, James Hudson, it differs from a sixth-century inscription about as much as modern English prose differs from a Shakesperean text.

Finally, it should be noted that Arthur's were not the only famous remains the monks purportedly discovered after the fire. Amongst others, they claimed to have disinterred St Patrick, St Gildas and, most incredibly of all, Archbishop Dunstan who had lain in peace at Canterbury for over two hundred years. These dubious relics were put on display at Glastonbury and attracted generous donations from those who came to worship at the abbey.

Today the affair of Arthur's bones is considered so suspect that few historians take it seriously. In all likelihood, the monks discovered an unmarked grave and subsequently some had the idea to claim it as Arthur's. An inscribed cross was fashioned as 'proof' and the announcement made to an eager public. Whatever actually occurred, we can be sure of one thing; pilgrims came flocking and the abbey was considerably enriched.

Much has also been made of Glastonbury's association with the

Holy Grail, but this too seems to have arisen following the 'discovery' by the monks. The Bible relates how Joseph of Arimathea laid the body of Christ in the tomb after the Crucifixion. According to the poem *Joseph d'Arimathie*, written by Robert de Boron in the late 1190s, the Grail was the vessel used at the Last Supper, which Joseph obtained from Pilate and used to collect the blood of the crucified Christ. In the poem, Joseph eventually embarks on a series of adventures, leading ultimately to the Grail being brought to Britain, to the Vale of Avalon.

Although Robert makes no reference to Glastonbury, the abbey's monks soon suggested that this was where the Grail was hidden. In 1247, the abbey produced a revised edition of the history of Glastonbury, compiled by William of Malmesbury a century before. Although in William's original treatise *De Antiquitate Glastoniensis Ecclesiae* ('On the Antiquities of the Church of Glastonbury'), written in 1130, he mentions nothing of Joseph of Arimathea, in the revised edition written at Glastonbury in 1247, the church at Glastonbury is said to have been founded by Joseph himself; unquestionably a fraud devised to reap benefit from Robert de Boron's popular poem. William of Malmesbury's original version said only that the church was thought to have been founded by disciples of Christ. He does not provide any evidence for the story, nor does he offer any names.

So the famous sites traditionally associated with Arthur do not withstand historical scrutiny. There is no contemporary document to prove Arthur's existence, and archaeologists have found nothing bearing his name. Considering that the medieval stories were simply romantic fiction, based to a large degree upon the less than reliable Geoffrey of Monmouth, what reason is there to look further? Is Arthur, after all, just a myth?

Even if Arthur is simply a mythical character, the legend is very old, which is in itself significant. From William of Malmesbury, the *Annales Cambriae* and the *Historia Brittonum*, three works definitely written before Geoffrey of Monmouth, which all mention Arthur, we know that the legend was well established by the early twelfth century. To discover how these legends arose, we must now examine any other early literary references to Arthur, to see if they predate Geoffrey of Monmouth.

Summary

Although Geoffrey of Monmouth's account of Arthur's life cannot be accepted as an historical work, he certainly did not invent King Arthur and some of his claims may well be based on truth. Yet when we try to locate Arthur, we find the stories at sites associated with him discredited as, at best, medieval legends and, at worst, deliberate fabrications.

1. In the *Historia Regum Britanniae*, Geoffrey makes many historical claims known to be inaccurate from reliable contemporary sources. For example, he denies that Britain was ever conquered by the Romans, and relates how the Saxons eventually invaded England with the help of an army of Africans. He should not therefore be taken too seriously as an historian.

2. Although there is little collaborative evidence to support the detail of Geoffrey's Arthurian story, the legend itself was already in existence. Some ten years before Geoffrey, William of Malmesbury makes a brief mention of Arthur. Furthermore, in the British Library, there are two manuscripts written, in their present form, around 1100, which name Arthur's battles: the *Annales Cambriae* and the *Historia Brittonum*.

3. The principal reason for the popularity of Geoffrey's Arthurian story was that it formed the basis of a medieval propaganda exercise for the English king, Henry I. The kings of England, of Norman blood following the battle of Hastings in 1066, needed to prove descent from a heroic pre-Saxon British king. The most appropriate contender was the fabled King Arthur.

4. If Arthur lived six centuries before Geoffrey, then the Arthurian tourist attractions do not withstand historical scrutiny. Tintagel Castle, Arthur's legendary birthplace, was not built until the twelfth century, and Winchester's 'Round Table' has been scientifically dated to the reign of Edward III, about 1344.

5. The discovery of 'Arthur's Grave' at Glastonbury Abbey in 1190 is considered by most historians to have been a medieval hoax to attract pilgrims. No evidence exists to suggest that anyone prior to 1190 associated Glastonbury with Avalon. On the contrary, early writers seem completely unaware of any such notion. There is also evidence of fraud on the part of the abbey concerning the Glastonbury Grail legend. A revised edition of William of Malmesbury's *De Antiquitate Glastoniensis Ecclesiae*, written in 1247 by monks from Glastonbury, includes mention of Joseph of Arimathea that was not in William's original version of 1130.

3

Arthur Before the Romances

Over the years, much has been made of King Arthur's inclusion in early Welsh literature, many writers having employed it in support of various Arthurian theories. Unfortunately, any examination of Welsh literature in the search for historical accuracy encounters a serious drawback: none of the surviving copies of those works mentioning King Arthur dates from a time before the Arthurian Romances had become firmly established. Nonetheless, can this Celtic poetry and prose provide us with insight into the status of the Arthurian legend as it existed when Geoffrey and his immediate successors composed their works?

The oldest surviving manuscript containing a Welsh poem that mentions Arthur is *Llyfr Du Caerfyrddin*, the 'Black Book of Carmarthen' (now in the National Library of Wales in Aberystwyth). Like a number of medieval Welsh manuscripts, this work takes its name from the colour of its binding. It was compiled around the mid-thirteenth century, probably by one scribe, and it consists almost entirely of poetry seemingly copied from earlier documents or oral accounts. Although Arthur is included briefly in a few of the poems within the manuscript (for instance, *Englynion y Beddau*, the 'Stanzas of the Graves', which remarks how Arthur's burial place remains a mystery), he is only spoken of in detail in one, the *Pawr yw'r Porthor*, commonly referred to as the 'Dialogue of Arthur and Glewlwyd Gafaelfawr'. In this poem, Glewlwyd Gafaelfawr is the guardian of a fortress to which Arthur attempts to gain entry, being made to prove his worth before being allowed inside. Unfortunately the tale supplies us with nothing concerning the historicity of Arthur, for the details concern only encounters with demons, monsters and mythical beasts. The only Arthurian inclusion within the 'Black Book of Carmarthen' with any historical pretensions concerns Arthur's presence at the battle of Llongborth (in *Englynion Geraint,* the 'Stanzas of Geraint') although, regrettably, the location can no longer be identified.

Slightly later than the 'Black Book of Carmarthen' is *Llyfr Taliesin*, the 'Book of Taliesin' (also in the National Library of Wales), a manuscript dating from around 1300 containing poems both attributed to and about a sixth-century poet of that name. Although it can be argued that Taliesin actually existed, the surviving manuscript is many times removed from the bard himself. Arthur is mentioned in several poems within the 'Book of Taliesin', but once again only in passing allusions, with the exception of one work, *Preiddiau Annwfn*, the 'Spoils of Annwn', a poem on the theme of a raid by Arthur and his men into the magical land of Annwn to steal its treasures, a fabulous cauldron and a magical sword.

We turn next to perhaps the most notorious of all the Welsh manuscripts to include Arthur, *Llyfr Čoch Hergest*, the 'Red Book of Hergest', compiled around 1400 and now in the Bodleian Library, Oxford. In this manuscript, two tales are of particular interest, *Breuddwyd Rhonabwy*, the 'Dream of Rhonabwy', and *Cyfranc Culhwch a Olwen*, the 'Tale of Culhwch and Olwen'. The former, the story of a warrior called Rhonabwy who is employed by the king of Powys to seek out his renegade brother, actually includes an historical event, the battle of Badon. During his journey, Rhonabwy experiences a vision of King Arthur's camp on the eve of a battle. Interestingly, the Arthurian Britain portrayed in Rhonabwy's dream is highly symbolic, and needs to be examined in detail at a later stage. 'Culhwch and Olwen', on the other hand, clearly has an ancient ambience. It was certainly in existence in 1325, for it survives in fragmented form in *Llyfr Gwyn Rhydderch*, the 'White Book of Rhydderch' compiled around that time (now bound in two volumes in the National Library of Wales). Moreover, linguistic analysis has produced evidence for 'Culhwch and Olwen' having originally been composed as early as the tenth century.

In the tale, the hero Culhwch bids for the hand in marriage of Olwen, the daughter of the giant Ysbaddaden. The giant, intent on preventing their marriage, imposes a series of impossible tasks on Culhwch, which he must complete if he is to win his bride. On the advice of his father, the hero travels to the court of Arthur and acquires his assistance. For much of the story it is Arthur himself who leads the quest on Culhwch's behalf: he rescues the god-king Mabon, hunts down a giant boar and attacks Ireland, carrying off a magical cauldron.

Essentially, this completes the outline of King Arthur in early Welsh prose and poetry. Although there are other Welsh tales that include him, they only exist in the form of later transcriptions, which are much too recent to be useful in drawing conclusions regarding the state of the Welsh Arthurian legend during the time of the medieval Romancers. There is, however, an additional area of Welsh literature which must be considered in relation to King Arthur: the Triads.

Taking their name from their groupings of themes or characters into threes, the Triads served as a mnemonic device summarising Welsh folklore. They were anonymously committed to writing during the Middle Ages by a group of Welsh writers, probably in the hope of preserving some of the Welsh oral tradition that was rapidly being lost. Not really poems in the true sense, they are basically outlines of what were obviously more detailed sagas. Sometimes they consist of only a handful of lines. King Arthur is referred to in a series called *Trioedd Ynys Prydain*, the 'Triads of Britain', which also include a number of known historical characters from the Dark Ages. (Although dispersed through many Welsh manuscripts, the 'Triads of Britain' were not brought together in one printed text until 1567, when they appeared in *Y Diarebion Camberäec*, which was the second edition of *Oll Synnwyr Pen Kembero Ygyd* ['All the Senses in a Welshman's Head'] by William Salesbury.)

The 'Triads of Britain' are intriguing in that Arthur is not always depicted as the epitome of majestic virtue, in fact far from it. One story in the Triads, the 'Three Wicked Uncoverings', has Arthur blamed for the ultimate defeat of the Britons, being guilty of removing the head of the god Bran that had been buried on London's Tower Hill as a talisman against foreign invasion. Worse still, in the 'Three Red Ravagers', Arthur is depicted as a curse upon the land itself; wherever he walks no grass will grow for seven years. Nor is he successful in his exploits. In the 'Three Powerful Swineherds' Arthur even fails dismally in an attempt to raid a herd of pigs belonging to a rival king. To add further confusion, his rank and position is often ambiguous; in the 'Three Frivolous Bards', for example, Arthur is included as one of the three bards. However, the traditional King Arthur is also found in the Triads. The battle of Camlann, for example, is mentioned in the 'Three Futile Battles', as a conflict between Arthur and Modred. Additionally, the tale of 'Culhwch and Olwen' is echoed in the 'Three Unrestrained Ravagings', where Arthur's court is sited at Kelliwic in Cornwall.

An examination of Arthur in Welsh literature would be incomplete without consideration of the *Mabinogion*. The *Mabinogion* is often believed to be an ancient Celtic manuscript, and as such, would be very important in the search for an historical King Arthur. In reality, it was the title used by the Lincolnshire diarist, Lady Charlotte Guest, for her

English translations of twelve medieval Welsh tales, published in three volumes between 1838 and 1843, later published in one volume in 1877 and subsequently re-published many times. The *Mabinogion* is made up of eleven tales from the 'Red Book of Hergest', together with a story of the bard Taliesin (apparently from another source). It includes tales such as 'Culhwch and Olwen', *Peredur* (see Chapter Four) and the 'Dream of Rhonabwy', which are indeed of Arthurian interest, but they are only translations of tales that can be examined at source. We discuss the *Mabinogion* to rectify the popular misconception that it is an original Arthurian manuscript.

The word Mabinogion comes from the *Pedair Cainc y Mabinogi*, the 'Four Branches of the Mabinogi', the name previously given to just four of the tales (*Pwyll, Branwen, Manawydan* and *Math*). The Welsh term *mabinogi* originally meant 'youth', but later came to mean 'a tale of youth' and finally 'a tale'. The *Mabinogion* is important in that it affords a wider readership to early Welsh literature, but from the Arthurian standpoint a study of the *Mabinogion* should be considered an investigation of tales within the 'Red Book of Hergest'.

Although there is a tendency for modern English and American writers to use the collective term 'Mabinogion' for the eleven tales from the 'Red Book of Hergest', they are not attributable to one author or era. The 'Red Book of Hergest' contains examples of every kind of Welsh literature (tales, Triads, poems and proverbs) that existed at the time it was compiled, between 1382 and 1410. Despite the fact that some pieces are written in other hands, it is mainly the work of one scholar who was simply copying various documents that appear to have survived from an earlier period.

What conclusions can reasonably be drawn from this early Welsh literature? Was Arthur interpolated into Welsh folklore after he had already become a theme of popular romance? Or was it from such tales that Geoffrey and the Romancers drew material to elaborate their own stories?

Trying to draw conclusions from the 'Triads of Britain' presents us with problems. Unlike the other poems, they do not offer linguistic grounds on which to date the original stories that the writers were attempting to outline. Much of the lore they contain may well date back to Roman or indeed pre-Roman times, but all that can be said with certainty is that the Triads reflect the state of Welsh Arthurian tradition by the thirteenth and fourteenth centuries, well after the Arthurian Romances had become firmly established.

In the Triads, Arthur's character is strange indeed, as he is often portrayed as incompetent. This could hardly be seen as an attempt to cash in on the themes of the Arthurian Romances and, as such, could constitute evidence of the survival of a separate Arthurian tradition. However, if pre-existing Welsh legends of Arthur had impugned his character by the twelfth century, it seems unlikely that he would have then become the central theme of medieval romance in England and elsewhere. It is more probable that England had come to claim King Arthur as its own, and so the Welsh may subsequently have considered it expedient to debunk his supposed exploits.

As regards the 'Dream of Rhonabwy', there is good reason to doubt that it was written earlier than Geoffrey, although it may have been composed before the the Romances, for the setting of the story can be dated with certainty. The king of Powys, who commissions the warrior Rhonabwy to seek out his brother, is named as Madog ap Maredudd, a known historical character who died around 1159. Based on this evidence, the 'Dream of Rhonabwy' was almost certainly composed later than Geoffrey's *Historia*. However, the tale's dream sequence is highly allegorical and may be based on an earlier war poem.

As 'Culhwch and Olwen' was probably composed as early as the tenth century, over a hundred years before Geoffrey's *Historia* was written, it may be the oldest surviving Arthurian tale. However, there are clearly parallels between the tale of 'Culhwch and Olwen' and others we have mentioned. The attack on Ireland to seize the cauldron is reminiscent of the raid in the 'Spoils of Annwn', and Arthur's ship is called Prydwen in both tales. Additionally, there is the name of Glewlwyd Gafaelfawr, the castle guardian from the poem in the 'Black Book of Carmarthen'. In 'Culhwch and Olwen', Glewlwyd Gafaelfawr is the porter to Arthur's own castle, and has been instructed to let no one pass unless he can satisfy certain conditions; conditions similar to those imposed on Arthur in the 'Dialogue of Arthur and Glewlwyd Gafaelfawr'.

It certainly seems odd that the hero of the story, Culhwch, suddenly disappears from a substantial section of the poem, while Arthur continues with the giant's series of tasks on his behalf. Surely we should expect Culhwch as the hero of the tale, to cross into Ireland to search for the cauldron himself. Might the 'Spoils of Annwn' have been interpolated into the tale of 'Culhwch and Olwen' at some point during its development? If so, it may be that the germ of the earliest Welsh Arthurian legend survives within the existing version of the 'Spoils of Annwn'.

In the extant 'Spoils of Annwn', we read of Arthur's theft of the cauldron and sword from the land of Annwn. It could have been from this poem that Geoffrey derived Avalon and the magical sword Caliburn, and Robert de Boron took his idea for the Holy Grail; both writers making attempts to medievalise ancient, mythological concepts. The similarities with the Grail and Excalibur legends cannot be ignored, particularly when Annwn is depicted as a land which lies across the water; a mystical land full of wonders and marvels that must surely bear some relationship to Geoffrey's isle of Avalon. In fact, the link between Annwn and Avalon is further substantiated when we see that within the poem the land is also called the 'fort of glass', a name associated with Glastonbury in the late twelfth century.

Five years after 'Arthur's remains' were unearthed by the monks at Glastonbury Abbey in 1190, a work entitled *De Principis Instructione* was written by the scholar Giraldus Cambrensis. In the text, Giraldus explains that the word Glastonbury meant 'fort of glass'. Although this assertion is unfounded (the name for the town more likely being derived from Glasteing, the personal name of the settlement's founder), it does suggest that the 'Spoils of Annwn' existed around a century before the surviving 'Book of Taliesin' was compiled around 1300, for it seems that Giraldus was using it in an attempt to bolster the town's claim to being the isle of Avalon. As such, Giraldus' assertion that Glastonbury was the 'fort of glass' demonstrates an acceptance by this time that Avalon and Annwn were one and the same.

Geoffrey's Avalon is so similar to the mystic land of Annwn that there must be some connection between them. For instance, in Geoffrey's work the enchantress Morgan is the head of a sisterhood of nine women who act as guardians of this isle; in the 'Spoils of Annwn' Annwn is the home of nine maidens who are custodians of the magical cauldron. In the 'Spoils' Arthur's ship is called Prydwen, while Geoffrey uses Prydwen as the name of Arthur's shield. Were Geoffrey and the subsequent Romancers trying to medievalise an ancient Celtic tale? Or was the Welsh writer of the 'Spoils of Annwn' attempting to Celtify a purely medieval story? In considering which came first, we must discover if any of these themes were ancient Welsh or Celtic traditions.

The idea of nine saintly women living in seclusion could certainly have been of Celtic origin. The first-century classical geographer Pomponius Mela, for instance, writes of nine priestesses living under a vow of chastity on an island off the coast of Brittany. These women were of a Celtic tribe similar to the Britons themselves, and were said to have the power to heal the sick and foretell the future. This is the only example currently known to historians but it could well represent a Celtic tradition that Geoffrey may have drawn upon in his construction of the Arthurian story. As regards the Grail (which, of course, is not mentioned by Geoffrey of Monmouth) there are many examples of magical cauldrons in Celtic literature, such as the Cauldron of Dagda (Dagda being chief of the Tuatha de Dannan) in Irish folklore, indicating that the cauldron of the 'Spoils' could tally with ancient Welsh mythology. In fact, in the tale of 'Culhwch and Olwen' it is to Ireland that Arthur went in pursuit of the cauldron. Moreover, the cauldron is said to belong to Di-wrnach, very possibly a Welsh rendering of the Irish Dagda.

It seems, therefore, that Geoffrey and the other Romancers may have used early Welsh tales, such as 'Culhwch and Olwen' and the 'Spoils of Annwn', as the source material for some of their Arthurian themes. But is there any supportive evidence that a tradition of Arthurian storytelling existed in Celtic Britain before the time of Geoffrey of Monmouth?

A number of writers have cited the so-called 'Saints' Lives' from the monastery of Llancarfan in Glamorgan. Compiled by various monks from the monastery, five of these medieval biographies of Welsh Dark Age saints include Arthur. In the 'Life of St Cadoc', Arthur assists the saint's mother in eloping, whereas in the 'Life of St Carannog', the saint helps Arthur defeat a giant serpent. We are told that St Illtud was Arthur's cousin and one-time fellow warrior, while St Padarn was Arthur's enemy who caused the earth to swallow him up. Finally, there is Caradoc's 'Life of Gildas', mentioned previously, which includes the saint obtaining Guinevere's release from King Melwas of Somerset.

Although nothing of historical value concerning Arthur can be gained from these works (for various reasons, such as the fact that the saints lived at different times spanning three centuries, and the clearly mythical nature of the events described), they have often been used as evidence for an early Celtic Arthurian tradition. Unfortunately, only one may predate Geoffrey, the 'Life of St Cadoc'. Although the surviving manuscript is a much later copy, the original work has been attributed to Lifris, who is recorded as teaching at the monastery in the late eleventh century. If this attribution is correct, then the mention of Arthur in the 'Life of St Cadoc' would predate Geoffrey's *Historia* by at least thirty-five years.

Aside from the *Historia Brittonum*, the *Annales Cambriae*, William of Malmesbury, and Cadoc's biography, there are three other brief references to King Arthur that may date from earlier than 1135. (In Chapters Thirteen and Seventeen we also examine two references to King Arthur in early British poetry, which may also predate the twelfth century: the *Gododdin* and the *Canu Llywarch Hen*.)

In 1113, a group of Church officials from the French city of Laon journeyed through England raising funds for the rebuilding of their cathedral. A few years later Hermann of Tournai wrote of the visit, describing the journey between Exeter and Bodmin. Somewhere along the route, he tells us, the local people informed the travellers that they were entering the land of Arthur. They drew attention to two landmarks, Arthur's Chair and Arthur's Ovens. Although we are not told what these were, they were more than likely rock formations. Hermann also mentions a Cornish legend that Arthur was still believed to be alive. The controversy surrounding this brief comment concerns the number of years after the event the description was written, the general consensus of expert opinion locating it between 1130 and 1140.

A manuscript preserved at Avranches in France, containing what remains of the chronicle of the monastery of Mont Saint Michel in Brittany, includes King Arthur in a brief entry. It relates that Arthur became king of Britain in 421 A.D. The chronicle is often historically inaccurate, so the date should not be afforded too much attention, but we must establish when the document itself was compiled. Was it before or after Geoffrey? Since expert analysis has revealed that the Arthur entry was written along with the records for the years around 1100, it would seem to predate Geoffrey. However, it has not as yet been possible to prove beyond doubt that these early twelfth-century records were actually written at the time they describe. They may not have been added until the late twelfth century, and therefore after Geoffrey.

On the north portal of Modena Cathedral in northern Italy, there is an archway called the Modena Archivolt, carved with figures that appear to be from an Arthurian scene. The scene depicts a woman held prisoner in a castle, with three mounted knights attempting her rescue. Beside one of the figures is the contemporary inscription *Artus de Bretania*, 'Arthur of Britain'. The cathedral was begun in 1099, although the Archivolt is generally dated by art experts as somewhere between 1120 and 1140. Even if we accept the later date, the Modena Archivolt is evidence that the Arthurian story had spread as far as northern Italy within a year or so of Geoffrey's *Historia*; the soundest indication thus far that the Arthurian legend was widely known at the time when Geoffrey of Monmouth was recording it.

These isolated references are tantalising, but the extent to which tales of King Arthur had been further disseminated throughout Europe by the time that Geoffrey was writing, and the precise nature of any Celtic Arthurian poems that then existed, are both now difficult to determine. All we really know about the Arthurian legend of the early twelfth century comes from William of Malmesbury, writing a few years before Geoffrey's works appeared, who says 'this is the Arthur of which the Britons speak such nonsense even today'.

From what we have been able to glean from an examination of the earliest Welsh literature – the 'Spoils of Annwn', the 'Tale of Culhwch and Olwen', and so on – William's 'nonsense' may have depicted a somewhat different Arthur to the King Arthur portrayed in the High Romances; a salt-of-the-earth warrior chieftain entangled in a mesh of Celtic mythology or a warlord engrossed in the pursuit of demigods, demons and mythical beings. Nonetheless, it is probably from such Celtic mythology that the substance of what became the Arthurian Romances was taken – as with Annwn, the cauldron and the nine maidens. With this in mind, we must therefore analyse the subject matter of the medieval Romances, in order to ascertain if any elements they contain could be of early Celtic origin, starting with the key characters in the drama.

Summary

We have attempted to trace any Arthurian allusions that predate Geoffrey of Monmouth's work. Apart from William of Malmesbury, the *Annales Cambriae* and the *Historia Brittonum*, none can be dated with certainty before 1135. However, there is other circumstantial evidence giving insight into the Arthurian legend that existed when Geoffrey wrote the *Historia*.

1. Over the years, researchers have made much of King Arthur in early Welsh literature. Unfortunately, none of the surviving copies of these works including King Arthur date from the time before the Arthurian Romances had become firmly established. However, there are indications that Geoffrey and the other medieval Arthurian writers may have based their stories on early Welsh legends.

2. In the 'Spoils of Annwn' (surviving copy, circa 1275), the

theme of the poem is a raid by Arthur and his men into the magical land of Annwn to steal its treasures, a fabulous cauldron and a magical sword. The similarities to the Grail and Excalibur legends cannot be ignored, particularly when Annwn is depicted as a land which lies across the water; a mystical land full of wonders and marvels that seems to bear some relationship to Geoffrey's isle of Avalon.

3. In the tale of 'Culhwch and Olwen' (surviving copy, circa 1325), the hero travels to the court of Arthur and acquires his assistance. For much of the poem it is Arthur himself who leads the quest on Culhwch's behalf, and attacks Ireland to carry off a magical cauldron. Again there are clear parallels with the isle of Avalon.

4. Five of the 'Saint's Lives', from the monastery of Llancarfan in Glamorgan, include King Arthur. Although nothing of historical value concerning Arthur can be gleaned from these works, one of them *could* predate Geoffrey; the 'Life of St Cadoc', which may have been written in the late eleventh century.

5. In 1113, a group of Church officials from the French city of Laon journeyed through England raising funds for the rebuilding of their cathedral. Some years later Hermann of Tournai wrote of the visit, mentioning Arthurian folklore in Cornwall. However, this account was not written until somewhere between 1130 and 1140.

6. A manuscript preserved at Avranches in France, containing what remains of the Chronicle of the monastery of Mont Saint Michel in Brittany, includes King Arthur in a brief entry. There is some evidence that this may have been added about 1100, although expert opinion is divided; some prefer a much later date, around 1200.

7. On the north portal of Modena Cathedral in northern Italy, an archway is carved with figures that appear to be from an Arthurian scene. Beside one of the figures is the contemporary inscription *Artus de Bretania*, 'Arthur of Britain'. The carving is dated by art experts as somewhere between 1120 and 1140. There is therefore a strong possibility that it predates Geoffrey of Monmouth.

8. Because of the widespread allusions to Arthur at, or just prior

to, the time of Geoffrey's writing, it seems certain that Arthurian legends were widely disseminated by his time. Geoffrey's role would therefore seem to have been to popularise them and locate them in an historical context.

4

The Arthurian Entourage

Before continuing our search for King Arthur himself, it is important to examine other members of his legendary court. Is there evidence that any of them existed as historical figures? We begin with Arthur's immediate family: his sister Morgan and his wife Guinevere.

Morgan le Fay, or Morganna as she was later called, first appears in Geoffrey's *Vita Merlini* as the leader of an order of nine holy women from the isle of Avalon. It is she who tends Arthur's wounds after the battle of Camlann and, according to Geoffrey, falls in love with Arthur and exacts his promise to stay. At this point in the evolution of the Arthurian legend, she is not his sister. As the story developed, Morgan remained a mystic and healer, but she came to assume the role of Arthur's sister only after Chrétien de Troyes first portrayed her as such. It may seem strange to those familiar with the modern Arthurian story that in the early Romances, Morgan was a kindly enchantress and not the malevolent witch she later became. It is primarily due to the *Vulgate Cycle*, compiled around a century after Geoffrey, that Morgan is transformed into the evil sorceress whose magic destroys the kingdom. Although she is still depicted as carrying off Arthur to Avalon, she despises Guinevere, seduces Lancelot, and constantly plots against both of them.

The principal reason for Morgan's fall from grace is that the *Vulgate Cycle* was something of a religious propaganda exercise. Indeed, the religious allegories in the *Vulgate* tales are so powerful that some scholars have suggested they were written under the direction of the Cistercian monks, a notably zealous order. The concept of a female prophet would have been close to blasphemy in the eyes of these monks, at a time when a great many churchmen were seriously debating the existence of the female soul.

There may have been even greater reason to denigrate her character. As we have seen, Geoffrey of Monmouth appears to have taken a variety of mythical characters and woven them into Arthur's life. This certainly seems to be the case with Morgan, for not only her name but also her prophetic and healing powers identify her with the Celtic deity Morrigan, the Earth Mother and goddess of health and healing.

Guinevere also appears to have been based on a Celtic goddess. In a number of Welsh poems of the Middle Ages (for example the *Y Tair Rhamant*, 'The Three Romances', from the 'White Book of Rhydderch') she appears under the name Gwenhwyfar, meaning 'White Spirit'. This suggests that she may have been derived from the Celtic goddess Epona, depicted as a white horse or white lady and worshipped widely throughout northern Europe in pre-Christian times. However, it is unlikely that Geoffrey himself created Arthur's queen from an ancient goddess. After all, the name Guinevere was Wace's addition (popularised by Chrétien); Geoffrey's queen was Ganhumara. According to Geoffrey, Ganhumara came from a noble Roman family. Unfortunately Geoffrey fails to provide specific details, and there is no historical record of a Ganhumara during the fifth or sixth centuries.

As regard Arthur's warriors, the three most famous Knights of the Round Table – Galahad, Lancelot and Perceval – all appear to be medieval literary inventions. Galahad was only introduced in the *Quest del Saint Graal* of the *Vulgate Cycle*, where he is the son of Lancelot who eventually succeeds in the Grail quest when all others have failed; a theme that was adopted by Malory in *Le Morte Darthur*. Perceval, although introduced into the Romances earlier than Galahad, also appears to have been born of artistic licence. He first makes an appearance in the *Conte del Graal*, by Chrétien de Troyes, as a simple country boy who eventually becomes the most successful of Arthur's knights. Thereafter, he remained a central character for nearly all the subsequent Romancers, who often cast him as the knight who discovers the Grail.

It is possible, however, that Chrétien based Perceval and his Grail quest on an old Celtic hero Peredur, although the argument for this rests solely with a medieval Welsh tale. Entitled *Peredur* (and preserved in the 'Red Book of Hergest'), it is virtually an exact rendering of Chrétien's story of Perceval, although the action is set in Wales and Celtic themes are included. For example, in Chrétien's poem Perceval witnesses a procession in which he sees the Grail; in *Peredur* the hero witnesses an identical procession, although the Grail is replaced by a head on a silver platter, a symbolic theme that often appears in Celtic art. Which came first? Did Chrétien plagiarise a Celtic folk-tale; or is *Peredur* an attempt to build a Welsh story from a romantic French poem? Unfortunately, the most probable conclusion is that the *Conte del Graal* came first, as the surviving copy of *Peredur* is two centuries later than Chrétien's work.

Chrétien also introduced Lancelot, whose love affair with Guinevere became pivotal in many of the later Romances. In Chrétien's original version, *Le Chevalier de la Charrete*, Lancelot simply makes love to the queen after an epic quest to rescue her. However, the *Vulgate Cycle* (and later Malory) elevates this brief affair into the cause of the rebellion which ultimately destroys the kingdom. Chrétien provides no background for his hero, besides referring to him as *Lancelot del lac* ('Lancelot of the lake'), and saying that he was raised by a fairy. He does, however, claim that the material for his story came from his patroness, Marie the Countess of Champagne, although it is unclear whether this implies that it was her invention. It is, of course, possible that Marie had supplied Chrétien with a character from a French folk-tale, whom he adapted for inclusion in the Arthurian poem. Unfortunately, once again, there is no way of knowing either way. Like Galahad and Perceval, Lancelot seems to be a later addition, having no association with the historical King Arthur.

Gawain, on the other hand, is one of Arthur's knights who is found in Geoffrey's *Historia*, where he appears as the brother of Modred. It was not for another two and a half centuries that Gawain really came into his own in the most famous of all Middle English Romances, *Sir Gawain and the Green Knight*. Composed by an anonymous writer from the North-West Midlands around 1400, the story has twice been made into a feature film. Unfortunately, it would appear that Gawain is yet another character with no association with the historical Arthur. There is considerable evidence that he was adopted by Geoffrey from a fictional French hero called Walwanus, who appears in a number of eleventh-century manuscripts and whose exploits echo Gawain's in many respects.

So these are the origins of the major Arthurian characters whom we have considered thus far. Guinevere and Morgan appear to be based on Celtic goddesses, although whether or not they were already associated with the legends of Arthur before Geoffrey is impossible to say. For the four principal knights: Galahad, Perceval, Lancelot and Gawain, there is evidence that they were French folk heroes, integrated into the Arthurian story at various stages of its development during the Middle Ages, though there is a slight possibility that Perceval originated as a Welsh hero.

However, a stronger case can be made for Welsh origins for two other members of Arthur's court. First there is Bedivere, who according to Geoffrey was Duke of Normandy and Arthur's right-hand man, and who by Malory's time is the knight who reluctantly casts Excalibur to the Lady of the Lake. Geoffrey introduces Bedivere as a skilled one-handed spearman, which is exactly as he is portrayed in the tale of 'Culhwch and Olwen', although here his name is given as Bedwyr. As we have seen, there is evidence to accept the bulk of 'Culhwch and Olwen' as a genuine Celtic poem composed much earlier than Geoffrey. Whether or not Bedwyr was associated with the legends of Arthur before the twelfth century is impossible to say. But it is very likely that he predates Geoffrey of Monmouth. The same can be said of Sir Kay.

Included by Geoffrey but only as one of many knights, Kay is brought to life by Chrétien as Arthur's steward. Under the Welsh spelling 'Cei', he appears more than any other Arthurian character in medieval Welsh literature, often separated from the Arthurian setting. His characterisation is in keeping with a legendary hero of the ancient Celts. In 'Culhwch and Olwen', for example, he has the power to breathe underwater, and instead of a horse he rides a salmon. It is possible that Cei was originally a British river god, whose folklore was fairly widespread. However, it seems unlikely that Geoffrey would knowingly have included Welsh gods and spirits to pad out his attempted portrayal of historical events. It is more probable that Cei, along with Bedwyr, Morrigan and possibly Gwenhwyfar, had been gradually absorbed into the legend of King Arthur during the half millenium that preceded the twelfth century. As the last defiant hero of the pre-Saxon Britons, it is a reasonable assumption that Arthur became the central figure to whom the old mythology adhered.

Unfortunately, these characters, whether Welsh heroes, Celtic goddesses, or French poetic inventions, are unlikely to have been based on genuine historical figures, let alone those who had any association with the real warrior Arthur. Of all King Arthur's romantic entourage, there are only four with reasonable claims to historical authenticity, including the one who might seem the most unlikely – Merlin the magician.

Geoffrey of Monmouth made much of Merlin, depicting him as the real power behind the throne. His two other Arthurian works include Merlin as the central character: the *Prophetiae Merlini* completed in 1130 while he was still writing the *Historia*, and the *Vita Merlini*, a long poem written around 1150. According to Geoffrey, Merlin's mother was Princess of Demetia (Dyfed in South-West Wales), although his father was an incubus, a spirit who seduced the royal daughter while she slept. This same theme was taken up by Robert de Boron around 1200, who provides us with an explanation of Merlin's peculiar origin. In his version, a group of devils devise a plan to create an Antichrist who would be half-human and half-demon. However, a priest intervenes and the woman chosen to bear the devil-prophet is blessed. Although the son, Merlin, is born with the gift of prophecy, he is inherently good. In Robert's poem, Merlin later repays the priest by revealing to him how Joseph of Arimathea brought the Holy Grail to 'the Vales of Avalon'.

It is quite clear that at least one of Merlin's supposed exploits has been taken from a legend originally associated with another character entirely. Geoffrey includes an account of how Merlin was able to outdo King Vortigern's magicians by revealing two dragons below the foundations of a fortress that the king was attempting to build. The tale is exactly the same as a legend in the *Historia Brittonum*, but in that account, Ambrosius was the young magician. Here the parallel between Ambrosius and Merlin ends. Merlin is certainly not based on Ambrosius, for not only does Geoffrey include him separately, but Merlin never becomes a king or warrior himself, as Ambrosius does.

It appears that the figure of Merlin was based on a Welsh bard called Myrddin. As the official court poets whose task it was to compose songs praising the exploits of their kingdom's warriors, in particular their chieftains, bards enjoyed considerable influence in early Welsh society. Moreover, they were often considered to possess the gift of second sight and were generally the most learned men of the tribe.

According to Geoffrey, Merlin was born in the city of Carmarthen, and in Welsh tradition the name means 'Myrddin's Town'. Merlin is often called Myrddin in early Welsh literature (although the surviving manuscripts that include these works postdate Geoffrey). Seldom in these tales is he the magician of the Arthurian stories; rather, he is a bard or poet, and a number of Welsh poems are actually attributed to him. Moreover, in a number of these folk-tales Myrddin has no connection with Arthur at all. The key to Myrddin's origin is possibly found in a poem entitled *Afallennau* (the 'Apple Trees'), from the 'Black Book of Carmarthen'. In this, the bard is reduced to a solitary existence of madness following an ill-fated battle at a place called Arfderydd. Not only is this battle referenced in the *Annales Cambriae*; Myrddin is actually named. An entry for the year 575 says:

'The battle of Arfderydd between the sons of Eliffer and Gwenddolau son of Ceidio; in which battle Gwenddolau fell and Myrddin went mad'.

It appears therefore that the *Afallennau* is an ancient Celtic poem about the bard Myrddin who actually existed, suggesting that at least some of the other traditions concerning him may also be authentic. Yet although Merlin may have been based on an historical figure, the Myrddin of history appears to have lived over a half a century after the real Arthurian period; Perhaps, then, he is another character erroneously drawn into the Arthurian saga.

By contrast, one character who may have been based on a real person who lived during the Arthurian era is one of Arthur's knights, Tristan.

The story of Tristan and Isolde became one of the most popular love stories of the Middle Ages. Tristan, the son (or sometimes the nephew) of King Mark of Cornwall, falls in love with his father's (or uncle's) new queen Isolde and tragedy ensues. He first appears in the poem *Ur-Tristan* as early as 1150, and actually becomes one of Arthur's Knights in the French prose story 'Tristan' around 1230. In Welsh poetry, which also includes a number of versions of this story, he is called Drystan, and a sixth-century memorial stone from Fowey in Cornwall actually bears the Latin version of this name. Over six feet tall, this inscribed monolith marked the grave of 'Drustanus, son of Cunomorus'. The argument that Drustanus is Tristan therefore relies on Cunomorus being King Mark.

Cunomorus has been convincingly located in place and time. He appears in the writings of Gregory, the bishop of Tours, in the late sixth century, and he can be identified from a number of Dark Age Cornish genealogies, where the name appears in the British rendering as Cynfawr, a king who ruled Dumnonia (Devon and Cornwall) during the early sixth century. The monolith, about a mile north of Fowey on the A 3082, stands close to Castle Dore, an Iron Age hill-fort which modern excavations suggest was the seat of Cunomorus. More importantly the ninth-century monk Wrmonoc, in his biography of Saint Paul Aurelian (the *Vita Pauli Aureliani*), refers to Cunomorus, and also calls him King Mark.

So both Tristan and King Mark seem actually to have existed, conceivably at the same time as Arthur i.e. in the sixth century. Moreover another character may well have been a contemporary of

Arthur: Modred, who according to the *Annales Cambriae* (c. 950), died with Arthur at the battle of Camlann.

In Geoffrey's version of events, Modred is Arthur's nephew, the son of his sister Anna. The *Vulgate Cycle* went on to make him Arthur's own son through incest with his half-sister Morgause (or Margawase), and in later Romances, Modred's mother becomes Morgan le Fey. However, nearly all the Romances are united in following Geoffrey's assertion that Modred rebelled against Arthur, bringing about not only Arthur's demise but his own as well, at the battle of Camlann. As we have seen, the *Annales Cambriae* support Geoffrey's notion that the two men fell in this battle, although Arthur's relationship to Modred is unspecified; they may even have fought on the same side.

Was Geoffrey correct about the family rivalry between them? Under the Welsh spelling of the name, Medraut (the same as in the *Annales*), Modred appears in a number of the Welsh poems as Arthur's opponent, although here they are seldom related; rather they are rulers of different kingdoms in their own right and feuding rivals. Which is nearer the truth – Geoffrey's version, or the Welsh poetic version? Which is the the better explanation for the brief comment in the *Annales* regarding the death of the two warriors at the battle of Camlann? Sadly, there is no way of knowing; the *Historia Brittonum* fails to mention Modred and no other Dark Age manuscript records him.

Drustanus, Cunomorus and Modred are therefore all possible contemporaries of the historical King Arthur, and we shall investigate all three in greater detail once we have extricated Arthur himself from myth and legend, starting with a close examination of Excalibur, the Holy Grail and Avalon.

Summary

We have examined the principal characters in the Arthurian Romances and analysed which, if any, could be based on historical figures. Of King Arthur's entourage, only four have some claim to historical authenticity: Merlin, Mark, Tristan and Modred.

1. It seems likely that Sir Kay, Sir Bedivere, Morgan le Fey and Guinevere were based on ancient Celtic deities: Cei, Bedwyr, Morrigan and Gwenhwyfar, who were probably absorbed into the legend of King Arthur by the twelfth century. Galahad, Lancelot,

Perceval and Gawain all appear to be medieval literary inventions, French folk heroes in their own right, integrated into the Arthurian Romance during its development in the Middle Ages.

2. Merlin seems to be based on a Welsh bard called Myrddin, who is found independently from Arthur in early Welsh literature. Bards enjoyed considerable influence in ancient Welsh society and were often attributed with the gift of second sight. In an ancient poem entitled *Afallennau*, Myrddin is reduced to madness following the battle of Arfderydd. Not only is the battle recorded in the *Annales Cambriae*, for the year 575, but Myrddin is actually named. The problem, however, is that the Myrddin of history lived at least half a century after the likely Arthurian period.

3. One character who may have been based on a real person who lived during the Arthurian era is one of Arthur's knights, Tristan, the son of King Mark of Cornwall. Welsh literature also includes the hero, giving his name as Drystan, and a sixth-century memorial stone from Fowey in Cornwall actually bears the Latin version of this name. Over six feet tall, this ancient stone monolith marked the grave of 'Drustanus, son of Cunomorus', a king who is known to have ruled in Cornwall during the early sixth century. Since the ninth-century monk Wrmonoc mentioned Cunomorus, who he also referred to as King Mark, it seems likely that both Tristan and Mark were based on historical figures.

4. In Geoffrey's version of events, Modred is Arthur's nephew who rebelled against him, bringing about not only Arthur's but his own demise at the battle of Camlann. The *Annales Cambriae* also say that Modred (under the Welsh spelling, Medraut) fell with Arthur at Camlann. However, the relationship between Arthur and Modred is unclear in the *Annales*, as it fails to specify whether or not they fought on opposite sides.

5

Magic and Mystery

Perhaps the most intriguing features in the Arthurian story are the three mystical elements that recur in nearly all the Romances: Excalibur, the Holy Grail and the isle of Avalon. Were these themes associated with the legend of King Arthur before the Middle Ages, or were they simply inventions of Geoffrey and his successors? First, we examine the origins of Arthur's sword, in the popular story the source of all his power.

The word Excalibur was an adaptation by Wace of Geoffrey's name for Arthur's sword, Caliburn, and nearly all the Romancers that followed continued to use the now familiar Excalibur. Although it has been suggested that Geoffrey's term derived from the Latin word *chalybs*, meaning steel, Welsh legends indicate another origin of the name. In a number of Welsh tales (such as 'Culhwch and Olwen') Arthur's sword is called *Caledfwlch*, from the old Irish *Caladbolg* meaning 'a flashing sword'. If Caliburn did come from *Caledfwlch*, then this would imply that the Excalibur theme may have been taken from an early Celtic legend.

The familiar story of Arthur's magical sword is not related by Geoffrey, who tells us only that it was forged on the isle of Avalon. It was not until a century after Geoffrey that the *Vulgate Cycle* introduced the Excalibur story we know today. In the *Vulgate* version, Arthur, who originally received Excalibur from a mysterious nymph, the Lady of the Lake, ultimately orders his knight Girflet to cast it into an enchanted pool as he lies dying on the field of battle. After twice disobeying the wishes of his king, the knight reluctantly consents. When the sword is thrown an arm rises from the lake, catches the weapon and takes it down into the watery depths. This, of course, is the incarnation of the tale later elaborated by Sir Thomas Malory, although in his version it is Bedivere and not Girflet who returns the sword to the Lady of the Lake. Although other Romancers cast Galahad, Lancelot, or even Perceval in this role, the event itself had become firmly entrenched in the saga by the end of the Middle Ages.

There are clear Celtic undertones to the Excalibur theme, suggesting that the writers of the *Vulgate* story may have been employing much earlier material. Archaeological excavations have unearthed many precious artefacts, including swords, that had been thrown into sacred lakes and pools by the Celtic people of Northern Europe as votive offerings to water deities. One such dig, on Anglesey in 1942, recovered no less than 150 items that had been preserved for centuries in the mud of the dried-up lake of Llyn Cerrig Bach. These artefacts were prized possessions, including cauldrons, horse trappings and brooches, and as such had clearly not been discarded; rather they had been cast into the water as offerings over a period spanning some 250 years until the end of the first century A.D.

Could the theme of Excalibur being thrown to the Lady of the Lake have therefore derived from the ancient Celtic practice of making a sacred offering to a water goddess, perhaps in the hope of restoring the king to health?

This hypothesis is further substantiated in the Romances, where the Lady of the Lake is given the name Viviane. This name could well have been an adaptation of a specific Celtic water goddess, recorded by Roman writers under the name Covianna. A shrine to Covianna, under the Romanised name Coventina, can still be seen today on Hadrian's Wall. A well at the shrine has been excavated to reveal numerous votive offerings, particularly coins. From discoveries such as those at Coventina's Well, it can be deduced that the imperial soldiers stationed in Britain began to adopt British customs, just as they did in other Celtic parts of their empire, such as Gaul. Where the British warriors had offered their prized possessions, the Roman soldiers threw coins into the sacred pools, a practice that has survived to this day in the tradition of wishing wells.

The tale of Arthur drawing the sword from the stone seems to be an entirely separate theme. Despite the popular notion of the nineteenth century, it was not Excalibur that was drawn from the stone in the original Romances, but a different sword entirely. In Malory's story, the sword and stone incident occurs well before Merlin takes Arthur to receive Excalibur from the Lady of the Lake. Malory simply says that the sword appeared in the churchyard of 'the greatest church in London'. In his words:

'There was seen in the churchyard a great stone like unto a marble stone and in the midst thereof was like an anvil of steel and therein stuck a fair sword naked by the point, and letters there were written in gold about the sword that saiden thus: "Whoso pulleth out this sword of this stone and anvil, is rightwise born the king of all England".'

The story of the sword in the stone actually entered the Romances somewhat earlier than the Lady of the Lake motif, although once more it can be seen that the original version is slightly different to the modern one, for the sword is not actually placed in the stone itself but rather in an anvil upon it. Robert de Boron was responsible for introducing this earlier theme, which Malory later paraphrased.

Robert may have based his conception of the sword and the stone on the traditions of the Celtic warrior elite. If a dispute arose concerning the election of a new tribal leader, or the commanding chieftain of an alliance, the matter was resolved in combat. More often than not it would be decided by a duel, not necessarily to the death, between the rival candidates. As a sign that the loser or his supporters would abide by the outcome, a symbol of authority was presented to the victor. This was usually a sword consecrated by the pagan priesthood and laid upon a stone altar throughout the contest. The warriors believed that once the victor had attained the symbolic artefact, it would inflict a curse on any who broke the covenant. Could this be the origin of the story of Arthur drawing the sword from the stone?

There is a second possibility. In Latin the word for a large stone or detached fragment of rock is *saxum*, a word that could have been confused with the word *Saxon*. Hence there may have been an original legend about Arthur having to prove himself worthy of leadership by showing he could take the sword, i.e. 'the fight', from the Saxons. Add to this the similarities between the word *anvil* and *Angle*, and it may have implied some notion of defeating both the Angles and the Saxons. The sword and stone theme could therefore have originated either through a misinterpretation, or more likely as a symbolic play on words.

So amongst the fanciful aspects of the Arthurian tales, the stories of Arthur's sword could well have genuine associations with an early Arthurian story originating in the Dark Ages.

Can the same be said of the Holy Grail? The Grail first appears in the *Le Conte del Graal* by Chrétien de Troyes, under the original spelling *graal*. In the story, Perceval, while at the castle of the Fisher King, witnesses a strange procession passing through the hall between the courses of a banquet. Heralded by a young boy carrying a bloodied lance, the procession surrounds a beautiful maiden holding an object which Chrétien describes simply as a *graal*. Although a few decades later Robert de Boron transforms the Grail into the cup used by Christ at the Last Supper, it is far from clear what Chrétien's *graal* is meant to be. In his description he says that 'the *graal* was worked with fine gold, and there were in the *graal* many precious stones, the finest and most costly in the world'.

Although this description could certainly refer to a cup or chalice, the Chrétien *graal* is more likely to have been some form of platter or dish, since the Fisher King is served a Mass wafer that had been placed upon it. Furthermore, Chrétien gives the impression that *graals* were relatively common objects in his day, for he simply refers to it as *un graal*, 'a *graal*', and not *le Graal*, 'the *Graal*', as Robert does later. In fact, Robert de Boron went on to describe it in even more venerating terms as *Le Saint Graal*, 'The Holy Grail'.

Chrétien's lack of detail infers that *graal* was a word familiar to his contemporary readership, although the meaning has since fallen from use, and the word does not occur elsewhere. However, *graal* could be derived from the word *gradale*. A number of medieval French inventories of household possessions refer to items under the name *gradale*, possibly from the Latin *gradus* meaning 'in stages', and probably applied to a dish or platter that was brought to the table at various stages during a meal.

If the *graal* was a platter, it would tend to dampen the argument that the story was originally Celtic. The suggestion that the quest for the Holy Grail in the Arthurian saga came originally from Celtic legends of magic cauldrons, such as the Cauldron of Dagda mentioned earlier, relies on the Grail being a chalice. If we knew more of Chrétien's *graal* we would be better placed to draw conclusions; unfortunately, the real significance of the *graal* in Chrétien's poem must remain a mystery, for *Le Conte del Graal*, his last work, was never completed. However, an epic poem does survive, from around the same period as Robert de Boron, which may provide us with a solution to the Grail story and its most likely origins. On this occasion it does not come from England, Wales, or even France, but from Germany and the pen of Wolfram von Eschenbach, one of the greatest German poets of the Middle Ages.

The Arthurian story had already found its way into Germany sometime around 1200 in the form of two poems, *Erec* and *Iwein*, by the poet Hartmann von Aue. A year or so later, around 1205, Wolfram composed his epic Arthurian poem *Parzival*, later to be immortalised in Wagner's opera *Parsifal*. It is essentially a reworking of Chrétien's *Le Conte del Graal*, although Wolfram provides many of the details absent from Chrétien's unfinished work. However, in Wolfram's story the Grail is not a platter, nor even a chalice, but a magical stone called the Lapsit Excillis, from the Latin *lapis exilis*, meaning, literally, a small stone. According to Wolfram, it was with this stone that God had banished the angels who failed to support him in his battle with Lucifer.

In *Parzival*, the stone is in the keeping of a noble family who are entrusted with its protection. In return, they live in splendour on the food and drink that it miraculously provides. Additionally, the stone has the power to heal and preserve the life of its guardians. Contained within the walls of an impregnable castle, the Grail is further protected by an order of knights, chosen as children when their names appear on the stone itself.

The story opens with Anfortas, king of the Grail Castle, being mortally wounded, although his protection by the Grail means that he cannot die. His only hope of freedom from the pain of his living death is to find a man to replace him. A message then appears on the stone telling the king that his heir, the son of his sister Herzelyde, will soon come to the castle. But only if the heir poses the right question will he prove himself worthy of succession.

Anfortas' nephew, and heir apparent, is none other than Parzival, although he has been raised unaware of his true lineage. When he arrives at the castle he witnesses the same procession as Perceval does in Chrétien's story, although the Grail is now the stone. After failing to ask the correct question, Parzival leaves and spends the remainder of the story acquiring wisdom by enlisting as one of Arthur's knights. Ultimately, Parzival returns to the Grail Castle and proves himself worthy of succession.

It is likely that the story of the Grail was an addition to the Arthurian legend, for the Grail of Chrétien and Wolfram has no connection with Arthur himself. Only much later in the development of the story does the Grail have any direct bearing on Arthur's life, when it becomes the vessel sought by Arthur's knights to rid the land of famine and plague. So where did the story originate? Fortunately Wolfram reveals his source. In his epilogue to *Parzival*, he refers to Chrétien's *Le Conte del Graal*, informing his readers that it fails to do justice to a tale that already existed. He goes on say that his own full and accurate portrayal of the original legend came from an Arabic manuscript discovered by his friend Kyot in Toledo, Spain.

If Wolfram is to be believed, then the original Grail legend appears to have been an Arabian story, probably adapted for a European readership by the crusaders. Many such poems were composed during the crusades by the visiting soldiers, who took Arabian tales and transformed them with medieval heroes replacing the original characters. There is additional evidence that the Grail story was originally an Arabian tale, for Wolfram actually tells us that the Grail Knights were the Knights Templar.

The Knights Templar came into existence in early twelfth-century France as a full-time military organisation, an international order of knights founded with the specific purpose of fighting for Christendom in the Holy Land. But the Knights Templar were more than simply knights, they were Cistercian monks trained to fight as crusaders. It is therefore possible that a crusader poet, possibly a Templar, adopted and adapted an Arab legend which later became amalgamated into the Arthurian cycle.

Having examined the legends of Excalibur and the Holy Grail, we turn next to perhaps the most haunting element of the Arthurian saga; Avalon and the mystery of Arthur's last resting place. We have already seen how Geoffrey could have based his Avalon on the Annwn of Celtic legend. However, there is nothing Celtic in Geoffrey's descriptions of Avalon, for here we are dealing with a blatant borrowing from Classical mythology. For example, when he talks of the vines of Avalon that sow themselves, and inhabitants who live for at least a hundred years, Geoffrey is clearly recounting the Greek myth of the Fortunate Isles, the islands of self-tending fruit and immortality.

Nonetheless, the Celtic element is certainly present. Not only are there nine holy women, and the Celtic goddess Morrigan appearing as Morgan; the name Avalon itself seems to be of Celtic origin. From Ireland comes an ancient cycle of poems involving the sea god Manannan, who rules over a magical island described by the Gaelic word *ablach*, meaning 'rich in apples'. Geoffrey goes as far as to refer to Avalon as the 'Isle of Apples' (*Insula Pomorum*) in his *Vita Merlini*.

Avalon is, therefore, primarily a Celtic notion, and so may have been associated with the original Arthurian legend. Trying to locate Avalon is a more complex issue. If it were based on a real island, it could have been almost anywhere. For instance, there is the Isle of Man, taking its name from the god Manannan and said to have been his home. Then there is Ireland itself, which the tale of 'Culhwch and Olwen' identifies as Annwn. In the South-West are the Scilly Isles, which appear in a legend dating back to the Middle Ages with Morgan as their queen. In Scotland, Iona was called the Isle of Dreams, a name applied to Avalon in more than one medieval Romance. The Welsh contender is Bardsey Island, for centuries the burial site of saints and other Christian holy men; a legend recorded as early as the thirteenth century relates how Merlin sleeps there in a cave, preserving forever a cauldron containing the treasures of the vanquished Britons.

But even if one of these sites has a feasible claim to be answered, it is evidently not worth seeking Arthur there. According to Geoffrey, Arthur goes to Avalon merely for his wounds to be healed; Geoffrey does not say where Arthur was laid to rest. It seems that the mystery surrounding Arthur's burial site was too well known for Geoffrey to fabricate a location. Before Geoffrey, William of Malmesbury wrote that Arthur's grave had still not been found and the Welsh poem the 'Stanzas of the Graves', which concerns itself with the burial sites of the Celtic heroes, admits that Arthur's burial site remains a mystery.

Faced with this problem Sir Thomas Malory, who attempted to amalgamate all the Arthurian legends, decided to hedge his bets. To begin with he follows Geoffrey's lead in portraying Arthur being taken to Avalon by ship, in order that his wounds can be tended (though he does not actually specify burial there). Then, a few lines later, Bedivere arrives at a chapel in Glastonbury, where he discovers a hermit mourning beside a newly dug grave. When he asks the hermit who is buried there the hermit answers: 'This same night, at midnight, here came a number of ladies and brought here a dead corpse and prayed me to bury him'. Bedivere assumes it is Arthur, although the hermit cannot confirm so. It would appear that Malory was endeavouring to satisfy his readership concerning Glastonbury Abbey but, unconvinced that Glastonbury could be described as an island, included Avalon separately. In fact, he does not really commit himself to Glastonbury at all, for he also includes another version of the story in which Arthur's grave remains to be discovered.

Speculation regarding Avalon and its connections with the historical Arthur has given rise to many intriguing theories about its origin. The barge episode in many Romances, for instance, could imply that Arthur was given a Viking-style burial at sea or alternatively, that he was given a boat burial on land, akin to that of the Sutton Hoo Man of East Anglia. The most feasible notion, however, is that the legend of Avalon derived from the *underworld* of Celtic mythology, since in Celtic mythology heroes are often taken bodily into the *underworld* of the gods and spirits. So the Avalon story could well have been a part of the original Arthurian legend as it existed before Geoffrey's time.

Unfortunately the tales of Avalon could lead anywhere and to just about any conclusion. All that can be deduced from the tales concerning Avalon, Excalibur and the Holy Grail is that there was a huge body of material that could be related to the Arthurian legend at a time when the first Romances were written. Having exhausted the material contained in Arthurian myth, legend and folklore, we must now return to historical sources and examine them in greater detail, to see what they may be able to tell us about the historical Arthur.

Summary

We have investigated the origin of the three mystical elements that recur in nearly all the Romances. In conclusion, it seems that the Excalibur story may reflect historical events associated with the real Arthur, the Holy Grail was a medieval invention, and Avalon was an early Arthurian legend taken from Celtic mythology.

1. The story of Excalibur being thrown to the Lady of the Lake originates in one of the *Vulgate* Romances around 1225, in which Arthur orders his knight Girflet to cast the sword into an enchanted pool as he lies dying on the field of battle. Here are strong Celtic undertones, suggesting that the writer may have employed much earlier material. Archaeological excavations have found many swords that had long ago been thrown into sacred lakes by the Celtic people of Northern Europe, as votive offerings to the water goddess, the goddess of healing.

2. The story of the sword in the stone was introduced in Robert de Boron's tale, where the sword was not actually placed in the stone itself but in an anvil upon the stone. In Latin the word for a large stone or detached fragment of rock is *saxum*, a word that could have been confused with the word Saxon. It is possible therefore that there was an original legend about Arthur having to prove himself worthy of leadership by showing he could take the sword, i.e. 'the fight', from the Saxons. Add to this the similarities between the word anvil and Angle, and it may allude to taking the sword from both the Saxons and the Angles. The sword and stone theme could therefore have originated either through a mis-interpretation, or more likely, a symbolic play on words.

3. The Grail first appears in Chrétien de Troyes under the original spelling *graal*. Although a few decades later Robert de Boron transforms the Grail into the cup used by Christ at the Last Supper, it is far from clear what Chrétien's *graal* is supposed to be. It appears to have been a type of plate or dish, since a Mass wafer is served from it. The word *graal* could be derived from *gradale*, as a number of medieval French inventories use this word for a platter that was brought to the table at various stages during a meal. The later story of the Grail as the holy chalice seems, therefore, to have been a medieval invention.

4. An explanation of the Grail story's origin is provided by Chrétien's contemporary, the German poet Wolfram von Eschenbach. In 1205, Wolfram composed his epic poem *Parzival*, which is very similar to Chrétien's story, except that the Grail is not a platter but a magical stone. In his epilogue to *Parzival*, Wolfram tells his readers that Chrétien had failed to do justice to a story that already existed. He goes on to explain that his own portrayal of the original legend came to him from an Arabic manuscript discovered in Spain. If Wolfram is to be believed, then the Grail story may originally have been an Arabian tale returned to Europe with the crusaders.

5. The isle of Avalon, Arthur's last resting place, is included in Geoffrey and nearly all subsequent Romances. It seems highly probable that this legend existed before Geoffrey. From Ireland comes an ancient cycle of tales involving the sea god Manannan, who rules over a magical island described by the Gaelic word *ablach*, meaning rich in apples. In fact, Geoffrey goes as far as to refer to Avalon as the 'Isle of Apples' in the *Vita Merlini*.

6

Historical Manuscripts

The historical evidence for King Arthur rests mainly with the *Annales Cambriae* and the *Historia Brittonum* as we saw in Chapter Two, but we must also consider the other historical sources covering the period in question, sources which unfortunately fail to include King Arthur.

First, there is the *Historia Ecclesiastica Gentis Anglorum* ('Ecclesiastical History of the English People'), which gives a reliable historical framework for the Dark Ages. Compiled around 731, this is the first English work that could genuinely be termed historical writing. Written by the monk Bede, at the monastery of Jarrow in Northumbria, it transformed the rough framework of existing material into an actual history book. Bede's work established the style for historians that followed; amongst other developments he was the first to employ the *Anno Domini* system of dating for historical purposes. His sources were primarily ecclesiastical documents from the region of Kent, together with the sixth-century monk Gildas and a wide variety of oral accounts.

The second important historical manuscript covering the events of the fifth and sixth centuries is the *Anglo-Saxon Chronicle*, of which a number of versions survive. Although it appears to be based on early West-Saxon monastic records, the surviving *Chronicle* was not compiled until the reign of Alfred the Great, between 871–899, seemingly under Alfred's personal supervision.

The fact that neither work contains reference to Arthur has long cast a shadow of doubt over his historical authenticity. However, Bede may not mention Arthur for the simple reason that he is writing an ecclesiastical history of the Saxons, and as such has no reason to include him. As for the *Anglo-Saxon Chronicle*, since this was most likely Alfred's attempt to promote the successful exploits of his own Saxon ancestors, it is reasonable to assume that he would not have wished to draw attention to the accomplishments of the opposition.

The few surviving writings of the foreigners who visited Britain during the apparent Arthurian period are chiefly travelogues describing events in which they were involved, rendering their omission of

Arthur irrelevant. As for the fragmentary monastic records, they almost entirely concern themselves with ecclesiastical affairs.

We come, therefore, to the most important work in the search for King Arthur, the *De Excidio Conquestu Britanniae* ('On the Ruin and Conquest of Britain'), written by Gildas in the mid-sixth century. Reputedly the son of a British aristocrat, Gildas appears to have attended a school in Wales founded by St Illtud. According to William of Malmesbury, Gildas eventually became a monk, spending some time at the monastery in Glastonbury. Since Gildas actually seems to have been alive either during the Arthurian period or immediately afterwards, the omission of Arthur from his work might, at first, seem damning. But as with Bede and the *Anglo-Saxon Chronicle*, there may well be another explanation for Arthur's exclusion.

Gildas' work was never intended as a straightforward textbook of history; indeed it is essentially a tirade. As the title suggests, it is primarily a criticism of his fellow countrymen, levelled at the petty squabbles which allowed the Saxons their superiority. He hardly mentions anyone by name prior to the time of his writing, except Ambrosius whom it seems he admired. Gildas verifies the victory of the Britons at the battle of Badon, mentioned in the *Annales Cambriae* and the *Historia Brittonum*, although he does not say that it was Arthur who triumphed there, omitting the name of the leader altogether. This omission is to some extent hopeful in the search for Arthur, for it means that the name of the British leader at the most important battle of the era is open to investigation.

Having briefly considered surviving sources contemporary with the era in which we place Arthur, at this point we need to return to writers of the twelfth century. How useful are the works of William of Malmesbury in the search for Arthur? William is considered by modern scholars to be a far more reliable historian than Geoffrey, and though William says very little of Arthur, he does provide us with a reasonable idea of the status of the Arthurian myth at the time that Geoffrey was writing the *Historia*. To begin with, William's *Gesta Regum Anglorum* tells us that a variety of Arthurian stories were in circulation. Unlike Geoffrey, William tends to regard these as fables, but he does not reject Arthur himself as an historical character.

From William's work it is evident that very little was known about Arthur. But William does provide us with a starting point. For instance, he tells us that Arthur aided the warrior Ambrosius Aurelianus in fighting the Angles. Although Ambrosius is named in the *De Excidio* of Gildas, as the leader of Britons who launched a successful counteroffensive against the Saxon invaders sometime during the 460s or 470s, almost nothing is reliably known about Ambrosius, including how or when he died.

William of Malmesbury goes on to say that Arthur triumphed at the siege of Mount Badon. Since Gildas also mentions the battle of Badon as the high point of the period of warfare initiated by Ambrosius, it would appear that William is implying that Arthur is the successor of Ambrosius. Whether or not the two ever fought alongside each other remains unclear. What is clear is that Arthur was believed to have been a Christian king, evidenced by William's description of Arthur bearing an image of the Virgin Mary during the battle of Badon.

On the other hand, William regarded much of what he heard about Arthur as suspect. He derided, for example, the legend that Arthur single-handedly defeated 900 of the enemy at Badon. It is apparent that Arthur had acquired a mythical status by the early twelfth century, and also that the hunting of Arthurian relics seems to have become fashionable. William mentions that someone claimed to have located the tomb of Arthur's nephew a few years earlier, although he goes on to say that Arthur's own tomb still evaded discovery.

What can be deduced from William's common-sense approach? Only that in the early twelfth century, Arthur was believed to have been a Christian king who lived some 600 years before. Any further information appears to have been confined to legend. William's message is one of caution, as we saw in Chapter Three. All the same, he clearly believes that there is enough evidence of his existence, for he adds that in his opinion Arthur is worthy of inclusion in authentic history as one 'who long sustained his failing country'. But where did William obtain *his* information?

Thankfully, a source that William may well have used has survived in the form of the *Historia Brittonum*. Now preserved in the British Library in a manuscript catalogued as 'Harley 3859', the *Historia Brittonum* is an early twelfth-century copy of an earlier document. The style of writing, together with older fragments of the work which still survive elsewhere, indicate a much earlier date for its original compilation – sometime around 830. The *Historia Brittonum* is generally believed to have been the work of a ninth-century monk from Bangor in North Wales called Nennius.

In the *Historia Brittonum*, Nennius claims to have compiled his history of the Britons by making 'a heap' of what he could find amongst old documents at his disposal. He tells us:

'I have heaped together all that I found, from the Annals of the Romans, the Chronicles of the Holy Fathers, the writings of the Irish and the Saxons and the traditions of our own wise men.'

Unfortunately, none of these sources can be traced. What Nennius derived from them is disorderly, but certainly appears to be a genuine attempt by the writer to reconstruct a history. On the subject of Ambrosius, Nennius says virtually nothing, but of Arthur he tells us the following:

'In that time the Saxons strengthened in multitude and grew in Britain. On the death of Hengist, Octha his son passed from the northern part of Britain to the kingdom of the Kentishmen and from him arise the kings of the Kentishmen.

'Then Arthur fought against them in those days with the kings of the Britons, but he himself was leader of battles.

'The first battle was at the mouth of the river Glein. The second, third, fourth and fifth upon another river which is called Dubglas, in the district of Linnuis. The sixth battle upon the river which is called Bassas. The seventh battle was in the Caledonian wood that is Cat Coit Celidon. The eighth battle was in Fort Guinnion in which Arthur carried the image of St Mary, ever virgin, on his shoulders and that day the pagans were turned to flight and a great slaughter was upon them through the virtue of Our Lord Jesus Christ and through the virtue of St Mary the Virgin, his mother. The ninth battle was waged in the City of the Legion. The tenth battle he fought on the shore of the river which is called Tribruit. The eleventh battle took place on the mountain which is called Agned. The twelfth battle was on Mount Badon, in which nine hundred and sixty men fell in one day from one attack by Arthur, and no one overthrew them except himself alone. And in all the battles he was the victor.'

It appears that William of Malmesbury took his information from Nennius, since his description of the battle of Badon corresponds with that in the *Historia Brittonum*, including an image of the Virgin (although ascribed to a different battle). William, however, does not take seriously the idea that Arthur alone killed over 900 men. This may only have been metaphorical, implying that no other British leader helped him in the fight; a possible indication that Arthur was let down, or that his army overcame considerable odds.

But how reliable is Nennius? There is much that is historically inaccurate elsewhere in the *Historia Brittonum*, which does nothing to bolster claims of historical authenticity. However, the content strongly suggests that not only William, but also Geoffrey of Monmouth, took Nennius as his source. For example, Geoffrey's story of Brutus the Trojan, plus many of his other fanciful themes, appear in Nennius, often quoted almost verbatim. Geoffrey, however, is far more imaginative than Nennius, who does not appear to be deliberately trying to pull the wool over anyone's eyes. Nennius introduces his work with the following:

> 'I ask every reader who reads this book to pardon me for daring to write so much here after so many, like a chattering bird or an incompetent judge. I yield to whoever may be better acquainted with this skill than I am.'

By his own admission he is artless, a confession which leaves one with the impression that the *Historia Brittonum* is an honest attempt by Nennius to present the information at his disposal.

So it seems that in Nennius we have not only William's source, but also the basic formula for Geoffrey of Monmouth. But where did Geoffrey find his account of other Arthurian episodes? It would seem that he took one from the *Annales Cambriae*. Now in the same composite manuscript as the *Historia Brittonum* at the British Library, the *Annales Cambriae* were also copied in their surviving form during the early twelfth century. The *Annales* appear to have originally been compiled on behalf of the kings of South Wales, for although they include a series of genealogies of a number of British rulers, they conclude with a more detailed family tree of the South Welsh kings of the ninth century. Fundamentally of Welsh interest, they are also an attempt to catalogue the events throughout Britain.

Although the contents of the *Annales* discuss events that date back to the mid-fifth century, it appears from the style and spelling of the earlier section that they were only kept as a contemporary record from around 800. In their present form, however, the fact that the last entry is dated in the 950s indicates that they were originally written at that time.

Regrettably the *Annales Cambriae* are little more than an incomplete chronology of dates, coupled with brief notations on important incidents that occurred. Written in Latin, they span a period of 533 years, but do not use the *Anno Domini* system of dating. The *Annales* can be dated, however, because of an entry in year nine saying

'Easter is changed on the Lord's day by Pope Leo, bishop of Rome'. This is known from other sources to have occurred in 455 A.D., so if the ninth year is 455 A.D. then the first year must be 446. Whenever this method of adjustment is tested against other dates, known to be accurate from reliable sources, it appears to be correct to within a year or so either way. Consequently, the entries relating to Arthur, being inserted in the years 72 and 93, can be taken as 518 A.D. and 539 A.D. The first of these, in 518, concerns the Battle of Badon, saying:

'The battle of Badon, in which Arthur carried the cross of our Lord Jesus Christ on his shoulders for three days and three nights, and the Britons were victorious.'

There is no reference to Arthur fighting alone, although we do see another mention of a holy relic on his shoulders. On this occasion, however, it is a cross and not an image of the Virgin. It is now generally agreed that there has been an early confusion between the Welsh word for shoulders, *ysgwydd* (pronounced 'scuith') and *ysgwyd* (pronounced 'scuit'), meaning shield which would explain one oddity. The important point is that the *Annales* speak of a cross and not the image of the Virgin, suggesting that the compiler of the *Annales Cambriae* was not reliant on the same source as Nennius.

The second and only other reference to Arthur in the *Annales* is the entry for the year 539:

'The strife of Camlann in which Arthur and Medraut perished, and there was plague in Britain and in Ireland'.

Since Nennius does not mention Camlann (probably because he is only concerned with Arthur's victories), it could well have been from the *Annales* that Geoffrey took his information concerning this battle.

Before collating the information that we can derive from the *Annales Cambriae* and the *Historia Brittonum*, we must examine in greater detail Geoffrey's claim to possess an 'ancient book' from which he learned the truth about King Arthur. There is certainly evidence for Arthurian legends surviving into the Middle Ages, but aside from the *Annales* and Nennius has Geoffrey drawn on any other historical sources?

Besides Geoffrey and William of Malmesbury, two historians who were their contemporaries also endeavoured to place Arthur in some kind of historical context. Less reliable than William, but more reliable than Geoffrey, they are Caradoc of Llancarfan and Henry of Huntingdon. Neither can be taken as a particularly reliable source of additional information on the historical Arthur. Henry bases his work concerning the Arthurian period primarily on Nennius and the *Anglo-Saxon Chronicle*. In his *Historia Anglorum*, written around 1135, he includes Nennius' list of Arthur's twelve battles, inserting them between the *Chronicle*'s entries for 527 and 530. He seems to have arrived at this dating because the *Anglo-Saxon Chronicle* indicates that the Saxon advance was halted for a time after 527. Caradoc, on the other hand, in his *Vita Gildae* ('Life of Gildas') circa 1140, includes Arthur in the life of the monk. Once again, the inclusion of Arthur is unreliable, since an earlier more accurate work (the *Vita Gildas* by the ninth-century Breton monk Rhuys) fails to include him.

The relevance of Henry and Caradoc relates to Geoffrey's 'ancient book'. In a postscript to the *Historia*, Geoffrey cautions them both, along with William, telling them to leave King Arthur alone, for only he (Geoffrey) has the 'ancient book in the British language'. Fine words maybe, but it is a lasting pity that he never seems to have produced the book, if it actually existed, as evidence. As regards Archdeacon Walter from whom, as we saw, Geoffrey claims to have acquired the book, other than his name, nothing relevant to our research now survives. Without this book, we are left with the *Historia Brittonum* of Nennius as the earliest document to provide us with any details concerning King Arthur.

Arthur does not appear to have been invented by Nennius. From the style of his writing, and his open confession of artlessness, he seems to have lacked the imagination or indeed the motive. He even includes a number of serious contradictions throughout his narrative, such as different versions of the same person's death. Nennius gives the reason for these discrepancies, explaining that he is offering all the information he has collected, presumably to allow the reader to decide between conflicting accounts. Additionally, there is the fact that Nennius provides no more detail of Arthur's life than the above passage. If he had invented Arthur, surely he would have presented us with more particulars. For these reasons, we are left with the impression of an honest scholar simply transcribing what he has discovered, where his referring to Arthur is concerned.

The same is true of Arthur's battles; Nennius is unsure of their precise locations. If he had invented the hero, why does he provide so

Principal Locations in the Search for Arthur.

little detail? This lack of detail, we believe, points to Nennius' list being derived from an old British war-poem commemorating the exploits of Arthur. After all, many such poems still survive (such as the *Canu Llywarch Hen*, discussed later), praising the battles of warriors who are known to have existed.

What does the list of battles tell us? Surely it must provide some idea where and when the events took place? Unfortunately not. Aside from the battle of Badon, none of the others are historically verifiable, although some might be located with a little informed guesswork. The River Glein, at the mouth of which the first battle was said to have been fought, is probably the River Glen in South Lincolnshire; Linnuis, where the next four battles were fought, may well be Lindsey, also in Lincolnshire; and the City of the Legion is probably Caerleon (the direct translation of the Welsh name), although Chester is called Caer Legion in the *Annales Cambriae*. Besides the battle of Badon, which must have been in the South of England (as will be reasoned shortly), the only other location that can be traced with any degree of accuracy is the battle of the Caledonian Wood. Since 'Caledonia' was the Roman name for Scotland, Cat Coit Celidon seems to have been fought somewhere in the far North.

What, then, are we to make of the account given by Nennius? At first glance the information is puzzling. The list of battles appears to involve him fighting all over Britain. If Arthur was fighting the Kentishmen of the South-East, why is he also in the far North? What was Arthur's role in contemporary military events? There are two likely possibilities.

The first would confirm William of Malmesbury's statement that Arthur aided Ambrosius in fighting the Angles. If Arthur was fighting in Lincolnshire, the probable area for the first five battles, he would indeed have been in an area occupied by the Angles by the late fifth century. Perhaps until Ambrosius' death Arthur was commissioned to fight in other parts of the country, while the main armies were busy in the South fighting the Saxons.

The second interpretation arises from a brief statement in Nennius concerning Arthur's rank. Arthur is introduced simply as the Britons' *dux bellorum*, 'leader of battles', implying that Arthur was not a king himself. This implication is echoed in Nennius' assertion that Arthur fought *cum regibus brittonis*, '*with* the British kings'. He does not use the word *rex*, 'king', and even the word *tyrannus*, 'chief', is absent. Elsewhere in the *Historia Brittonum* (see below), where Nennius mentions a legend concerning Arthur's dog, he describes Arthur simply as *Arthuri militis*, 'the warrior Arthur'. This ambiguity concerning Arthur's status prompts speculation that he may have been a foreign mercenary, which may account for his fighting in such widely spread locations, presumably for whoever was paying him at the time. Conversely, he may have been the commander-in-chief of Ambrosius' armies.

This raises more questions than it answers, and all that can be safely deduced at this stage is the legendary status of Arthur during the lifetime of Nennius. There are two legends of Arthur in an appendix of *Mirabilia* (Marvels) in the *Historia Brittonum*. One concerns a stone marked with a paw print of Arthur's dog, Cabal, said to lie on a pile of rocks in the region of Buelt (Builth) in Central Wales. According to Nennius, if anyone removes the stone it magically returns of its own accord. The other concerns a tomb which was said continually to change its size. It was in the district of Ercing (modern Weston-under-Penyard, near Ross-on-Wye), and was thought to contain the body of Arthur's son Amr. These two inclusions do seem to suggest that Arthurian legends had become firmly established by the time of Nennius in the early ninth century.

So, what can reasonably be surmised from the *Historia Brittonum* concerning the Arthurian legend that existed around 830 A.D.?

1. By the ninth century Arthur already featured in folklore.

2. Arthur was believed to be a Christian warrior who fought the invading Saxons and perhaps the Saxon allies, the Angles in the East, or even the Picts of the North.

3. Arthur was believed to have consolidated a successful counteroffensive initiated by Ambrosius Aurelianus sometime during the late fifth and early sixth centuries.

4. The battle of Badon, seemingly the result of a siege lasting three days, was considered Arthur's most important victory.

5. Arthur does not appear to have been thought of as a king at all; rather as some form of war leader or commander-in-chief, perhaps the nearest equivalent in more recent history being the Japanese Shogun.

This, then, is all we know of the status of the Arthurian legend in the ninth century. Although considerably earlier than the Middle Ages version of Geoffrey of Monmouth, it derives from an account written more than three centuries *after* the actual events appear to have taken place.

Having said that, we need to pinpoint the Arthurian era with greater accuracy. When exactly was it? As we saw earlier in this chapter, Nennius tells us that it was directly after the death of Hengist, a figure who is generally considered by historians to have existed. Not only is Hengist mentioned by Bede, but he is also recorded as dying in 488 in the *Anglo-Saxon Chronicle*. However, although the *Chronicle* confirms Hengist's existence, the accuracy of its dating requires further proof as we will show. At this stage then, the only sure indicator of the period of Arthur is the battle of Badon, an historical event attested by Gildas himself who wrote within living memory of the conflict. As the only historically verifiable event which has been associated with Arthur, it is therefore crucial to ascertain precisely when the battle of Badon occurred.

Summary

We have examined the few historical sources which cover the late fifth and early sixth centuries, the period that King Arthur is thought to have lived, in search of hard evidence for his existence. One battle in which Arthur is said have fought historically occurred, and two warriors associated with him are known to have existed.

1. There are two important Anglo-Saxon historical sources that cover the Dark Ages: the *Historia Ecclesiastica Gentis Anglorum* ('Ecclesiastical History of the English People'), written by the monk Bede around 731, and the *Anglo-Saxon Chronicle*, compiled during the reign of Alfred the Great, between 871–899, seemingly under Alfred's personal supervision. The fact that neither work contains reference to Arthur has long cast a shadow of doubt over his historical authenticity. However, Bede may not mention Arthur because he was writing an ecclesiastical history of the Saxons, whereas the *Chronicle* was Alfred's attempt to promote the successful exploits of his own Saxon ancestors.

2. The most important work in the search for King Arthur, the

De Excidio Conquestu Britanniae ('On the Ruin and Conquest of Britain'), was written by the monk Gildas in the mid-sixth century. Gildas fails to mention Arthur, although he does verify the victory of the Britons at the battle of Badon without naming their leader.

3. Writing just before Geoffrey, William of Malmesbury is a reliable historian. In the *Gesta Regum Anglorum* he tells us that Arthur aided the warrior Ambrosius Aurelianus in fighting the Angles. Ambrosius is named by Gildas as the leader of the Britons who launched a successful counteroffensive against the Saxon invaders sometime during the 460s or 470s. William of Malmesbury also says that Arthur triumphed at the siege of Mount Badon.

4. The *Annales Cambriae* were completed in the 950s. Regrettably, the *Annales* are little more than a list of dates, coupled with brief notations. However, there are two entries relating to Arthur: the first in 518, saying that Arthur was victorious at the battle of Badon; the second in 539 saying that Arthur and Medraut perished in the battle of Camlann.

5. The *Historia Brittonum* was compiled sometime around 830 A.D. Written by a monk named Nennius, it tells us that Arthur fought against the Saxons on the death of the Saxon king Hengist, whom, the *Anglo-Saxon Chronicle* confirms, died in 488. Nennius also provides a list of twelve battles in which Arthur fought, including the battle of Badon. The most surprising element in Nennius is that he does not refer to Arthur as a king, but simply as a 'warrior' who was merely a 'leader of battles'.

6. From the *Historia Brittonum*, the *Annales Cambriae* and the *Gesta Regum Anglorum*, we discover that Arthur was a warrior who led the Britons against the Anglo-Saxons during the late fifth or early sixth centuries. Three elements these documents collectively associate with Arthur provide good evidence of his existence: The battle of Badon, the British leader Ambrosius and the Saxon warrior Hengist. Badon and Ambrosius are both mentioned by Bede, and more importantly by Gildas, who wrote within living memory of the period in question, while Hengist is referred to by Bede and the *Anglo-Saxon Chronicle*.

7

Dating the Events

It might appear obvious that the battle of Badon took place around 518, as given in the *Annales Cambriae*. However, the entries concerning Arthur must be treated with some caution, since they are two of a small number of British entries in the first century of the *Annales Cambriae*, and are found amongst a series of extracts from Irish annals. It could well be that although the annalist was familiar with these events involving Arthur, and perhaps the timescale separating them, he was uncertain where they should be inserted in the chronology.

Since Gildas wrote at least 350 years before the *Annales* were compiled, almost certainly within living memory of the battle, he is probably the most reliable source. Unfortunately, Gildas does not supply dates, creating problems for us when we try to place the events he describes in an accurate historical chronology. Despite this, he does supply a vital clue to when the battle of Badon may have occurred, as we shall see.

The translation of languages depends on the interpretations of the translator. It is unlike deciphering a mathematical code, where each symbol has a precise meaning. Consequently, translation often involves a degree of artistic licence. Not only is it a matter of tense and syntax (grammatical structure in sentences), but also the understanding of an individual writer's use of symbolism and metaphor. With Gildas this is not easy; his idiosyncratic style and poetic use of Latin creates many problems. Particular problems arise concerning the section in his *De Excidio* relating to the battle of Badon, a passage in which Gildas says:

Usque ad annum obsessionis Badonici montis, novissimaeque ferme de furciferis non minimae stragis, quique quadragesimus quartus, ut novi, orditur annus mense iam uno emenso, qui et meae nativitatis est.

Since there has been much controversy concerning the interpretation of this passage, it is important to be aware of the meanings of the individual words:

Usque (this continued – continually) *ad* (until) *annum* (the year of) *obsessionis* (the blockade of – the siege of) *Badonici montis* (Badon Hill – Mount Badon), *novissimaeque* (the last) *ferme* (virtually) *de* (applicable to – originating from) *furciferis* (the rascals) *non* (not) *minimae* (very small) *stragis* (slaughter), *quique* (and this) *quadragesimus* (the fortieth) *quartus* (the fourth) *ut* (inasmuch as) *novi* (I know) *orditur* (in turn) *annus* (year) *mense* (month) *iam* (by this time) *uno* (one) *emenso* (to pass through a space of time), *qui* (which) *et* (also) *meae* (belonging to me) *nativitatis est* (of birth).

The syntax and precise content of Gildas' Latin does not automatically transpose into a modern English equivalent. The most direct translation, minus any poetic meaning that may have been intended by Gildas, reads:

'This continued until the year of the Siege of Badon Hill, virtually the last defeat of the rascals, and certainly not the least. And this the forty-fourth year, inasmuch as I know, with one month by this time having passed and it was also the year of my birth.'

Confusing indeed. What is Gildas actually saying?

A number of historians have attempted to resolve this ambiguity, their solutions depending on different interpretations of the passage, and providing varying translations into English of what Gildas may have meant. Of these, there are two which must be examined now if we are to pin down the date of the battle of Badon.

Some scholars adhere to the first interpretation, which has Gildas saying that the battle occurred forty-three years earlier, i.e. he was now forty-four and the battle had occurred sometime during the first year of his life. A slight variation on this theory is that it took place exactly forty-four years and one month before the time of his writing. The translation thus reads:

'This continued until the year of the Siege of Badon Hill,

virtually the last defeat of the rascals, and certainly not the least.
That was the year of my birth; as I know one month of the forty-fourth year since then has already passed.'

Gildas' *De Excidio* is thought to have been written in the 540s, as the work was composed before the death of Maglocunus, king of Gwynedd in Wales, whom Gildas addresses personally and whose death occurred during a plague that affected Britain in the late 540s which is recorded in the *Annales Cambriae*. The *Annales* insert the death of Maglocunus in 549, and independent Irish records evidence plague in Britain at this time. From Gildas' references to the exploits of Maglocunus, his criticism must have been compiled shortly before the death of that king. If we date the *De Excidio* to about 545, then according to this first interpretation, the battle of Badon would have occurred sometime around the year 500.

The second interpretation of Gildas' confusing Latin is more convincing. It suggests that the battle took place in the forty-fourth year of a specific era. The translation would thus read:

'This continued until the year of the Siege of Badon Hill, virtually the last defeat of the rascals, and certainly not the least. And this was the forty-fourth year with one month having passed. I know this because it was also the year of my birth.'

What era could Gildas be referring to? The answer is provided by Bede in the *Historia Ecclesiastica*. Bede was familiar with Gildas' *De Excidio*, for in one passage he writes: 'Among other most wicked actions, not to be expressed, which their own historian, Gildas, mournfully takes notice of, they added this – that they never preached the faith to the Saxons.' Bede even quotes Gildas word for word on occasions. In similar fashion to Gildas, Bede talks of: '. . . the siege of Badon Hill, when they [the Britons] made no small slaughter of those invaders about forty-four years after their arrival in England'.

These invaders, explains Bede, were the Anglo-Saxons. Although it is clear that Bede is quoting Gildas in this passage, he must also have been employing an additional source, as he identifies the era as Anglo-Saxon, which Gildas neglected to do. If this interpretation is correct, then, we must date the arrival of the Anglo-Saxons before we can fix the battle of Badon. To do that, we need to look at the fate of Roman Britain.

The early years of the fifth century heralded the end of the Roman Empire in the West. Although it struggled on for a few more decades, the imperial establishment had all but collapsed. Its demise began with a hotbed of trouble brewing amongst the Huns of central Asia. Driven at first by a series of disastrous crop failures, these fierce and warlike barbarians surged towards the western Goths, who were in turn driven from their own lands. Consequently, the vanquished Goths crossed the Danube and the Rhine, compelling other nations to migrate still further westwards. With Rome on the defensive, the barbarian hordes across Europe began to break through the frontiers of the empire. The Alans, from what is now Georgia, were driven onto the plains of Hungary, the home of the Sueves and the Vandals, causing all three tribes to push westwards. One barbarian chief, Alaric, king of the Visigoths, reached Italy in 401, and by 408 was laying siege to Rome itself. To meet this challenge, the Romans were compelled to withdraw troops from the colonial outpost of Britain.

With the Roman forces severely diminished, it was not long before problems arose on British soil. In the North the Picts of Scotland began a series of increasingly daring raids across Hadrian's Wall, and in 410 the British administration appealed for reinforcements from Emperor Honorius in Rome. But the emperor had troubles of his own, for in the same year Rome itself was sacked by Alaric's Visigoths. Not only did the British receive no reinforcements, but they also lost the legions they still possessed. With the empire in tatters, the Roman army totally withdrew from Britain.

Britain had been part of the empire for three and a half centuries, the fabric of its government long reliant on its military support. This had provided stability for longer than anyone could remember. Now, suddenly, it was gone and anarchy threatened the country. Every freeborn Briton had long been a Roman citizen, and few would have danced in jubilation on the White Cliffs of Dover as the last boat-load of soldiers disappeared over the horizon.

Precise records during this period of British history are few and far between, but an overall picture can be gleaned from St Germanus, the bishop of Auxerre in Burgundy, who visited Britain in 429 as an envoy of the Catholic Church. According to his biographer Constantius, although there were serious troubles in the North, an organised Roman way of life persisted in the numerous British towns. Even so, matters were growing progressively worse and over the following two decades central administration seems to have collapsed. In many parts of the country the Britons reverted to tribal allegiances, and regional warlords soon established themselves. With continual territorial squabbles, the island slid inexorably into anarchy and the Dark Ages.

In these troubled times few records were kept, and almost none have survived for us to examine today. The principal reason that so little is known of this period of British history is that the break from Rome removed Britain from the field of the Mediterranean writers from whom we acquire much of our earlier information. It is, therefore, far from certain exactly what took place during the third decade of the fifth century, the key historical sources being limited to Gildas, Bede, Nennius and the various incarnations of the *Anglo-Saxon Chronicle*. Although recorded history is imprecise, the basic picture appears to be that the North was suffering repeated incursions from the Picts, while the West was being invaded by the Irish. But the greatest problem for the majority of the Britons was the struggle for regional supremacy between their own native chieftains. It was upon this fragmented country that the Anglo-Saxons stamped their indelible mark.

As a result of the attack by the Huns on the Goths, there were mass migrations westwards right across the European continent in an unprecedented domino effect which continued until Attila, the king of the Huns, was ultimately defeated by a joint Roman/Visigoth army at Chalons sur Marne (in Gaul) in 451. As a result of this general move westwards, coastal dwellers from what is now part of Denmark and North Germany began to cross the Channel to settle in eastern Britain. These people were of mixed tribal groupings, Jutes, Angles and Saxons, later collectively called the Anglo-Saxons, or just Saxons. It appears that rather than attempt to repel these unwelcome migrants, many of the British chieftains began to enlist their services as mercenaries. Payment included land on which they could settle.

From what can be gathered from all the historical sources, by the mid-fifth century one British chieftain organised a massive influx of Germanic and Scandinavian mercenaries, settling entire tribes and their families in parts of the South-East. A large part of Britain came under his control. The identity of this man, and his precise status, is something of a mystery, although it seems that in some respects he could be considered to be the British equivalent of Attila the Hun.

Gildas blames this leader for the eventual ruin of Britain but fails to name him, referring to him only as the *superbus tyrannus*, the 'proud tyrant'. Bede, on the other hand, calls him Vertigernus, while Nennius and the *Chronicle* use the name Vortigern. This is unlikely to have been his true name; rather it was a title of some sort, which seems to have been derived from the Latin word *vertifernus*, meaning 'overlord'.

Whatever his real name was, it appears that for sometime, Vortigern was virtually the absolute ruler of Britain, suppressing his fellow chieftains and repelling the Picts and the Irish.

The reason that Gildas blames the 'proud tyrant' for the ruin of Britain is that it was on his initiative that the Anglo-Saxons, who eventually conquered all England, were first invited to Britain to fight as mercenaries. Both Gildas and Bede recount how the first of the Saxons arrived on British soil in three boat-loads. This is certainly an oversimplification, for archaeological evidence indicates that these people had been settling in England for some time, the Britons almost certainly having enlisted their help in the past in an ad hoc manner. However, it would appear that the three boat-loads were the first to be deliberately invited as reinforcements from abroad, and to avoid confusion, the term 'Saxon advent' is usually applied to this particular event. As Bede himself took the Saxon advent as the first arrival of the Anglo-Saxons, the dating of the advent is crucial in the dating of Badon.

According to Bede's *Historia Ecclesiastica* the advent occurred as follows:

'In the year of the Lord 449, Martian being made [Roman] emperor with Valentinian, and the forty-sixth from Augustus, ruled the empire for seven years. Then the nation of the Angles, or Saxons, being invited by the aforesaid king [Vertigernus], arrived in Britain.'

Is Bede accurate in his dating of the Saxon advent? The picture is confusing, and different dates can be derived from the *Annales Cambriae* and Nennius. This confusion seems to have arisen as a result of an original ambiguity concerning the date of a specific British plea for help mentioned by Gildas. According to him, some years after the Romans left Britain, events took such a turn for the worse that:

'The miserable remnants sent off a letter again, this time to the Roman commander Agitius in the following terms: "To Agitius, thrice consul: the groans of the British". Further on came the complaint: "The barbarians push us back to the sea and the sea pushes us back to the barbarians; between these two kinds of death, we are either drowned or slaughtered". But they got no help in return.'

The reference to this letter is very important, as it is a rare dateable event from the narrative of Gildas. Although Gildas calls the Roman commander Agitius, he is actually referring to an officer named Aetius, who was consul in Gaul. This conclusion can be drawn not only from the similarity of the two names, but also from the reference to 'thrice consul'; Aetius was the only man to acquire a third consulship (other than an emperor) for over 300 years. As his third term began in 446, and the fourth in 453, the plea for help must have occurred at some point between these two years.

So exactly how long after this appeal was the Saxon advent? The events that follow the Aetius letter are described by Gildas:

> 'Meanwhile as the British feebly wandered, a dreadful and notorious famine gripped them, forcing many of them to give up without delay to their bloody plunders, merely to get a scrap of food to revive them. Not so others: they kept fighting back, basing themselves on the mountains, caves, heaths and thorny thickets. Their enemies had been plundering their land for many years; now for the first time they inflicted a massacre on them. . . .' [With the Britons now on the offensive] 'the impudent Irish pirates returned home, though they were shortly to return, and for the first time the Picts in the far end of the island kept quiet from now on, though they occasionally carried out devastating raids of plunder. So in this period of truce the desolate people found their cruel scars healing over.'

This is probably the period of Vortigern, the about turn of events seemingly being a result of his ruthless efficiency. Following this there is a time of peace in which as Gildas says, 'the island was so flooded with abundance of goods that no previous age had known the like of it'. Unfortunately, this age of abundance did not last. Gildas tells us that 'a deadly plague swooped brutally on the stupid people, and in a short period laid low so many people, with no sword, that the living could not bury all the dead'.

The problems that this natural catastrophe created weakened the country to such an extent that the Pictish and Irish raids recommenced. The Britons were thus forced to seek external assistance by convening 'a council to decide the best and soundest way to counter the brutal and repeated invasions and plunderings'. Together with their leader, the 'proud tyrant', they decide to hire the Anglo-Saxons to fight for them as mercenaries.

These events which, in Gildas' account, separate the letter from the Saxon arrival must span at least a decade, perhaps two. This would allow time for the Britons to rally, probably under Vortigern, time for a period of wealth, and time for a plague to once again weaken the island. By this reckoning, the Saxon advent occurred sometime between 460 and 470. So why does Bede locate it in 449? We believe it is possible that Gildas inserted the passage on the Aetius letter in the wrong place in his text.

The evidence for this error comes from Gildas himself. It is possible to date the plague he refers to; an epidemic known from many foreign sources swept across the entire Roman world during the late 440s. As the plea to Aetius occurred during the consul's third term, between 446 and 453, it could not have been made a decade or two *before* the plague, as Gildas' order of events requires it to have been.

The letter to Aetius must therefore have been sent after the plague had weakened the country. Gildas tells us that the Pictish and Irish invasions recommenced at this time, and that the British were forced to seek external assistance. In all probability Gildas acquired a copy of the letter, which he could see referred to the invasions by the Picts and the Irish. Aware of the two periods during which the appeal may have been made, he wrongly attributed it to the former. It would seem, therefore, that the appeal to Aetius was made before deciding to invite in the Saxons, a decision that was forced upon the British after the consul refused them aid.

This appears to have been the conclusion eventually reached by Bede, even though he used Gildas as his source concerning the letter. If we compare his version of events with Gildas' passage, we can see that Bede is quoting him almost verbatim. In Bede's words:

'To him the wretched remains of the Britons sent a letter which began "To Aetius, thrice Consul, the groans of the Britons." And in the sequel of the letter they thus express their calamities: "The barbarians drive us to the sea; the sea drives us back to the barbarians: between them we are exposed to two sorts of death; we are either slain or drowned." Yet neither could all this procure any assistance from him.'

So after all this, are we any closer to a reliable date for the Saxon advent? From our analysis of Gildas we know it was soon after the plague in the late 440s. We have also reasoned that the appeal to Aetius must have been despatched at about the same time, no earlier than 446 when his third consulship began. So we arrive at a date between 446 and about 453, the year Aetius completed his term as consul. Finally there is the evidence of the *Anglo-Saxon Chronicle*, which actually gives the date of Vortigern's invitation to the Saxons as 449.

When all this evidence is combined, it would appear that Bede's dating is correct when he explains that the Saxon advent occurred in 449. So, from the second (and more convincing) interpretation of Gildas' oblique statement concerning the battle of Badon, by adding the forty-four years to our estimates we arrive at a date of 493. The further evidence of the *Anglo-Saxon Chronicle*, also dating the advent to 449, confirms that the most probable year in which the battle of Badon was fought is 493.

Summary

To derive an accurate dating of the Arthurian period we have dated the battle of Badon to the year 493. To do so, we have examined the arrival of the Anglo-Saxons and the background to this turbulent period.

1. Although the *Annales* record the battle of Badon in the year 518, the writer seems to have been consulting Irish records for that period and so may be inaccurate regarding events in Britain. We turn, therefore, to the more reliable Gildas. Although from his writing it is evident that the battle took place in the year of his birth, because of his awkward style of Latin it is uncertain whether he is saying that this was forty-four years earlier, or in the forty-fourth year of some specific era.

2. As Gildas wrote his work around 545, the first interpretation places the battle around 500. However, the more likely explanation is that the battle took place forty-four years after the Saxons were first invited into Britain, as mentioned by Bede.

3. After the Romans legions abandoned Britain in 410, central administration collapsed and in many parts of the country the Britons reverted to tribal allegiances. With continual squabbles over territorial control, the island slid into anarchy. Consequently, coastal dwellers from parts of Denmark and North Germany began

to cross the Channel to settle in Eastern Britain. These people, Jutes, Angles and Saxons were later collectively called the Anglo-Saxons, or just Saxons.

4. From cross-referencing the available historical sources, we deduce that by the mid-fifth century one British chieftain hired a great many Saxon mercenaries, settling entire tribes and their families in parts of the South-East. Gildas, Bede, Nennius and the *Anglo-Saxon Chronicle* all include this warlord, Nennius and the *Chronicle* referring to him as Vortigern, meaning 'overlord'.

5. Gildas does not date the arrival of these mercenaries, but Bede tells us that it took place in 449. This, together with the *Anglo-Saxon Chronicle* dating of the Saxon arrival as 449, means that the most feasible year for the battle of Badon is forty-four years later, 493.

8
The Anglo-Saxons

Having dated the battle of Badon, we must establish exactly where it occurred. To do so, we must reconstruct a picture of Britain as it was in the final decades of the fifth century, beginning with the major influx of Anglo-Saxons around 450.

The picture is somewhat confused, but it appears that in addition to the Saxon settlements in the South-East, the Angles began to arrive in large numbers, establishing a hold on the area of the Wash in Lincolnshire and Norfolk. Although in the ensuing decades they were able to establish their own colonies as far south as Suffolk, they may well originally have been recruited as reinforcements of Vortigern's northern army.

The archaeological evidence, in the form of pottery from Yorkshire, Lincolnshire and East Anglia, tells us that the newcomers began arriving around 450. These people, the Angles, exhibit a slightly different culture from the southern colonists, one that indicates that they were originally from Schleswig in the northernmost part of Germany. Bede gives this area as their homeland, a territory which was then called Angeln.

Although the colonists in the South-East of England are almost invariably described simply as Saxons, the very first of these settlers were the Jutes, from Jutland in Denmark. Bede tells us that it was the Jutes who initially established the kingdom of Kent, suggesting that the three boat-loads were not Saxons at all. Alternatively, they may have been the first of the Saxons, invited to settle in the Jute colony. Either way, in the following decades the influx of true Saxons from the estuary of the river Elbe (adjacent to Angeln) overwhelmed the Jutish population, the minority being forced to integrate with the Saxons within a very short period.

In many ways the Jutes, Angles and Saxons were closely related to one another, the area from which they originally came being no larger than modern Wales. For most purposes, therefore, the term Anglo-Saxon can safely be applied to the entire culture. Indeed the variations

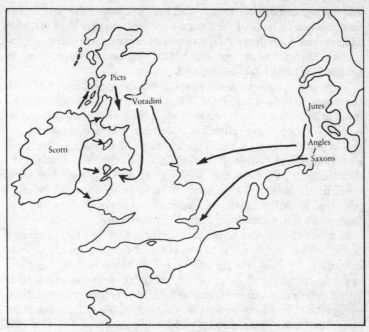

Invasions and Migrations in the Fifth Century

amongst them were tiny in comparison to the massive cultural gap between themselves and the Romanised British, many of whom were practising Christians. The Pagan newcomers had their own religious customs, which the majority of the Britons would probably have found abhorrent. In Roman terms the Britons were civilised, the Anglo-Saxons barbarians. With such cultural differences, problems were bound to arise.

Trouble began around 455, when the Saxon colonies in the South-East revolted against the British. There were doubtless many reasons for the rebellion, although Gildas informs us that it arose over a question of payment for the mercenaries. He provides no details, but does explain the severity of the insurgence, saying that cities were destroyed and British inhabitants killed, enslaved or forced to flee. Bede gives the same account, although he adds the names of the revolutionary leaders; two brothers called Hengist and Horsa.

The Angles in the North also joined the rebellion, for Bede tells us that having 'entered into league with the Picts, whom they had by this time repelled by force of their arms, they began to turn their weapons against their confederates'. The degree of organisation in the Anglian revolt is difficult to ascertain. It is fairly certain, however, that the British were completely unprepared.

The rebellion appears to have begun with the overthrow of a British contingent in the north of Kent. The *Anglo-Saxon Chronicle* includes this initial Saxon victory under 455, saying that it took place at Aegaeles Threp, most probably Aylesford. Good fortune did not persist for the Saxons, as the *Chronicle* tells us that one of their leaders, Horsa, died in the battle. Nonetheless, this Saxon victory marks the establishment of the independent kingdom of Kent, since Hengist is proclaimed its king. The battle is also mentioned by Nennius (although he calls it Episford), who says that not only Horsa but also Vortigern's son, Cateyrn (discussed later) perished.

As to the fate of Vortigern, Gildas gives us nothing to go on, except that in one passage he refers to him as the 'ill-fated tyrant'. Since Bede also offers no clues, we are left only with Nennius. Unfortunately, Nennius' 'heap' of all he could find includes almost as much from legend as it does from any written records he may have acquired. Even within these broad constraints he contradicts himself, in one place saying that after Essex, Sussex and Middlesex are conceded to the Saxons Vortigern dies a broken man, whereas elsewhere he is consumed by fire.

Many scholars have deduced from Nennius, together with the various surviving legendary accounts, that Vortigern's failed policy with the Saxons, plus the general unrest in a nation debilitated by plague, brought about his overthrow in civil war. One way or the other, he appears to have gone by 460. Nennius, for example, suggests that one Vitalinus was in charge after Vortigern's death, probably a member of Vortigern's family since Vortigern's grandfather bore the same name. Whoever was actually leading the Britons at this stage, they certainly suffered a massive defeat.

When the literary and archaeological evidence is pieced together, it seems that by the time the rampage eventually ceased, the Saxon influence extended westwards from Kent, through Sussex and into Hampshire, and northwards through Middlesex to Essex. The Anglian influence, on the other hand, stretched northwards from the Wash, through Lincolnshire and Humberside, and southwards to Saxon Essex. Remarkably, it also extended as far west as Warwickshire. Defending an area half the size of England must have placed considerable strain on the Anglo-Saxon forces, for it appears that they retreated soon after the successful routing of the Britons. This must have provided the British with a breathing space in which to organise their forces, since sometime around 465 they seem to have mustered a counteroffensive. Gildas says:

'After a time, when the cruel plunderers had gone home, God gave strength to the survivors. . . . Their leader was Ambrosius Aurelianus, a gentleman who perhaps alone of the Romans had survived the shock of this notable storm. . . . Under him the people regained their strength and challenged the victors to battle. The Lord assented and battle went their way.'

Of the same period Bede says:

'When the victorious army, having destroyed and dispersed the natives, had returned home to their settlements, the Britons began by degrees to take heart, and gather strength. . . . They had at that time for their leader, Ambrosius Aurelius, a modest man, who alone, by chance of the Roman nation had survived the storm. . . . Under him the Britons revived, and offering battle to the victors, by the help of God came off victorious.'

Once again, Bede is clearly using Gildas as his source, although he gives Ambrosius' second name as Aurelius and not Aurelianus. Unfortunately, there is nothing more concerning Ambrosius. Aside from the fact that he is the only Briton of the period whom Gildas names, he remains as mysterious as Arthur himself. Whether or not he actually overthrew Vortigern (or his successor) or simply succeeded him is uncertain. All we know is that he began to turn the tide on the Anglo- Saxons.

It is reasonable to assume that this occurred somewhere around 465, for the *Chronicle* lists no battles between 465 and 473. This must have been a time of consolidation on both sides, when defences were prepared and personnel organised; a preparation for the decisive struggle that followed, an all-out confrontation which culminated in the battle of Badon.

Unfortunately, everything we know of this all important period of conflict from Gildas is contained in just two lines:

'From then on victory went now to our countrymen, now to

their enemies. This lasted right up till the siege of Badon Hill.'

Bede cannot help us, for he simply paraphrases Gildas:

'From that day, sometimes the natives, and sometimes their enemies, prevailed, till the year of the siege of Badon Hill.'

We are left, therefore, with the *Chronicle* (which provides us only with the Anglo-Saxon side of the story) and Nennius, whose only mention of Badon is as the twelfth battle in his list of Arthur's battles (see Chapter Six).

It appears that once the war was underway it was the Saxons who went on the offensive, consolidating their hold over Middlesex and moving westwards. According to the *Chronicle*, in 473 Hengist and his son Oisc fought against the Britons and captured 'innumerable spoils', the enemy fleeing from them 'as they would from fire'. From the archaeological evidence, it seems that they consolidated their position in Surrey, pushing along the Thames Valley into Berkshire. However, the Britons seem to have held the advance at this stage and there appears to have been an uneasy stalemate in the South-East for the next decade. The war then shifts to a second front, in the East, against the Angles.

Here the fighting appears to have gone in favour of the Britons, and the Angles in the Warwickshire area seem to have fallen quickly under British control. The archaeological evidence indicates a continuity of British presence throughout this period, an undisturbed ceramic sequence together with uninterrupted burials. In Lindsey and Kesteven, respectively the northern and southern parts of Lincolnshire, archaeological discoveries indicate a survival of British power until the late sixth century. Many of the great dykes that dominated the south-western approaches to East Anglia were dug at this time to mark a fixed frontier. The linear earthwork known as King Lud's Bank, near Grantham in Lincolnshire, for example, may represent a British attempt to control any further invasion, as it blocked the ancient route way known as Sewestern Lane.

It was in the far North, however, that the fiercest fighting seems to have occurred, where Bede tells us that the Anglo-Saxons fought together with the Picts. Here the archaeological evidence clearly shows that the initial colonies failed to establish themselves before the Britons totally reoccupied the area.

It is during this period that Arthur first appears in Nennius' account. As we saw in Chapter Six, he tells us that:

'When Hengist was dead, Octha his son passed over from the northern part of Britain to the kingdom of the Kentishmen. Then Arthur fought against them in those days.'

When exactly was this? From the *Chronicle*, the death of Hengist is dateable to 488. But a problem arises concerning the historical existence of Octha. The *Chronicle* makes no mention of him, talking instead of Hengist's son Oisc. Octha *is* mentioned by Bede, who says that he was the son of Oisc, but the *Chronicle* disagrees, having Oisc succeeded by someone called Eormenric.

How reliable is the *Chronicle* on this point? In one surviving copy we are told that Oisc succeeded Hengist in 488, and reigned for 24 years until 512; in another that he reigned for 34 years until 522, so it appears that there was some confusion. Two possibilities might account for this contradiction. Either Oisc and Octha are the same person or, more likely, the chroniclers had no documentation relating to Octha's reign. If the latter is the case, perhaps these two men reigned one after the other (one until 512, the other from 512 to 522), accounting for the two separate dates in the *Chronicle*. If so, which man came after Hengist?

The dilemma appears to be solved by a ninth-century manuscript known as the *Cotton Vespasian*. Now in the British Library, it offers a list of the kings and bishops of the Dark Ages, including the names of Hengist, Oisc and Octha. It gives the order as Hengist, father of Octha, father of Oisc. Weighing the evidence, it seems that Hengist's son was Octha, as Nennius says.

Nennius says that Octha was in command of the Saxon forces in the North, which suggests a working alliance between the Angles and the Saxons at this time. This being the case, perhaps Octha was forced to retreat after defeat in the North, regardless of the death of his father. Either way, there seems to have been fighting in the North around or just prior to 488.

The most likely locations of Arthur's battles from Nennius' list seem to tally with what can be concluded from this assorted evidence. It would appear that the first five on the list, fought on the River Glein and in Linnuis, took place in Lincolnshire (on the River Glen and in Lindsey). This may have been the period in which the British reasserted control and the construction of the great dykes was undertaken. Following this there is a battle in the far North (in 'the Caledonian Wood'), presumably against the Picts and their Angle allies. Then follows the eighth battle, a particularly important victory judging from the fact that 'the pagans were put to flight on that day and there was a great slaughter upon them'. This, the battle of Castellum (Fort) Guinnion, could be almost anywhere, although it may well have been the final battle in the North, possibly forcing Octha and his Saxon expeditionary force to return home.

This eastern and northern stage of the war may well have been the period of which William of Malmesbury wrote, when Arthur fought against the Angles. However, it is the ensuing period of the conflict which is most confusing; the period in which Ambrosius appears to have been succeeded by Arthur himself as the leader of the British forces.

We have no way of knowing what really happened to Ambrosius, as his demise is not recorded in any surviving documents. However, Nennius provides evidence of a civil conflict at this juncture, based on the possible locations of the following three battles. If the 'City of the Legion' is Caerleon in South Wales, it was certainly not against the Anglo-Saxons or the Picts. The same would apply even if the 'City of the Legion' was Chester in North-Central England. It may, therefore, represent an internal power struggle that arose after the death of Ambrosius, perhaps against the Vortigern family. Alternatively, Arthur may even have taken up arms against Ambrosius himself.

The fact that the eleventh battle took place on a mountain (called Agned) tends to rule out a conflict against the Saxons, since there are no mountains in South-East Britain. (The location of the battle of Agned is considered in Chapter Seventeen). The tenth battle is said to take place on the shore of a river (called Tribruit), which suggests a fairly wide estuary of some kind, perhaps the mouth of the River Severn, only a few miles south of Caerleon. If this conjecture is correct, then the time that Arthur spent in the Caerleon area may have been the original source of Geoffrey of Monmouth's statement that Arthur held his court in that city between campaigns.

This brings us to the battle of Badon itself, a battle fought sometime around the end of the fifth century, and one that was definitely against the Anglo-Saxons, as we know from Gildas. The battle marked a decisive defeat of the Saxons, resulting in a truce that was to last for more than half a century; in fact, right up until the time that Gildas was writing, as he tells us that after Badon, war with the Anglo-Saxons had ceased.

In the half century that followed Badon, until the time of Gildas' writing, Britain enjoyed a period free from external attack. Indeed, there is archaeological evidence of a reverse Anglo-Saxon migration; considerable numbers returned to the continent of Europe, uncertain, no doubt, of their precarious foothold in Britain. Several types of characteristic English Anglo-Saxon pottery have been discovered in parts of Germany, dating from the early to mid-sixth century, indicating that these regions received newcomers direct from Britain. Gildas also tells us that there was considerable civil strife amongst the Britons during this period, which he saw as heralding the ultimate ruin of Britain. Bede, less vehement than Gildas, expresses it more lucidly:

'In the meantime, in Britain, there was some respite from foreign, but not civil war. There still remained the ruins of cities destroyed by the enemy, and abandoned; and the natives, who had escaped the enemy, now fought against each other.'

Unfortunately for the Britons, Gildas was correct in his assessment of the situation; their new superiority over the Anglo-Saxons was not to last. Soon after 550 the Saxons were again pushing westwards, opening with a victory at a battle near Salisbury. It was not long before what is now Buckinghamshire was overwhelmed, and in 577 the Britons in the South-West were cut off from the rest of Britain following a Saxon triumph at the battle of Dyrham, when Bath, Cirencester and Gloucester were lost. For a time, the Britons appear to have struggled on in the Somerset marshlands, but in 614 the Saxons moved into Devon and by 682 were in effective control of the entire South-West peninsular, apart from Cornwall (which remained independent until 926).

Broadly speaking, south of the Thames the invaders were predominantly Saxons, while to the north they were Angles. In the latter areas, the Midlands and the North of England, the Angles were on the move westwards slightly later than the Saxons, around the beginning of the seventh century. In the far North, the powerful kingdom of Northumbria soon grew from the smaller Anglian kingdoms of Bernicia and Deira. In the eighth century, however, Northumbria was eclipsed by the central English kingdom of Mercia, which rose to prominence under its famous leader Offa, who pushed the remaining Britons back into the Welsh mountains. The final Anglo-Saxon phase was the growth of the Saxon kingdom of Wessex, which first achieved prominence under Alfred the Great in the ninth century. It was his successor, Athelstan, who effectively united all the Anglo-Saxons into a single kingdom around 927. This large Anglo-Saxon nation, first called Angelcynn and then Englaland, came eventually to be known as England.

The native British were gradually driven from most of England and reduced to three remnants of Celtic civilisation: Wales, Cornwall and the North-West, while others fled across the Channel and settled in Brittany. Ultimately, even Cornwall and the North-West were conceded to the Anglo-Saxons, leaving only the area we now call Wales as the surviving homeland of the native Britons. The Anglo-Saxons gained so much control over what is now England that they began to refer to the native Britons as 'Welsh', deriving from the Saxon word *weala*, meaning foreigners. The Britons, on the other hand, began to call themselves *cymru*, meaning 'fellow countrymen'. From the tenth century onwards it was no longer a matter of Anglo-Saxon and native Britain, but two separate countries, England and Wales.

It was this division that enabled the stories of King Arthur to survive primarily in Wales and Cornwall. This could explain why the *Annales Cambriae* (the 'Annals of Wales') mention Arthur, while the English *Anglo-Saxon Chronicle* does not, and why the Welsh monk Nennius makes reference to him, whereas he is omitted from the work of the English monk Bede. Certainly it is in the areas of Cornwall and Wales that the folklore of King Arthur is most evident, where his name and exploits appear to have survived until the period of the medieval Romancers. This could well explain why Geoffrey of Monmouth places Arthur's birth and death in Cornwall and his court in Wales.

The battle of Badon, then, at the end of the fifth century, was the last great British victory over the Anglo-Saxon forces, one which led to a temporary period of British ascendancy before the Anglo-Saxons recommenced their piecemeal conquest of the whole of England. Badon, as we have shown, is an essential element in the hunt for the historical Arthur; the problem is to discover where the battle of Badon was fought and against whom. The evidence points towards any of three Saxon kingdoms: Kent, Sussex or Wessex, and these we will investigate in the next chapter.

Summary

We have reconstructed a picture of Britain as it was in the final decades of the fifth century, to allow informed speculation on the location of Badon. In this period the native British and invading Anglo-Saxons were battling for control of the island.

1. The Anglo-Saxons who first arrived around 449 were very different from the Romanised Britons, many of whom were practising Christians. The Pagan newcomers had their own religious customs that the majority of the Britons would probably have found abhorrent. In Roman terms, the Britons were civilised, the Anglo-Saxons barbarians. With such cultural differences, problems were bound to arise.

2. From the *Anglo-Saxon Chronicle* we learn that trouble began in 455, when the Saxon colonies in the South-East went into revolt. There were probably many reasons for the rebellion, although Gildas informs us that it arose over a question of payment for the mercenaries. Although he provides no specific details, he says that cities were destroyed and the Britons were forced to retreat. Bede gives the same account, although he names one of the revolutionary leaders as Hengist, the warrior who, Nennius tells us, died when Arthur's leadership began.

3. Of the fate of Vortigern, Gildas and Bede say nothing. From Nennius, however, we gather that his failed policy with the Saxons brought about his overthrow in civil war. Whatever happened, by cross-referencing the various sources, we can deduce that he was no longer in power by 460.

4. When the literary and archaeological evidence is pieced together, it seems that by the time the rampage eventually ceased, the Saxon influence extended over much of South-East England. But within a few years there was stalemate, for the *Chronicle* lists no battles between 465 A.D. and 473 A.D. When fighting recommenced it was an even match for the next twenty years. From Gildas and Bede we learn that the man who led the Britons at this time was Ambrosius Aurelianus, the son of a Roman official.

5. William of Malmesbury records that Arthur had fought alongside Ambrosius against the Angles, who we know from the archaeological evidence occupied the northern part of East England. From Nennius we learn that Arthur fought against the

Saxons when Hengist died and Hengist's son Octha retreated from the North. As the *Chronicle* places the death of Hengist in 488, it seems that this is when Arthur took over the leadership of the British forces from Ambrosius.

6. This brings us to the battle of Badon, a decisive defeat of the Saxons resulting in a truce that was to last for more than half a century; right up until the time that Gildas was writing, as he tells us that after Badon war with the Anglo-Saxons had ceased. Unfortunately, soon after 550 the Saxons were again pushing westwards and the Britons were eventually divided and forced into Wales and Cornwall. The large Anglo-Saxon nation that resulted was eventually called England and the Britons, whom the Saxons referred to as *weala* (meaning 'foreigners'), became known as the Welsh.

9

The Battle of Badon

The first and most obvious kingdom that the British might have fought against at Badon is Kent, since its king, Octha, is mentioned by Nennius. Unfortunately, apart from what Nennius tells us, there is nothing substantial to go on concerning Octha, or his kingdom, a decade either side of the year 500. From the archaeological evidence, however, the kingdom of Kent appears to have suffered defeat during this period. Archaeologists can pinpoint the locations of particular tribal groups from the pottery they leave behind, as each culture created individual ceramic styles. The pottery can be dated according to its exact position in the layers of soil and other material accumulated at a site. The changes in the types of pottery found are called ceramic sequences. In the areas of Essex, Hertfordshire and much of Buckinghamshire, there is a break in the ceramic sequences of the Saxons, indicating that they withdrew into Middlesex, Surrey and Kent around the turn of the century.

Nonetheless, prior to this time there was a considerable build up of Saxon influence in the South of England, a significant increase in manpower that began originally in 477. According to the *Anglo-Saxon Chronicle*, that year saw the arrival of a new wave of Saxon warriors who landed in strength at a place called Cymenesora, probably the Selsey Peninsular just to the east of Portsmouth. Led by the warrior Aelle, they quickly overpowered the Britons in the district, forcing them to flee. In 485, the *Chronicle* again records Aelle defeating the Britons, this time at the River Mearcredesburna (possibly the Alun). Thereafter, Aelle seems to have gone from strength to strength until 491, when he besieged the fort at Anderida (modern Pevensey). During this battle, the *Chronicle* tells us, his men slaughtered all those who had taken shelter within its walls, a massacre that marked the final defeat of the British in the area, and saw the establishment of the Saxon kingdom of Sussex (South Saxons). Aelle had now reached the easternmost limits of his campaign, for he was now sharing borders with Octha's kingdom of Kent.

What happened next is unknown, although Bede tell us that Aelle became the first high king of Saxon-occupied Britain; a position the *Chronicle* refers to as *bretwalda*, meaning 'wide ruler'. The term may well infer that he was the senior partner in an alliance with the kingdom of Kent.

Unfortunately for Aelle, his kingdom did not survive for long. The literary and archaeological evidence clearly shows the virtual annihilation of Saxon Sussex. The *Chronicle* makes no further reference to Sussex, or its kings, for another one and a half centuries, while archaeology has discovered no Saxon burials in the area between the late fifth and sixth centuries.

This reversal of Saxon Sussex, together with the withdrawal of Octha's Kentish Saxons from the Thames Valley, can only be explained by a major British offensive sometime during the 490s, an offensive which tallies completely with what Gildas tells us of the battle of Badon: the Saxons on the offensive until 491, Aelle establishing himself as chief Saxon warlord, and an eclipse of at least half the Saxon South-East within a few years. A major decisive battle fought sometime in the mid-490s fits perfectly.

However, an anomaly occurs in the closing years of the fifth century; a new Saxon influx that hardly seems possible so soon after a major British victory, and which forms the only feasible argument against the battle of Badon being fought before the turn of the century.

According to the *Chronicle*, in 495 a new warlord named Cerdic arrived in Britain. Landing near Southampton, Cerdic and his warriors fought a series of successful battles in a fan-shaped movement towards Salisbury. Reinforcements from the Continent arrived over the next few years, and by 508 they had defeated the British king Natanleod and seem to have established control over an area around the size of modern Hampshire. The Saxon command of this area appears to have been considerable, for the *Chronicle* records a further group of settlers arriving in 514.

In 519, a final battle was fought to establish the kingdom of Wessex (West Saxons) at a place called Certicesford, a few miles south of Salisbury on the River Avon, which can safely be identified as Charford, since the name appears in Norman times as Cerdeford, meaning Cerdic's Ford. Here the New Forest Heath gave way to the open Chalk Downs of Wiltshire, indicating that the Saxon forces lacked sufficient strength to confront the British in the open. It seems, therefore, that both the northern and western boundaries of Cerdic's Wessex were roughly the natural borders which now exist between

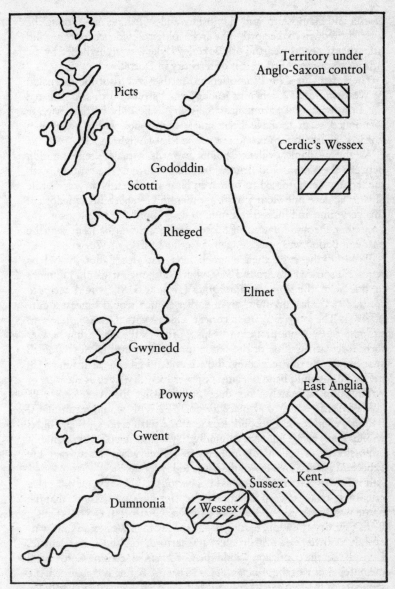

Britain at the Time of Badon

Dorset and Hampshire, and Hampshire and Wiltshire; the Avon to the west, the Downs to the north. The archaeological evidence for this stand off is that the nearby earthwork Bokerley Dyke was strengthened by the Britons to prevent further loss of territory in Dorset.

Thereafter, the *Chronicle* offers no further record of the extension of Wessex until 552, when its leader Cynric struck north and defeated the Britons at Old Sarum near Salisbury. The only battles that are mentioned seem to have been minor skirmishes within their own borders, apart from the conquest of the Isle of Wight in 530.

As the available evidence points towards a major confrontation between the Saxons and Britons around the turn of the century, with the Saxons being forced to retreat in large numbers, how was Cerdic able to achieve one victory after another and establish his kingdom at this very time and indeed continue to do so until 519? Perhaps it was only *after* the annihilation of Sussex and the defeat of Kent that the battle of Badon was fought, against Cerdic's forces of Wessex.

If this is the case, then a much later date for Badon would be required: somewhere around 520, which, although it would fall more in line with the *Annales Cambriae* (around 518), would seem to contradict Gildas' account, given earlier (which would suggest a date of 493). The only way to reconcile Gildas with the *Annales* is to propose a *third* interpretation of his words, to the effect that he was forty-three at the time of the battle (one month into his forty-fourth year of life). By this reckoning, if the battle did take place around 518, then Gildas would be in his late sixties or early seventies at the time of writing. Unfortunately, this does not fit what the *Annales* say of Gildas' death, which they place around 572. This would mean that if Badon was in the late second decade of the sixth century, then Gildas would have to be almost a hundred when he died. Although not impossible, this was highly unlikely at a time when the average life expectancy was much lower than it is today.

If we are to place Badon in this later period i.e. 518–520, we must also attempt to read between the lines of the *Chronicle*, and assume that the battle was fought around the same time as Charford (i.e. 519). Thus a British victory at Badon, halting the advance of the Wessex Saxons, was rapidly followed by a British defeat at Charford, resulting in a stalemate. Considering the confusion within the *Chronicle* concerning Cerdic, and the unreliability of the *Annales* as far as precise dating is concerned, the sequence of the two events could even have been reversed: a victory for the Saxons at Charford followed by defeat at Badon.

If Cerdic's forces were able to push just a few miles to the west of the

Avon, they could have established an excellent strategic position at the hill-fort known as Badbury Rings, a major contender for the site of Badon. A possible explanation of the battle of Badon in this scenario is that Cerdic may have overrun this British outpost and later Arthur retook it, forcing Cerdic to retreat beyond the Avon; a renewed offensive by the British at Charford a few years later failed, and then both sides dug in. Alternatively, Badbury hill-fort may have been an important British stronghold that survived the siege of Cerdic who, suffering such a damning defeat, was forced to withdraw, perhaps even dying in the battle.

After a consideration of this mass of confusing, and at times conflicting material, what conclusions can sensibly be drawn regarding the battle of Badon, its date, the location and the likely identity of the Saxon leader who fought there? Although the argument for Cerdic as leader of the Saxon forces at the battle of Badon around 520 tallies with the account given in the *Annales Cambriae*, it conflicts with all the other evidence:

1. There is archaeological and historical evidence showing that military activity halted, apart from in Hampshire, by the turn of the century.

2. By 500 the kingdom of Kent suffered a major setback, while the kingdom of Sussex virtually ceased to exist, until it was established again well over a century later.

3. Both Aelle of Sussex and Octha of Kent posed a very real threat, far greater than the newly arrived Cerdic who was only marauding in an area of no strategic significance.

The evidence weighs against Cerdic, but he does nevertheless present something of a mystery, landing at the time of Badon (if we accept a date of around 493 for Badon) and achieving a series of military victories. But we must remember that it is not known how many British kingdoms were actually allied to Ambrosius or Arthur. Perhaps the district of Hampshire was not included, and it could be that Cerdic landed there at a time when the principal protagonists in the struggle for Britain were busily engaged fighting one another elsewhere.

All points considered, the battle of Badon appears to have been fought against a Sussex/Kent alliance, indicating a possible strategic position in the Swindon area, which was about as far as the advancing Saxon forces had reached. If so, then a possible site for the battle of Badon could be Liddington Castle, a prominent Iron Age hill-fort not far from Swindon, overlooking the village of Badbury. It is one of many such hill-forts reoccupied during this time, and lies in a central position between the main Anglo-Saxon settlements (as they existed in the 490s), and the British areas controlled by the cities of Gloucester, Cirencester and Bath. Moreover, it stands on a major trading route junction of the period, at the intersection of the Roman road, Ermine Street, running to the south, and the ancient Ridgeway, cutting right across Central England.

Unfortunately, there is a major stumbling block in the case for Liddington Castle. As with Badbury Rings, the argument is reliant on the name similarity between the village of Badbury and the word Badon. There are, in fact, over half a dozen places still called Badbury in Britain today, their names deriving from the Old English *Baddanbyrig* or *Baddanburg*, meaning the 'fort of Badda'. Since Badda is a Saxon name, probably a god or hero, it follows that these sites were so named by the Saxons. It is difficult to imagine Gildas, a native Briton writing within living memory of Badon, referring to the battle site by the name the foreigners used.

If then, we discount 'Bad' place names derived from Saxon antecedents, could there be a British source for this important element? In the British tongue, the name may not have been pronounced Badon at all, but Bathon. Many words in the British language, which later evolved into modern Welsh, employed the syllable *th*. The Roman alphabet, in which English is still written today, had no single letter for this sound; although we now use the combined letters T and H, this is a comparatively recent development. As late as the Middle Ages, English writers employed a variant of the letter Y for the *th* sound, resulting in today's common misconception that our ancestors said 'Ye' for 'the', pronouncing it 'Yee'. The truth is that 'the' was always pronounced with a TH and not with a Y. In the Dark Ages, however, there was no standard way of conveying TH in writing; some Latin writers used the letters T and H, while others used the Greek letter *Theta*, (θ) which is pronounced 'th', but which has no Latin equivalent.

The problem is further compounded by a lack of standardised pronunciation. With certain place names and some personal names, the *th* syllable was pronounced with a different stress. To distinguish between these sounds, scribes would often employ a double D for 'th'; this practice has survived to this day in modern Welsh: the county of Gwynedd is pronounced as Gwyne*th*, and the village of Beddgelert as Be*th*gelert. To make things worse, writers sometimes dropped the double D, even when 'th' was meant, in favour of a single D. If this were the case with Badon, it would have been pronounced Ba*th*on. Following this argument and seeking modern names which are similar to Ba*th*on in the search for the battle site, we turn to the city of Bath.

The city, called by the Romans *Aquae Sulis* (meaning 'The Waters of Sul'), was eventually named Bath by the English. Although it is believed that they named the city after the Roman baths still to be seen there, Bath may simply have been a shortening of the British name Bathon. It is illuminating that when the *Anglo-Saxon Chronicle* talks of the capture of Bath in 577, it calls it Badanceaster, the 'City of Badan'. Perhaps the letter D is being used here for the *th* syllable; perhaps the name was pronounced as it is spelt. Either way, the fact that the city of Bath is referred to in the *Chronicle* as Badanceaster makes it a candidate for the battle site of Badon.

If the battle of Badon was fought somewhere in the vicinity of Bath, it would mean that the Saxons had reached a position some thirty miles further west than Liddington Castle. If so, the British would have been in serious trouble, since the Saxons would then have been less than fifteen miles from the Bristol Channel, thus threatening to cut the entire British nation in two. This may explain why the battle of Badon was so crucial, for the whole future of the country was at stake.

Bath is also precisely where Geoffrey of Monmouth tells us that Arthur fought his most celebrated battle. If this is not mere guesswork, what was the source of Geoffrey's information? Nennius, it seems. In the *Historia Brittonum* we find persuasive evidence that the battle of Badon was fought at Bath. As well as citing it in his list of Arthur's battles, Nennius mentions Badon elsewhere in his writings, this time giving us two vital clues to its location.

In the list of 'Marvels', at the end of Nennius' work, he tells us of a wonder of Britain which is a 'hot lake, where the baths of Badon are, in the country of the Hwicce'. These baths of Badon (in Nennius' original Latin, *balnea Badonis*) must be the Roman baths in the city of Bath. Although there may have been other Roman bath sites still visible during the time of Nennius, they are unlikely to have had a hot geothermal lake in the vicinity. The Roman baths of Bath, heated by natural springs of hot, subterranean water, were unique in Britain. Moreover, there is further evidence in Nennius' mention of 'the country of the Hwicce'. The Hwicce were an Anglo-Saxon tribe recorded in the 'Tribal Hidage', a Mercian document originally compiled about 661 which listed peoples subject to the Mercian king. This tells us that the kingdom of the Hwicce covered the Worcester and Gloucestershire areas, along with what is now part of the county of Avon, including the city of Bath.

From this assorted evidence we can conclude that the battle of Badon was almost certainly fought in the vicinity of Bath. But where? Although the *Annales Cambriae* refer only to the 'battle of Badon' (*bellum Badonis*), both Nennius and Gildas are more specific. Nennius tells us of the battle 'on Mount Badon' (*bellum in monte Badonis*), while Gildas talks of the 'siege of Mount Badon' (*obsessionis Badonici montis*). These references to a mount, together with the reference by Gildas to a siege, imply that the battle was fought for the possession of a hill-top site, probably one of the hill-forts that were reoccupied at this time. If Badon was a hill-fort in the Bath area, vital for control of the city, then the most likely contender would be the huge triangular hill-fort on Little Solsbury Hill, overlooking the city just to the north-east. Indeed, excavations have shown that this fort was refortified by the British during the late fifth century.

It seems therefore that at Bath the advancing Saxon forces failed to take the hill-fort, and during the resultant siege a counterattack by the British succeeded in routing the enemy. With the Saxon superiority broken, the way was open for a massive counter thrust into the South-East. Aelle may have been the Saxon commander at Badon, since Bede asserts that he was the 'high king' of Saxon Britain. Conversely, as the *Chronicle* seems to have excluded all mention of Octha, it could well have been him; perhaps the Saxon people had chosen to forget the name of the man who had led their army into the most damaging defeat of the entire era.

Summary

The location of Badon and its principal protagonists have long remained a mystery. We have investigated the historical evidence for Badon to determine that the battle was almost certainly fought near the city of Bath, against an Anglo-Saxon alliance, led by Octha, Aelle, or both.

1. From the archaeological evidence, the Saxon kingdom of

Artist's impression of fifth-century Viroconium, the Dark Age capital of Powys. The real 'Camelot'.

The ruins of Viroconium.

Viroconium, the underfloor heating system.

Viroconium, the baths complex.

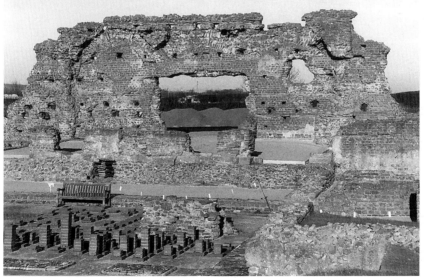

The 'Old Work' at Viroconium.

Reconstructed Roman stockade at the Lunt, near Coventry. The defences of fifth-century Viroconium would have been similar in design.

Reconstructed garrison building at the Lunt, similar to those that once stood at Viroconium in the fifth century.

n illo tempore saxones inualescebant in
multitudine & crescebant inbrittannia·
Mortuo aut hengisto octha fili' ei' transi
uit de sinistrali parte brittannie ad reg
nu cantorii· & de ipso orti s' reges cantor·
  unc arthur pugnabat contra illos·
millis dieb; cu regib; brittonu· s; ipse dux erat
bellorii· Primu bellu fuit inostiu flumi
nis quod dicit' glein· sedm & teriu & qr
tu & quintu· sup aliud flumen quod
dicit' dubglas· q: inregione linnuis·
Sextu bellum sup flumen quod uoca
e bassas· Septimu   fuit bellu
in silua celidonis· id: cat coit celidon·
Octauum fuit bellu incastello guinni
on· Inquo arthur portauit imagine
sce marie ppetue uirginis sup hume
ros suos· & pagani uersi s' infuga in
illo die· & cedes magna fuit sup illos
p uirtutem dni nri ihu xpi & p uirtute
sce marie uirginis genitricis ei? Nonu
bellu gestu: inurbe legionis· Decimu
gessit bellu inlitore fluminis· quod
uocat' tribruit· Vndecimu factu:
bellu inmonte qui dicit' agned· Duo
decimu fuit bellu inmonte badonis·
inquo corruer inuno die n genti sexa
ginta uiri de uno impetu arthur·

The earliest mention of Arthur, in Nennius' *Historia Brittonum* now in
the British Library.

The Berth near Baschurch in Shropshire, the sixth-century burial site of the kings of Powys and the real King Arthur.

The ramparts of the Berth.

The sacred enclosure. In the sixth century, the causeway (right foreground to middle-ground) would have provided the only access across the mere surrounding the Berth.

Berth Pool, where the real 'Excalibur' may have been cast as a sixth-century votive offering.

The Wrekin. The Iron Age hill-fort at its summit was probably reoccupied as the capital of Powys when Viroconium was abandoned around 520 A.D.

The Pillar of Eliseg in Valle Crucis, Llangollen, North Wales, on which a ninth-century inscription recorded the descent of the rulers of Powys from the British king Vortigern.

Kent, ruled by Octha, must have suffered defeat around the year 500, as there is a break in the sequence of Saxon ceramics, indicating a withdrawal from territory occupied in South-Central England.

2. According to the *Chronicle*, the Saxon kingdom of Sussex was founded in 477, when Saxon warriors landed near Portsmouth. Led by the warrior Aelle, they quickly overpowered the Britons in the district and established a power base. However, Sussex did not survive for long. The *Chronicle* makes no further mention of the kingdom or its kings after 491, until it was re-established over a century later. Additionally, archaeology has discovered no Saxon burials in the area between the late fifth and late sixth centuries.

3. The problems experienced by these two adjacent kingdoms can only be explained by a major British offensive sometime during the 490s. A crucial British victory sometime in the mid-490s tallies perfectly with what Gildas tells us of the battle of Badon.

4. Although a third warlord, Cerdic, is reported by the *Chronicle* as landing in the Hampshire area about the time of Badon, there is no archaeological evidence to suggest that his kingdom of Wessex had any real influence for another fifty years.

5. All the evidences considered, the battle of Badon appears to have been fought against a Sussex/Kent alliance (under the leadership of Octha, Aelle, or both) somewhere near the Bristol Channel, which according to the archaeological evidence is as far as the Saxons had pushed. As Bath is called Badanceaster, 'City of Badan', in the *Chronicle*, it is an excellent candidate for Badon. Not only is Bath precisely where Geoffrey of Monmouth tells us that Arthur fought his most celebrated battle, but Nennius's *Historia Brittonum* mentions the 'Baths of Badon' in a summary of British marvels at the end of his work. These are almost certainly the old Roman baths in the city of Bath.

6. As both Gildas and Nennius refer to the battle of 'Mount Badon', it must have been fought for the possession of a hill-fort. If the fort was vital for control of the city, then it was probably the huge triangular hill-fort on Little Solsbury Hill, overlooking the city just to the north-east. Indeed, excavations have shown that it was

occupied by the British during the late fifth century. The most plausible conclusion, therefore, is that in 493 the Saxon forces failed to defeat the British on Little Solsbury Hill and a counter-attack by Arthur drove the enemy back to the East.

10

Vortigern

We have so far investigated the state of the Anglo-Saxon kingdoms of the late fifth and early sixth centuries; but what of the Britons? If we are to uncover Arthur's origins, we must discover much more about the British and their leaders in the period leading up to the battle of Badon.

During Roman times, Hadrian's Wall divided the unconquered Picts of Scotland from the conquered Celtic tribes in England and Wales. There were around sixteen in all, each led by a chief or king. Following the usual Roman policy, these occupied tribal zones became Roman administrative districts called *civitates*. But once the Romans left, at the beginning of the fifth century, central government came under strain and regional control gradually reverted to the tribal chieftains. One of these chiefs, who seems to have been the most successful, was Vortigern.

Aside from Gildas, Bede and the *Annales Cambriae* (see below), the *Anglo-Saxon Chronicle* also records Vortigern as the leader of the British forces who fought Hengist and Horsa in 455. The only other inclusion of Vortigern in a Dark Age manuscript appears in the *Historia Brittonum* of Nennius. Here he is portrayed as reigning in some unspecified period after the end of Roman rule, when the Saxon brothers Hengist and Horsa land with three ships. Vortigern allows them to live on the isle of Thanet, and invites other Saxons to join them if they will aid his struggle against the Picts and the Irish who are harassing Britain. Ultimately, Vortigern is tricked by Hengist into arranging a conference, at which many of his nobles are massacred.

In the *Historia Brittonum* we are given a clue to the original province of Vortigern, since Nennius suggests that he is descended from 'Gloiu, who built a great city upon the banks of the River Severn that in British is called Caer Gloiu, in Saxon Gleucester'; in other words, Gloucester. This implies a connection with the Cornovii tribe, who occupied an extensive area in the West Midlands and East Wales. Since the Cornovii province became the kingdom of Powys soon after

Roman rule, Vortigern seems originally to have been the king of Powys, an excellent strategic position from which to gain control of Britain.

The most important Dark Age reference to Vortigern, which supports the conjecture that he ruled Powys, is an inscription on the Pillar of Eliseg, in Clwyd, North Wales. The Pillar of Eliseg is all that remains of an ancient stone cross standing in the Vale of Llangollen near the medieval abbey of Valle Crucis. Although the inscription is no longer visible, some of it was legible in 1696 when the Welsh antiquarian, Edward Lhuyd, translated what could then be discerned.

'Concenn son of Cattell, Cattell son of Brohcmail, Brohcmail son of Eliseg, Eliseg son of Guoillauc. Concenn, who is therefore great-grandson of Eliseg, erected this stone to his great grandfather Eliseg. Eliseg annexed the inheritance of Powys ... throughout nine [years] from the power of the English, which he made into a sword land by fire: whosoever shall read this hand inscribed stone, let him give a blessing on the soul of Eliseg: it is Concenn who ... with his hand ... to his own kingdom of Powys ... and which ... the mountain ... the monarchy Maximus ... of Britain ... Concenn, Pascent ... Maun, Annan: Britu moreover [was] the son of Vortigern whom Germanus blessed and whom Severa bore to him, the daughter of Maximus, the king, who killed the king of the Romans. ...'

In this inscription, Concenn commemorates the emancipating exploits of his great grandfather, proudly celebrating his line of descent from Vortigern himself. Concenn was the king of Powys, whose name appears in Dark Age Welsh genealogies under the Welsh spelling Cyngen. He is also named in the *Annales Cambriae*, where he is recorded as dying in Rome in 854. Although there is some speculation as to exactly when and why this cross was erected (it appears to be of Mercian design, from the late tenth or early eleventh century), it shows quite clearly that the rulers of Powys of the late Dark Ages considered themselves descendants of Vortigern, the founder of their kingdom.

Together with the evidence from Nennius, the inscription on the Pillar of Eliseg means that the kingdom of Powys is the most likely seat of Vortigern. However, the Pillar poses a problem, in that it suggests an earlier date for Vortigern than the bulk of evidence implies. The inscription states that Vortigern's wife, Severa, was the daughter of

Maximus. Maximus was a Roman officer who seized control of the Western Empire in the last quarter of the fourth century. To understand the implications of this reference, we need to look again at the later history of the Roman Empire.

In 376, Gratianus, emperor of the western half of the empire, ruled from Rome, ordered his main rival, Theodosius, to be executed on a charge of high treason. Gratianus was considered by many high ranking soldiers to be incompetent, and it was Theodosius they looked towards as his replacement. The only other threat to Gratianus came from one of his generals, Magnus Maximus, but not daring to risk another execution, the emperor played safe. He ensured that Maximus remained posted in command of the imperial forces on the far-off island of Britain.

Not long afterwards, Gratianus made one mistake too many and the army came close to revolt. By 383, the pot boiled over and Maximus was proclaimed emperor by the legions under his command. Taking his troops, he left Britain and sailed for Europe. He won the support of the legions in Gaul, conquered Italy and marched on Rome. Gratianus was soon assassinated and Maximus took his place.

The Eastern Empire, however, refused to recognise Maximus, instead proclaiming the son of Theodosius, also named Theodosius, as emperor. In the ensuing civil war, Maximus was killed and his armies defeated.

After the war the Western Empire was in tatters and Theodosius continued to rule from Constantinople. But there were many in the West who still regarded the family of Maximus as the rightful heirs to the imperial throne. Theodosius, on the other hand, did not perceive them as a threat, and not wishing to risk another campaign, took no action.

After the defeat of Maximus, his young daughters appear to have become imperial wards, so perhaps the marriage of one of them to the British king may have been contrived as a political manoeuvre. If Vortigern did become the late usurper's son-in-law, around the time of Maximus' death in 388, was he the same man who was fighting the Saxons in 455 as we read in Bede and the *Chronicle*?

The Pillar of Eliseg may thus hint towards an altogether different view of the early fifth century. The reign of Vortigern may have occurred much earlier than the evidence of Gildas, Bede and the *Chronicle* suggests; perhaps as early as the 420s, the period that falls in line with the *Annales Cambriae*.

A set of chronological computations, which act as a preface to the *Annales* themselves, say that:

> 'Vortigern held rule over Britain in the consulship of Theodosius and Valentinian. And in the fourth year of his reign the Saxons came to Britain in the consulship of Felix and Taurus, in the 400th year from the incarnation of Our Lord Jesus Christ.'

If Vortigern's reign began in the first consulship of Theodosius and Valentinian, which the Romans record as 425, then the fourth year of Vortigern's reign would have been 428, the recorded term of Felix and Taurus. The year 428, however, is 400 years from the traditional date of the Passion (the crucifixion) and not the Incarnation (the birth) of Jesus. (Due to an original miscalculation in the *Anno Domini* calendar, Christ was considered to have been born in 4 B.C.) Once again, this is an indication of the problems that arose though alternative systems of dating.

The answer to this riddle of Vortigern's particularly long reign may be provided by Nennius, who offers two basic versions of the demise of Vortigern. In one version, Nennius tells us that St Germanus attempted to convert the king to Catholicism and separate him from an illicit union with his daughter, until:

> 'Vortigern withdrew in disgrace to the fortress of Vortigern, which is in the country of the Demetians, on the river Teifi. Saint Germanus followed him, as before, and stayed there fasting with all his clergy for three days and as many nights to achieve his end, and on the fourth night about midnight, the whole fortress was suddenly destroyed by fire sent from heaven, and the fire of heaven burned. Vortigern was destroyed with all who were with him, and all his wives.'

Reading between the lines, Vortigern appears to have died in some natural catastrophe which was perceived as an act of divine vengeance. After this passage, Nennius goes on to tell the reader that this is only one version of how Vortigern perished. He then relates a second account of the king's death.

> 'When he was hated for his sin, because he received the English people, by all men of his own nation, mighty and humble, slave and free, monk and layman, poor and great, he wandered from

place to place until at last his heart broke, and he died without honour.'

Since Nennius has included both accounts of Vortigern's death, it seems unlikely that he is attempting any kind of fabrication. Indeed, he admits he is simply including the different versions he discovered. It is therefore reasonable to assume that during the lifetime of Nennius two separate stories of Vortigern's demise existed, one suggesting that he died in some natural catastrophe, the other that he died in exile after being deposed.

A possible explanation for these two different tales is found elsewhere in the *Historia Brittonum*. Nennius tells us that:

'From the [beginning of the] reign of Vortigern to the quarrel between Vitalinus and Ambrosius are twelve years, which is Guoloppum, that is Cat Guoloph [the battle of Guoloph].'

In Nennius' genealogy of Vortigern's family, Vortigern's grand-father is also named Vitalinus, Moreover, Guoloph has been identified as the River Wallop in Shropshire, which falls within part of the kingdom of Powys. This may mean that Vitalinus was a member of the Vortigern family whom Ambrosius fought in order to seize power. If this occurred around 460, then Vortigern's reign must have begun in the late 440s.

Conversely, we have also evidence that Vortigern's reign *ended* in the late 440s. If, as Nennius describes, Vortigern died whilst Germanus was present in England, this must have been in 447, which is the year of the saint's second and final visit to Britain, according to Bede. But if Vortigern had died during Germanus' visit, he could not then have been alive for the Saxon revolt which occurred about 455. Apart from Nennius, both the *Chronicle* and Bede also insist that he was still in power. If someone called Vortigern was still on the throne at this later date, then he must have been a second Vortigern.

Nennius' conflicting accounts of Vortigern's death may be evidence of two different legends originally attached to two separate kings both bearing the same name or title. Perhaps later generations, hearing of the exploits of the 'overlord', assumed the term applied to one man. The theory of two Vortigerns is supported by another passage in Nennius, in which he describes Pascent as the son of 'Vortigern the Thin'. Since no such epithet is applied to anyone else named in the *Historia Brittonum*, the writer may have transcribed a section of some earlier work, now lost, in which there was an intention to distinguish this king from another of the same name. Additionally, Nennius' assertion that Vortigern withdrew to the 'fortress of Vortigern' further implies that the name was a dynastic title. So there may have been *two* Vortigerns, one who came to power in the mid-420s and a second in the late 440s. In other words, the Vortigern who fought the Saxons was successor to the man referred to as Vortigern on the Pillar of Eliseg.

If this is the case, we can deduce from the Pillar of Eliseg the name of the first Vortigern's successor: Britu, the grandson of Maximus, who was blessed by Germanus. If Germanus blessed or anointed him personally, then this would confirm that his (Britu's) reign commenced around 447 when Germanus was present in Britain, corresponding with Vortigern's death in one of Nennius' accounts. It could be argued, therefore, that Britu was the second Vortigern or 'overlord' of Britain.

Bearing in mind this line of argument, let us consider what Nennius tells us of Vortigern's family:

> 'He had three sons, whose names are Vortimer, who fought against the barbarians, as I have described above, the second Cateyrn: the third Pascent, who ruled in two countries called Builth and Gwerthrynion after his father's death by permission of Ambrosius, who was great king among all the kings of the British nation. A fourth son was Faustus, who was born to him by his daughter.'

Here Nennius gives the name Pascent, which also appears on the Pillar of Eliseg as a descendant of Vortigern. As Nennius includes a family name from the Vortigern dynasty, it lends credence to his list of Vortigern's sons. He fails to include Britu as a son of Vortigern; but the solution may lie in the name Vortimer, which was probably derived from the same word as Vortigern. As Vortigern meant 'overlord', then Vortimer may also have been a title, perhaps for the heir apparent or crown prince. Consequently, Vortimer may have been Britu's title before he succeeded his father to become the 'overlord', Vortigern.

Although Nennius includes the death of Vortimer *before* Vortigern's death, there is clear evidence elsewhere that the lives of the two men had been confused with one another. An entry in the *Anglo-Saxon Chronicle* for the year 455 states:

> 'In this year Hengist ... fought against King Vortigern

at a place which is called Egelesprep and his brother Horsa was slain.'

If we compare this with a passage from Nennius, which clearly includes the same battle in which Horsa died, we find an important discrepancy:

'Vortimer fought four keen battles against them. The first battle was on the river Darenth. The second battle was at the ford called Episford in their language, Rhyd yr afael in ours, and there fell Horsa.'

Here it is not Vortigern fighting the Saxons but Vortimer, implying that Nennius, the writer of the *Chronicle*, or their individual sources had indeed confused Vortigern and his son.

If there were *two* Vortigerns, which of Nennius' two accounts of Vortigern's death relates to which of the rulers? Since the Pillar of Eliseg implies that Germanus approved of Britu, he cannot have been the Vortigern who came into conflict with the saint and died in the fire.

Moreover, there is evidence from Nennius that Vortimer found favour with Germanus, which further supports the theory that Vortimer was Britu. In his narrative he tells us that before Vortimer died:

'He told his followers to set his tomb by the coast, in the port from which the English had departed, saying "I entrust it to you. Wherever else they may hold a British port or may have settled, they will never again live in this land." But they ignored his command and did not bury him where he had told them: for he is buried in Lincoln. But if they had kept his command, there is no doubt that they would have obtained whatever they wished through the prayers of Saint Germanus.'

Not only does this passage imply that Vortimer found favour with Germanus, but also that he was discredited in the eyes of his countrymen, who failed to carry out his burial wishes. This suggests that it was the *second* Vortigern who was deposed and died in disgrace, and so the first Vortigern must have died in the fire. This makes 447 the date of accession, as it is the only year when one of the rulers could have died being hounded by Germanus, while the other received his blessing.

Britu probably subsequently lost power by 459, as according to Nennius the struggle between Vitalinus and Ambrosius occurred twelve years after Vortigern (i.e. Vortigern II) began his reign. Perhaps after the Saxon revolt forced Britu's overthrow, Vitalinus assumed control until Ambrosius made his bid for power.

So what, in the light of our theory that there were two Vortigerns, are we to make of the specific mention in the *Annales* that the Saxons came to Britain in 428 during the reign of Vortigern? This must refer to the first Vortigern, but the concept of Saxons arriving in 428 is not inconsistent with Bede's statement that the Saxons were invited in 449, because the Saxons seem to have arrived in waves before the specific advent of 449 (the arrival of Hengist). As we have seen, the archaeological evidence suggests that the arrival of the Anglo-Saxons first began in the second quarter of the fifth century i.e. predating 449. The British warlords seem to have been deploying them as mercenaries well before the invitation to Hengist and his warriors. It is very likely, therefore, that both Vortigern and his successor had used them in their armies, although for the latter the policy backfired.

The sequence of events seems to be as follows: Vortigern I of the Cornovii founded the post-Roman kingdom of Powys in the 420s, and assumed control over a large area of the country by 425. He continued to reign until 447, dying in some catastrophe (seen as an omen) during the time of Germanus' second visit to Britain. His son Britu then ruled the island until his pact with the Saxons backfired and he was driven into exile. Another member of the Vortigern family, Vitalinus, may then have assumed control for a short time, until 459 when Ambrosius made his bid for power.

The allusion to a clash between the king and Germanus may hold an important clue to the religious climate of Britain during the first half of the fifth century. In the *Historia Brittonum*, Nennius relates how Vortigern had committed a major heresy in the eyes of Germanus, who 'preached at Vortigern, to convert him to his lord'. Although he is accused of incest with his daughter, there appears to be a much greater, but undisclosed, sin involved. Why was Germanus so opposed to Vortigern? The answer appears to be the reason for Germanus' visit itself, which was to combat the ecclesiastical heresy of Pelagianism.

Pelagianism takes its name from the priest Pelagius, a Briton who devised a humanistic doctrine in opposition to the established Church. Sometime around 380 Pelagius left Britain for Rome, where he came into conflict with the fundamental Catholic doctrine of St Augustine.

Although he disagreed with the Establishment on a number of issues, it was his teaching regarding mankind's personal responsibility for salvation that aroused the greatest anger, for he was denying the doctrine of original sin.

In some respects Pelagius was a fourth-century forerunner to Martin Luther, as his writings attack both the riches of the Church and its position as the State religion of the empire. In 416, the Church responded by proclaiming the teachings of Pelagius a heresy. Not only the Church but the State itself stood to suffer if such dangerous ideas took hold, as they were doing in Britain and Gaul. At this time Catholic Christianity was virtually all that was holding the empire together. Therefore, in 425, Emperor Honorius was persuaded by the pope to issue an imperial command to the Pelagian bishops of Gaul. They were told to renounce their heresy before the bishop of Arles within twenty days, or face the severest consequences.

Although the policy was successful elsewhere, the problem remained in the isle of Britain over which Honorius had no direct control. The rich and powerful bishop of Auxerre, Germanus, was thus despatched to combat Pelagianism in Britain. Prosper of Aquitaine, who dedicated himself to attacking Pelagianism, wrote of the year 429:

'The Pelagian Agricola, son of the Pelagian bishop Severianus, corrupts the churches of Britain by insinuating his doctrine. But at the suggestion of the deacon Palladius, Pope Celestine sends Germanus bishop of Auxerre as his representative, and after the confusion of the heretics guides the Britons to the Catholic faith.'

According to Germanus' biographer, Constantius of Lyon, the bishop's deputation to Britain was received in St Albans by a delegation of clergy from the city, who were soon reconverted. With the success of St Albans under his belt, Germanus moved on to preach across the country, converting not only the laity but also the troops. It would therefore seem inevitable that at some stage the saint came into conflict with the chief British warlord Vortigern who, in all probability, was sanctioning the Pelagian heresy. Unfortunately for Germanus, it was only a matter of time before the British Church reverted to Pelagianism and he was impelled to make a second visit in 447. On this occasion he had greater success, evidently persuading Britu to renounce Pelagianism. There is considerable evidence for a swing towards the Roman Church at this time; Bede, for example, tells us that the faith 'continued long after, pure and untainted'.

As we will see, this return to the Catholic Faith was not only instrumental in the downfall of the Vortigern dynasty, but also paved the way for a new and powerful leader: Ambrosius Aurelianus, the last of the Romans.

Summary

In order to discover Arthur's origins we must examine the British leaders who preceded him. It seems that for the half century from the Roman withdrawal (around 410) to the time of Ambrosius (around 460), Britain was ruled by one family: the Vortigerns, of which there were two, or possibly three, successive kings.

1. When the Roman legions left Britain at the beginning of the fifth century, central government came under strain, with regional control gradually reverting to the tribal chieftains. According to all the available sources, the most successful of these was Vortigern who became supreme ruler of Britain.

2. From the *Historia Brittonum* we discover Vortigern's original province. Since Nennius says he is descended from Gloiu, who founded the city of Gloucester, it was probably the kingdom of Powys which covered the West Midlands and Central Wales. Additionally, Nennius implies that Ambrosius eventually fought against Vortigern's authority in Shropshire, in the very heart of Powys. That Vortigern was the king of Powys is confirmed by the Pillar of Eliseg in Llangollen, North Wales. Erected about 850, an inscription on the pillar reveals that Vortigern actually founded the kingdom of Powys.

3. But when did Vortigern rule? In the *Annales Cambriae* we learn that the fourth year of his reign fell in the Roman consulship of Felix and Taurus. As this is known from accurate Roman records to have been 428, then Vortigern's reign began around 425. However, Nennius tells us that Ambrosius fought with Vitalinus (a member of the Vortigern family) twelve years after Vortigern came to power. As this could not have been much before 460 (the time of Ambrosius), Vortigern's reign must have begun in the 440s. Add Nennius' conflicting accounts of Vortigern's death and we have

evidence that two successive leaders bore the title Vortigern ('overlord').

4. The most compelling evidence for two Vortigerns is that in one of his accounts Nennius says Vortigern died while Saint Germanus was present in Britain. This must have been in 447, the year of the saint's second and final visit to Britain. Yet Nennius, the *Chronicle* and Bede all insist that Vortigern was alive to fight the Saxons in 455. If a Vortigern was ruling in 455 he must have been a second Vortigern. If the first Vortigern died, to be succeeded by the second in 447, then a precise date for Ambrosius's struggle for power is 459 (as Nennius says that it was twelve years after the start of Vortigern's reign).

5. The second Vortigern was probably Britu, who is shown to be Vortigern's successor on the Pillar of Eliseg. There is also evidence that Britu was Vortigern's son Vortimer. Nennius' account that the Saxon warrior Horsa died fighting Vortimer is contradicted by the *Anglo-Saxon Chronicle*, which states that he died fighting Vortigern. The name Vortimer, however, was probably a title for the heir apparent; as Vortigern meant 'overlord', the word Vortimer was probably of similar origin.

6. Nennius provides us with evidence of religious dispute in Vortigern's Britain. Although he fails to give the reason for a bitter clash between Vortigern and Germanus, it was almost certainly due to Pelagianism, a doctrine that opposed the established Church. As Germanus was sent to Britain to combat the Pelagian heresy, he would inevitably have come into conflict with Vortigern himself, just as Nennius describes.

7. The most likely events of the Vortigern era are that Vortigern himself founded the post-Roman kingdom of Powys in the 420s, and came to control a large part of the country by 425. He broke away from the Catholic Church and continued to reign until 447, when he died in a fire during Germanus' second visit. Britu then ruled Britain until the Saxon revolt of 455 forced his overthrow and he was driven into exile. Vitalinus may then have assumed control for a short time until 459, when Ambrosius made his bid for power.

11
Ambrosius

After half a century of Vortigern rule which had seen both the deleterious effects of the Saxon advent, and waves of internal strife brought about by the rise of Pelagianism and subsequent attempts to control it, Britain experienced a drastic change of leadership.

Sometime around 460, a new and altogether different type of leader appeared on the scene; a man who appears to have reorganised the country and turned the tide on the invading Saxons. He is someone who Gildas not only seems to have admired but, uncharacteristically, he even names. Although he only mentions him once, Gildas says:

> 'Their leader was Ambrosius Aurelianus, a gentleman who, perhaps alone of the Romans, had survived the shock of this notable storm: certainly his parents who had worn purple, were slain in it.'

Bede, who once again is paraphrasing Gildas, clarifies this passage, saying:

> 'They had at that time for their leader, Ambrosius Aurelius, a modest man, who alone, by chance, of the Roman nation had survived the storm, in which his parents, who were of the royal race, had perished.'

Other than Gildas and Bede no other surviving Dark Age manuscript includes him, apart from Nennius. Since Nennius' story of Ambrosius is clearly legend (see below), we have only these few remarks from Gildas and Bede with which to reconstruct a reliable picture.

Although it only amounts to a brief mention, Gildas' entry tells us something about Ambrosius, including that his parents wore purple. Since purple was the royal colour of the Roman emperors, this statement implies that he was a member of a high ranking family, as

Bede points out. We see that his parents died during the storm, which can be taken to mean the Saxon onslaught that Gildas previously referred to. Furthermore, since Gildas seems to have had some admiration for this 'gentleman', who was 'alone among the Romans', we can only assume that he stood for some alternative viewpoint to Vortigern the 'tyrant'.

In addition, many surviving medieval Welsh legends tell of a clash between Vortigern and Ambrosius, and although they do not constitute evidence in their own right, they do appear to have been in existence in some form at the time of Nennius (around 830). Nennius names Ambrosius as the main rival of Vortigern and includes a legend concerning their first meeting, which we paraphrase here.

In Nennius' story, Vortigern is attempting to construct an impregnable fortress high in the Welsh mountains in the kingdom of Gwynedd, following his defeat by the Saxons. However, the work is constantly disrupted by a strange series of disasters. The king summons his magicians, who advise him that in order to complete the work he must sacrifice a boy and sprinkle his blood on the site. Eventually, such a child is found, but in order to save himself the boy challenges Vortigern to tell him what lies beneath the foundations. When he cannot do so, the boy reveals a pool containing two dragons, one red and one white, which proceed to fight one another. Interpreting this mysterious omen, the boy tells Vortigern that the two creatures represent the Britons and the Saxons, and the victory of the red beast means that the Britons will eventually triumph. The king's admiration is assured when it is revealed that the boy's name is Ambrosius, the son of a Roman consul. At the end of the passage, Vortigern is persuaded to give Ambrosius authority over the western part of Britain.

What does this legend tell us? First, it clarifies what Gildas and Bede say about Ambrosius' royal family ties, since we are told that he is the son of a Roman consul. Second, it infers that Ambrosius was brought up in secret, being kept hidden from Vortigern for some reason. And third, that Ambrosius was to have sway over the western part of Britain. Does any of this correlate with what is known of the historical situation at the time?

To find a clue to the family to which Ambrosius belonged, we now return to the twelfth-century account of Geoffrey of Monmouth. According to Geoffrey, the father of Ambrosius was Constantine, a prince from the kingdom of Armorica in northern Gaul. In Geoffrey's account, Constantine is invited into Britain to help defend the country from marauding barbarians. After his mission is successfully accomplished he is rewarded by the Britons, who offer him the Crown. As we saw in Chapter Seven, Geoffrey's Constantine is probably based on the Roman pretender Constantine III (around 400). Although there is no evidence that Constantine III had sons called Uther or Ambrosius, he certainly had one called Constans, who at one stage became a monk, just as Geoffrey describes, and whom he calls Ambrosius' brother. To shed more light on Ambrosius we must therefore examine Constantine.

The instability throughout the Roman Empire during the first years of the fifth century brought about an inevitable backlash in Britain. During 407, the Roman officer Constantine was proclaimed emperor by the British legions, just as Maximus had been two decades earlier. Constantine, assuming the title of Constantine III, wasted no time in crossing the Channel to defeat the invading barbarians in eastern Gaul. At first Emperor Honorius did nothing, assuming that Constantine would be defeated. However, when Constantine went on to capture the city of Arles in modern Provence, the imperial government sent a Goth, Sarus, against him. After Sarus failed to defeat Constantine and returned to Italy, Constantine's son Constans occupied Spain, leaving his general Gerontius in charge.

It was then that Honorius, harassed by the Visigoth Alaric, promised to abdicate in favour of Constantine if he offered aid in the defence of Rome. Constantine agreed, but when he crossed the Alps the emperor had a change of heart, forcing Constantine to withdraw into Gaul. Problems then began for Gerontius in Spain, as trouble flared up over his policy of allowing barbarian mercenaries to guard the Pyrenees. The legions of Gerontius, who were loyal to Constantine, eventually revolted, and as a result, Gerontius installed his own son Maximus (not to be confused with Magnus Maximus) as puppet emperor.

For a while a ludicrous (and very confusing) situation existed where there were no less than six separate individuals all claiming to be the legitimate Roman emperor: Theodosius in the East, Honorius at Ravenna, Maximus at Tarragona, Constantine and Constans (father and son claiming to be joint emperor) at Arles, and Attalus (set up by Alaric) in Rome. It was not long before they all began to clash with one another.

Gerontius was the first to go on the offensive, forming an alliance with the Vandals, Sueves and Alans who had been ravaging Gaul. Constans retreated before this force, was captured at Vienne to the south of Lyons and was put to death. Gerontius then besieged Arles. Meanwhile, Honorius sent an army, under the command of Flavius

Constantius, and Gerontius quickly made his way back into Spain. His own troops, feeling betrayed, besieged his house, whereupon Gerontius committed suicide.

Constantine held out for more than three months in Arles, until his Frankish general, Edobich, who had been despatched to enlist barbarian reinforcements from beyond the Rhine, was defeated en route. With no further hope of victory, Constantine fled to the sanctuary of a monastery, where he was arrested and despatched to Honorius. Although he was offered safe conduct, Honorius soon changed his mind and ordered Constantine killed in September 411.

In Geoffrey of Monmouth's account, Constantine is assassinated after reigning in Britain for ten years, which is clearly at odds with the known history of Constantine III. However, where Geoffrey portrays Constans being enticed to give up his life as a monk in return for the throne, he is close to the historical Constans, who was called from his monastery to become joint emperor.

Geoffrey appears to have pieced together myth, legend and some historical fact in creating his pre-Arthurian period. For Constans, in particular, he appears to have employed a fairly reliable source. It is relatively easy to unravel fact from fable when we have an accurate record of the period in question, but very difficult when there is no such documentation. All that can be assumed, therefore, is that the half-truths purveyed by Geoffrey, reflected in his treatment of the era of Constantine, are also to be found in his descriptions of the generations that followed. The problem is sifting the wheat from the chaff.

Bearing that problem in mind, let us examine the account of subsequent events in Geoffrey's *Historia*. After Constans is also assassinated, Vortigern seizes the crown, while Constans' brothers, Ambrosius and Uther, flee to Brittany. When the two princes reach adulthood, they return and depose Vortigern, and Ambrosius succeeds him. Although this storyline is certainly inaccurate we do, once again, see an allusion not only to Ambrosius succeeding Vortigern, but also being raised in exile. The most interesting question, however, concerns the relationship between Ambrosius and Constantine. Although Ambrosius is certainly a generation too late to have been Constantine's son, he may have been a descendant of the would-be emperor's family. Is this why Gildas says that his parents wore purple, the imperial colour?

In addressing this question we must consider more closely the Roman withdrawal from Britain. Although 410 is more often quoted as the date for the end of Roman rule, the true picture is considerably more complex. As we know, both Maximus and Constantine took large sections of the army with them when they returned to the Continent in pursuit of their imperial ambitions. Whatever army still remained by 410 must have been considerably weakened, creating a marauding opportunity for the Picts and Irish. Unfortunately, in that year Emperor Honorius, having enough troubles of his own, withdrew the remaining legions and ordered the British to organise their own defences. The chief source for the period of the Roman withdrawal is Olympiodorus (an Egyptian Greek, born circa 365) who dealt in his twenty-two books of history with the years 407–25. Olympiodorus is a reliable chronicler, whose assertions are often supported by confirmatory evidence. However, his version of events, outlined amongst others by Gildas and Bede, is challenged by the Greek historian, Zosimus.

With reference to the end of Roman rule Zosimus says that 'the people of Britain, therefore, took up arms and braved every peril, freeing their cities from the attacking barbarians'. He then tells us that the British actually expelled 'the Roman officials' and established 'a civil policy according to their own inclination'.

Zosimus is not the only one to tell us that the British expelled the imperial administration. Nennius also says that 'the Britons overthrew the dominion of the Romans'. If there is any truth here, then the Roman civil administration continued to exist after the departure of the legions in 410. If it did, then a Roman administrator must have been installed for a time before the British rebelled against him. It is quite possible that Honorius appointed such a man when his most immediate troubles were over. In fact, there is good evidence that he did. In the *Notitia Dignitatum*, the Roman register of imperial officers, there is reference to the *Comes Britanniarum* (Count of the Britons) a new position created sometime shortly after 410. This officer appears to have been the commander of an auxiliary field force, despatched to Britain sometime during the second decade of the fifth century.

The office of *Comes Britanniarum*, in effect the Roman military governor in Britain, appears to have been withdrawn around 418. An entry in the *Anglo-Saxon Chronicle* for that year reads:

'In this year the Romans collected all the treasures which were in Britain and hid some in the earth so that no-one afterwards could find them, and some they took with them into Gaul.'

This entry indicates a hasty evacuation and an attempt to remove anything of value, perhaps due to the British uprising referred to by Nennius and Zosimus. There is certainly archaeological evidence pointing towards a short term reoccupation, consisting primarily of Roman coins dating from the late second decade.

Could the *Comes Britanniarum* have been Ambrosius' father? Might he also have been related to Constantine? After all, Constantine would have been something of a hero to the ruling elite of the island and it may have been a shrewd political gesture for the emperor to install a member of Constantine's family as *Comes Britanniarum*, providing the loyalty of that person could be guaranteed.

If the last vestige of Roman administration was thrown out around 418, it would seem that the next move by the Britons was to establish some form of ruling council or senate. Since Gildas mentions such a body in connection with the invitation to the Saxon mercenaries, it may well have been recalled on various occasions throughout the turbulent period which followed the Roman withdrawal. However, any hopes of founding a British republic would have been dashed with the breakdown of order which resulted in the rise of Vortigern by 425.

Behind Nennius' legend of Ambrosius' parentage having been kept from Vortigern may lie an allusion to the *Comes Britanniarum* finding asylum in some sympathetic kingdom in Britain. Since the tale of Ambrosius growing up in exile is echoed in Geoffrey, perhaps a legend survived to this effect. If so, where would this exile have been?

It would be unrealistic to suggest that the entire population of Britain was happy to see the Romans leave. It seems more reasonable to assume that two factions emerged: one standing for an independent Celtic Britain, the other wishing to continue as part of the empire: the nationalists and the imperialists. In fact, just such a division of interests is reflected in archaeological discoveries of the period. Although much of Britain reverted to pre-Roman tribalism, Roman civilisation persisted in many areas. Not only was there a split in the civil and administrative lifestyles, but there also appears to have been a fundamental religious division, as we saw in Chapter Ten: orthodox Catholicism and radical Pelagianism. The imperialists supported the former, the nationalists the latter.

To summarise, it appears that for a few years after 410 a new Roman governor was installed in Britain, who could well have been a member of the Constantine family. However, his military backup seems to have been negligible, so that sometime around 418 the Britons were able to remove him from office and establish their own administration, perhaps a republic. It was not long before the central government fell apart and the Midlands warlord Vortigern seized power, and by 425 he appears to have dominated a large area of Britain. Judging from the mission of Germanus, Vortigern seems to have supported the ostracised Christian sect founded by Pelagius.

Considering Gildas' admiration for Ambrosius, together with the statement that he was 'alone of the Romans', Ambrosius almost certainly stood for the pro-imperial faction surviving in Britain. Gildas' and Bede's references to royal Roman connections, alongside Nennius' statement that Ambrosius' father was a Roman official, implies that he may have been the son of the *Comes Britanniarum*.

As for the *Comes Britanniarum* himself, what is known of Constantine's sons makes it unlikely that he was one of them. However, he may have been a son-in-law, bearing the family name of Aurelianus or Aurelius. Any son, even merely by marriage, of the last Roman governor may have been seen as a figurehead for the pro-Roman faction in Britain. It may have been this that also prompted Vortigern to marry a daughter of Maximus and legitimise his own dynasty. Consequently, Britu would have been the grandson of Emperor Maximus, as opposed to Ambrosius being the grandson of Emperor Constantine.

The subsequent failures of the Vortigern family, and the devastating invasion by the Anglo-Saxons in the mid-to-late 450s, may well have created a backlash in Britain and a renewed nostalgia for the halcyon days of Roman rule. After the deposing of Vortigern, or more likely Britu (who appears to have tried to fall in line with the Roman revival by reconverting to Catholicism) the pro-Roman faction seems to have seized power and Ambrosius became leader. In opposition to Vortigern, Ambrosius stood for Roman interests, for the Catholic faith and for the imperial government, a stand reflected in the new mood of the people. After the recent defeat of Attila the Hun, (in 451), there was a period of hopeful expectation throughout the entire Roman Empire. Some form of Roman revival certainly occurred in Britain during the Ambrosius period, since a British contingent is recorded fighting for Emperor Anthemius in northern France in 470, during an attempt to restore Roman authority in Gaul.

Armed with this outline of events of the early fifth century, we turn to looking for Ambrosius' kingdom of origin. Although it could be argued that he returned from exile abroad, there are indications that he had remained in Britain, in one of the minority pro-Roman kingdoms. If we begin with Nennius' statement that he first gained dominion over the West of Britain, initially from the kingdom of

Gwynedd in North Wales, and look towards the evidence provided by archaeology, we discover that Gwynedd is precisely where the most Romanised form of lifestyle had continued though the first half of the fifth century. Tombstones, for example, imply a continuity of Roman society, bearing inscriptions such as *magistratus* (magistrate) and *civis* (citizen). Such Roman terms would be meaningless unless a Roman style of civilisation still survived.

From the standpoint that Ambrosius' power base was in northern Wales we return to the *Historia Brittonum*, where Nennius also calls Ambrosius Gwledig Emrys; *Gwledig* meaning prince, and *Emrys* the Welsh rendering of Ambrosius. This version of his name is found in connection with Dinas Emrys, an Iron Age hill-fort in Snowdonia in North Wales, (about a mile to the north-east of Beddgelert) where *Cyfranc Lludd a Llefelys*, the 'Tale of Ludd and Llefelys' in the 'White Book of Rhydderch' locates Ambrosius' power base. Although the surviving copy is fourteenth-century, circa 1325, linguistic analysis has shown that the story is very much older. The fort was certainly reoccupied around the right period and was perhaps the most important in the area. Between 1954 and 1956, Dr H. N. Savory of the National Museum of Wales undertook an excavation of the hilltop fortifications, which revealed that a rich and powerful British chief was in possession towards the close of the fifth century. Whether or not Ambrosius himself was this warlord, this part of Britain, the kingdom of Gwynedd, is the most feasible location for Ambrosius' powerbase.

Unfortunately, all optimism for the continuation of a Roman way of life was doomed. When the imperial campaign failed in Gaul, it signalled the end of Roman militarism and the Western Empire collapsed entirely. In Britain, however, quite the reverse was happening; the dawn of a nationalist heyday, arguably the most intriguing period in British history. Was this the true age of King Arthur? This is the period in which Nennius places Arthur. If it really was the age of the historical Arthur, where might he have originated?

Summary

By 460, a new and altogether different type of leader emerged; Ambrosius Aurelianus, who reorganised the country to fight back against the Anglo-Saxons. All we know about Ambrosius is contained in a few lines by Gildas and Bede, plus a legend recounted by Nennius. These tell us that he was the son of a high ranking Roman official.

1. From both Gildas and Bede we learn of Ambrosius' background, including the fact that his parents wore purple. Since purple was the royal colour of the Roman emperors, this statement implies that he came from a landed Roman family. Additionally, his parents died during the Saxon onslaught. Also, since Gildas affectionately refers to Ambrosius as a 'gentleman', he must have represented some alternative viewpoint to Vortigern, the 'proud tyrant'. Finally, Nennius names Ambrosius as Vortigern's main rival, but more importantly tells us he was the son of a Roman consul.

2. There is evidence that after the legions departed in 410, Emperor Honorius appointed a senior official to represent Roman interests in Britain. In the *Notitia Dignitatum*, the Roman register of imperial officers, there is reference to the *Comes Britanniarum* (Count of the Britons) a new position created shortly after 410. This officer appears to have been the commander of an auxiliary field force despatched to Britain during the second decade of the fifth century. The *Comes Britanniarum* could well have been Ambrosius' father.

3. The *Comes Britanniarum* must have been removed in 418, for the *Anglo-Saxon Chronicle* says that in that year the Britons overthrew the last of the Romans. Thereafter, according to Gildas, the British established their own republic. Unfortunately, Britain soon fell into disorder, resulting in the rise of Vortigern by 425. From what we can ascertain from Nennius, at this time the consul's son, Ambrosius, found asylum in a sympathetic province.

4. After the Romans had departed two factions emerged, one standing for an independent Celtic Britain, the other wishing to continue as part of the empire: the nationalists and the imperialists. Such a division of interests is reflected in archaeological finds from the period. Although a large part of Britain reverted to pre-Roman tribalism, Roman civilisation persisted in some areas. There was also a major religious division: the Catholics supported by the imperialists and the Pelagianists supported by the nationalists.

5. Considering that Gildas was a Catholic monk, his admiration

for Ambrosius, together with his statement that he was 'alone of the Romans', infers that Ambrosius stood for the imperialist faction. After the failures of the Vortigern family and the Saxon revolt in the mid-450s, the imperialists may have seized power and Ambrosius probably became the new British leader. It is likely that a pro-Roman revival occurred in Britain during the time of Ambrosius, since a British contingent is recorded fighting for the emperor Anthemius in 470.

6. Nennius says that Ambrosius first gained dominion over the West of Britain, initially from the kingdom of Gwynedd in North Wales. This is precisely where archaeology has discovered that the most Romanised lifestyle continued through the first half of the fifth century. Additionally, an early Welsh legend sites Ambrosius' base camp at Dinas Emrys, an Iron Age hill-fort in Gwynedd. Between 1954 and 1956, archaeological excavations showed that a rich and powerful British chief was in occupation in the late fifth century. This may have been Ambrosius himself.

12
Roots

Sometime during the 480s, with military stalemate between the Britons and the Saxons in the South of England, the Angles in the East of Britain appear to have suffered a series of crushing defeats. With Ambrosius busy refortifying the defences along the Thames Valley, the conflict further north may well have been left under the command of one of his most able officers. One theory is that this lieutenant was a warrior whose achievements under Ambrosius eventually gained him complete command of the British forces. Was he a warlord who was destined to be omitted from the pages of recorded history – the legendary King Arthur?

Someone must have succeeded Ambrosius in the late fifth century, and he must be a candidate for the role of the true, historical Arthur. Unfortunately, the most important writers covering this period, Gildas and Bede, fail to say who the leader was. To discover whether this leader really was the legendary King Arthur, we must address some very important questions. What faction did he represent? Which religion did he support? Into which family was he born? In short, who was he?

As we have seen, it appears that there were many divisions amongst the squabbling warlords of the various kingdoms, the majority leaning towards one or another of the two political factions. Both factions were supported by a different Christian creed, and both creeds supported one of two separate dynasties; the Vortigern family on the one hand, the Aurelianus family on the other. Where might Arthur fit into this? Was he a nationalist or an imperialist? A Catholic or a Pelagian? A Vortigern or an Aurelianus? Somewhere in the confusion of the late fifth century we must search for the historical Arthur.

First, let us return to the earliest reference to Arthur, the *Historia Brittonum* of Nennius. As we learned in Chapter Six, when we read the *Historia Brittonum* regarding the status of this enigmatic leader, the information given is unexpected, considering that Arthur has become one of the world's most legendary kings. It appears that he may not have been a king at all, for Nennius merely calls him 'the warrior Arthur'. He may not even have been a Briton. We are told that he merely fought *cum regibus brittonis*, 'with the British kings', which infers that he was not one of them. All the same, his position is one of high office, since he was the *dux bellorum*, the 'leader of battles'.

This ambiguity concerning Arthur's status has prompted speculation that he may have been a Saxon mercenary. This is very unlikely. It is difficult to imagine the mass of the British nation giving their wholehearted support to an Anglo-Saxon so soon after the disastrous consequence of their dealings with Hengist and Horsa; furthermore, it was the Anglo-Saxons that the British were fighting.

Whoever was commanding the Britons by the last decade of the fifth century was without doubt a formidable leader. The fact that the Britons were stronger and more united than ever before during this period is evidenced not only in Gildas, Bede and the *Anglo-Saxon Chronicle*, but also by archaeology. For example, there are the huge fortifications in the form of dykes that were constructed at this time, such as those previously mentioned in Lincolnshire and East Anglia. The positioning of the ditch to the eastern side of the dyke is clear evidence that the dykes were intended to defend against attacks from the east. Excavations show that the builders used Roman style pottery and wore boots with hobnails of the Roman kind. In other words, it was the Britons who built them, to counter any further advances by the Angles. On the Saxon front there are the linear earthworks around the Thames Valley, built by the Saxons to mark a fixed frontier. The British, who they were digging in to resist, were certainly not the same disorganised rabble who had been routed only a few years before. The British forces were now a formidable threat.

Not only do the massive British fortifications indicate large reserves of manpower, and the Saxon earthworks attest to the Britons having a powerful army, but both these factors suggest a united British nation and, more importantly, a strong and determined leader. Where could he have come from?

First, he seems to have been one of Ambrosius' commanders, as William of Malmesbury claimed that Arthur fought alongside Ambrosius. Second, there is nothing in Nennius concerning any clash between Ambrosius and Arthur, as there is between Ambrosius and Vortigern. So did Arthur continue to represent only the imperialist faction after the demise of Ambrosius probably around 480? (The precise date of the death of Ambrosius is unknown, but Arthur was certainly active by 488 (as Nennius tells us).) Unlikely, as by the 480s any imperialist notions were outdated concepts; there was no imperial institution to belong to. The tottering empire in the West had finally collapsed in 476 when the German leader, Odovacer, overthrew Emperor Romulus Augustulus and become king of Italy. Only the Eastern Empire survived in South-East Europe, where it came to be called the Byzantine Empire. However, there was a later attempt to recapture the West by the Byzantine emperor, Justinian I, beginning in the 530s. Italy and part of Spain were recaptured for a short time but were soon lost, and no new form of empire emerged in the West until 800 when the pope crowned Charlemagne of the Franks as emperor. Although this institution later came to be called the Holy Roman Empire, it was very different to the empire of the Romans of several centuries before, and had no direct effect upon life in Britain.

With the empire gone, it follows that the imperialist faction in Britain was left without direction. On the other hand, following the disgrace of the Vortigern family, it seems most unlikely that the Britons would have rallied readily around the nationalist flag. If Arthur was the leader of the Britons during the last decade or so of the fifth century, then what did he represent: some form of nostalgic Romanised nationalism, or perhaps a transient compromise forced upon the divided British by the Anglo-Saxon threat? After all, the enemy was not only a common one but a pagan one. Both of the British factions, no matter what their differences, were Christian.

With the fall of the empire and the self-inflicted Saxon invasion, both political factions in Britain must have suffered an irreversible setback. Moreover, the petty differences between the tribal kings must have been overshadowed by the dangers of barbarian conquest. Nonetheless, any unifying leader would either have to reflect all their views, or more likely would need to be neutral; an outsider. Is this what Nennius means – a warrior who fought with the British kings as their leader of battles? Even if his name was not Arthur, whoever led the British at this time must certainly have fitted this description. For convenience (until we have examined the subject further) we will continue to refer to him as Arthur. The immediate task is to consider this leader's place of origin.

In the century following the departure of the Romans, most of the old British tribes had re-established themselves as kingdoms. Wherever he came from originally, Arthur's power base would probably have been one of these. But which?

The Cantii tribe in Kent were completely conquered by the Saxons, as were the Trinovantes of Essex. Further north in Suffolk and East Anglia the Iceni, once the tribe of the warrior queen Boudicca, had been overwhelmed by the Angles, as had the Coritani and the Parisii to the north and east of them. Since these tribal areas had been effectively neutralised we must, therefore, turn to the tribal regions which remained independent from the Anglo-Saxons in the mid-480s.

The state of the far North was as follows: the Novantae tribe to the west of the country had established themselves as the kingdom of Rheged, and the Brigantes, to the south of them, had founded Elmet. These areas were not only suffering repeated incursions by the Picts, but were being continually subjected to raids by the Irish. Neither of these areas could have mustered the political and military muscle to unite and lead the rest of Britain. As far as the South was concerned, the Atrebates of Wiltshire and Berkshire had established a number of smaller kingdoms, as had the Durotriges of Dorset, the Belgae of Somerset and the Regenenses of Hampshire. Since these kingdoms were too small and fragmented to have supplied any form of strong leadership, we must examine the larger, more stable ones of the Midlands, the South-West and Wales.

Aside from a few tiny mountain kingdoms of South-Central Wales, such as Buellt and Brycheiniog, only five other kingdoms appear to have remained. In the west of Wales: Gwynedd in the north, the old tribal area of the Deceangli; and Dyfed in the south, the old tribal area of the Demetae. In the east of Wales: the Silures tribe in the southern kingdom of Gwent; and in the northern and central part of the province the massive Cornovii kingdom of Powys, which also included a large section of the western Midlands. The remaining kingdom was Dumnonia, of the Dumnonii tribe, in Devon and Cornwall.

Since little is known of these kingdoms, we will begin by considering the one which was the most powerful by the time of Gildas. In the *De Excidio*, Gildas addresses himself to the five most influential kings. These were almost certainly from these five kingdoms. Of one of them he says:

> 'What of you, dragon of the island, you who have removed many of these tyrants from their country and even their life? You are last on my list, but first in evil, mightier than many both in power and malice, more profuse in giving, more extravagant in sin, strong in arms but stronger still in what destroys a soul.'

Tribes of Roman Britain.

This king, the most powerful of all, he calls Maglocunus, the king who died of the plague in the 540s. As usual, almost nothing is known of him aside from his mention in the Welsh genealogies and selected comments from Nennius. In both he is called Maelgwn, the Welsh rendering of his name. In the *Historia Brittonum* Nennius says that 'Maelgwn ruled as a great king among the Britons, that is in the region of Gwynedd'. Some important indications concerning the status of the kingdom of Gwynedd can be gleaned from the clues supplied by Gildas in the above passage.

The term used by Gildas to describe Maglocunus is the 'dragon of the island'. Even without the genealogies, or the evidence of Nennius, this would place him very much in the kingdom of Gwynedd, for it was here, during the mid-fifth century, that the rulers of the kingdom adopted the symbol of the red dragon as their tribal emblem. This emblem, which was eventually adopted by the whole of Wales, was originally the standard of the later Roman emperors. Its use by the kingdom of Gwynedd is very much in keeping with what we have seen of their strong imperial loyalties. In fact, the kings of Gwynedd are often found in early Welsh poetry being referred to as the 'dragons of Britain' or the 'head dragons'.

Surely it is no coincidence that Geoffrey of Monmouth calls Arthur's father Pendragon, from the Welsh meaning 'head (or chief) dragon'. Of course this may not necessarily mean that Geoffrey had access to some record, or knew of some legend associating Arthur's family with Gwynedd; it could simply be implying a king of Wales generally. However, when this allusion is considered with the apparent strength of Gwynedd in the post Arthurian era, together with Ambrosius' association with the kingdom and its imperialist leanings, it certainly indicates the importance of this area in our search for Arthur's background.

Pendragon's forename, Uther, almost certainly derives from the Welsh word *uthr*, meaning 'terrible' (as in 'frightening'), so his name must mean the 'terrible head dragon'. Once again, it would appear that like Vortigern, the 'overlord', Uther Pendragon is yet another by-name or designation. It is tempting to speculate that Geoffrey of Monmouth knew only the title of Arthur's father, whom he claims became king upon the death of Ambrosius, and from it constructed his name. However, as we have seen, Geoffrey was forever mixing his historical characters and ascribing relationships out of time and place, as he did when he stated that Constans was the brother of Ambrosius. Nevertheless, we have also found useful half-truths in Geoffrey's work, such as Constans being the son of Constantine.

What was the relationship between Uther and Ambrosius? Although they may not have been brothers (as Geoffrey portrays them) Uther could have assumed the regency of Gwynedd when Ambrosius became the overall British leader. The most important issue, however, concerns the ruler of Gwynedd's relationship to Arthur, be he Uther or anyone else: did Arthur succeed as king of Gwynedd? Nennius' oblique statements seem at first to rule this out. As we have said, he tells us that Arthur fought 'with the British kings', which could imply that Arthur was not a king himself. However, there may be another explanation for this remark. Is Nennius telling us that although Arthur was a king, he was not a native Briton? If he was not a king why does Nennius not simply say that Arthur '*led* the British kings', instead of saying 'he fought *with* the British kings', which infers he was their equal. Could Nennius be implying that Arthur was a king, but a foreign one? This hypothesis draws us once again to the kingdom of Gwynedd. The kings who ruled this area do not appear to have been Britons in the strictest sense of the word, but came from Manau Guotodin, to the north of Hadrian's Wall in what is now Scotland. They were British inasmuch as they inhabited the isle of Britain, but they were not Britons, the name for the inhabitants of what is now England and Wales. Returning to Nennius' passage concerning Maelgwn (Maglocunus), he goes on to say:

> 'His ancestor, that is Cunedag, with his sons, eight in number, came previously from the northern part, that is from the region that is called Manau Guotodin one hundred and forty six years before Maelgwn ruled and expelled the Scots with a very great slaughter from these regions.'

The tenth-century Welsh genealogies at the end of the *Annales Cambriae* also refer to this ancestor of Maglocunus and his occupation of North-West Wales, though here he is called Cunedda. The *Annales* say that the newly adopted Welsh kingdom stretched 'from the river that is called Dubr Duiu [the Dee] up to the river Tebi [the Teifi, which joins the sea at Cardigan]'. In the *Annales*, however, we find a contradiction of Nennius' specific dating. Here we are told that Cunedda was Maglocunus' great-grandfather, meaning that only two generations separate the two men; surely a period of time much shorter than Nennius would have us believe.

Let us first consider the time in which the *Historia Brittonum* places the arrival of Cunedda and his men, 146 years before Maglocunus ruled. Although the precise date of the beginning of Maglocunus' reign is unknown, the general consensus places it sometime around 520. Going back 146 years takes us to the mid-370s, just prior to the time of Magnus Maximus. Concerning this period, archaeological excavations of the fortress of Segontium (Caernarvon), the principal Roman garrison of North-West Wales, have revealed that its final buildings were erected about 370 and intensive occupation ceased around 385, when Magnus Maximus departed Britain to conquer the empire.

This *could* have been the time of the arrival of Cunedda's men. Perhaps they were invited to settle in the area to help guard it until the regular army could be strengthened. This was the general policy of the empire in its latter days; invite in one friendly barbarian army to secure the area against hostile tribes. However, there is a persuasive argument against this having occurred in North-West Wales at this time. The historical evidence concerning the district of Gwynedd would make it incompatible with what Nennius says. He tells us that Cunedda and his sons 'expelled the Scots with a very great slaughter from these regions'. The Scots referred to in this passage are the Scotti, a Roman term for the Irish meaning 'raider' or 'bandit'. In the latter days of the empire, the Scotti were settling in considerable numbers in South-West Scotland, and by the ninth century they had conquered the entire country; indeed, it is from the Scotti that Scotland derives its name. Any notion that the Irish had managed to settle in North-West Wales, while Segontium was still being garrisoned, is unlikely considering the Roman military presence. Furthermore, the archaeological evidence shows that it continued to be garrisoned, although with a smaller force, until the final departure of the legions in 410.

So if the timescale given by Nennius is inconsistent with archaeological evidence, what can we learn from the *Annales*, which tell us that Maglocunus was the great-grandson of Cunedda? As Cunedda's son Enniaun Girt (Maglocunus' grandfather) was old enough to fight with Cunedda (we know this from Nennius), we can assume that *his* son (Maglocunus' father) was born within thirty years of landing in Gwynedd. Add to this, say, another thirty years before the birth of Maglocunus, plus another thirty before the time of his reign, and we arrive at a generous ninety years, a hundred at the very most. This takes us back as far as the 430s. By this time, Gwynedd was certainly suffering repeated Irish raids. Perhaps, therefore, it was Vortigern who invited in Cunedda.

However, this date was arrived at by deducing the longest period of time that could have elapsed between Cunedda's arrival and the commencement of Maglocunus' reign. It is far more likely that

Maglocunus' father was born within ten years of Cunedda's arrival in Gwynedd, and Maglocunus himself within twenty-five years of this. Adding another twenty-five years before the start of his rule gives a more reasonable calculation of somewhere around sixty years in all. If this were the case, then it would take us back to sometime around 460, the time of Ambrosius, a far more likely period. From the evidence of Gildas and Bede, it can be deduced that the western part of Britain had been troubled by the Irish, on and off, throughout the first half of the fifth century after the Roman legions left. If the kingdom of Gwynedd was to have supplied the power base for Ambrosius in this later period, which it certainly appears to have done, some aid against the Irish must have been forthcoming.

According to the *Annales*, well before Maglocunus' reign, his grandfather, Enniaun Girt, became king of Gwynedd. The Cunedda family therefore ruled the kingdom for at least two generations before Maglocunus came to power, around 520. If Arthur ruled in the 490s, and if Arthur's roots were in Gwynedd, (seemingly the most powerful British kingdom of the era), he is almost certain to have been a member of the Cunedda family. So we must now look at the origins of the Cunedda dynasty in greater detail.

Summary

We have endeavoured to establish who King Arthur really was. The most plausible contender is a prince of Gwynedd, who unified the nationalist and imperialist factions of late fifth-century Britain.

1. That the Britons were stronger and more united by the last decade of the fifth century is not only shown in Gildas, Bede and the *Anglo-Saxon Chronicle*, but is also reflected in archaeology. For example, there are sophisticated forifications constructed by the British at this time all across the East of Britain. Although this suggests a strong and determined leader, no surviving document for the next three centuries names him. Nennius' *Historia Brittonum* is the first to do so, telling us that the leader's name was Arthur.

2. Of the British kingdoms free from Anglo-Saxon occupation, only five were sufficiently strong to have been Arthur's power base: Gwynedd in North Wales, Dyfed and Gwent in South Wales, Dumnonia in South-West England, and Powys in the West Midlands and Central Wales. The evidence to determine the most

powerful of these kingdoms derives from Gildas. When he was writing, some fifty years after the battle of Badon, the most powerful kingdom was Gwynedd. This, coupled with Ambrosius' connection with the area before Arthur, means that Gwynedd must have been a leading power throughout the era, making it a strong contender for Arthur's original kingdom.

3. Further evidence for Gwynedd being Arthur's kingdom comes from Geoffrey of Monmouth, when he names Arthur's father as Uther Pendragon. From the Welsh, the name means the 'terrible head dragon'. During the mid-fifth century, the rulers of Gwynedd had adopted the symbol of the red dragon as their emblem, and in Dark Age Welsh poetry the kings of Gwynedd are often referred to as the 'dragons of Britain', or the 'head dragons'. When Gildas addresses Maglocunus, the king of Gwynedd, he calls him 'dragon of the island'. If Uther Pendragon really was Arthur's father, then Arthur would appear to have been the son of the king of Gwynedd.

4. Nennius seems to imply that Arthur was not a native Briton. If he was, why does Nennius not simply say that Arthur '*led* the British kings', instead of saying that's 'he fought *with* the British'. Nennius appears to be drawing attention to some peculiarity. Could this imply that Arthur was a foreign king? This possibility draws us once again to the kingdom of Gwynedd. The kings who ruled this area do not appear to have been Britons at all. Both Nennius and the *Annales Cambriae* say that the kings of Gwynedd descended from Cunedda, a warrior from the Scottish district of Manau Guotodin.

5. From the *Annales* and Nennius we can deduce that Cunedda was Maglocunus' great-grandfather, who was invited by the people of Gwynedd to protect them from Irish raiders. From the archaeological evidence, together with Gildas and Bede, the most likely period for this to have occurred was about 460. Since this is the time that Ambrosius made his bid for power, it is possible that Cunedda also helped him overthrow the Vortigern family.

6. Since the genealogies attached to the *Annales* record Cunedda's son, Enniaun Girt, becoming king of Gwynedd after Cunedda's death, it seems that the Cunedda family assumed control of the kingdom sometime during or shortly after the Ambrosius period. Given that this period of Cunedda ascendancy lasted until the time of Gildas, it is very possible that Arthur was a member of this family.

13

The Votadini

Manau Guotodin, where Cunedda originated, was an area around the Firth of Forth in the region of Edinburgh, about the size of modern Lothian, forming the northern part of the Celtic kingdom of Gododdin. Although its people were predominantly Pictish, they were of a tribe called the Votadini who, during the days of the empire, were the northern tribe most favourably disposed towards the Romans. This was because their kingdom fell within an area that, for the period of the Roman occupation of Britain, was never truly Roman or Pictish. According to the second-century Greek geographer Ptolemy, the kingdom of the Votadini tribe extended from the Firth of Forth as far south as the River Wear. Modern excavations have suggested that the Votadini tribal capital was at the Yeavering Bell hill-fort at Wooler near Bamburgh.

The word Pict does not denote a particular tribe; rather it is a Roman term meaning 'painted men', and was used to refer to anyone of the British tribes that fell outside the limits of the empire. Since the ancient British warriors who fought against the Roman invasion painted themselves in woad (a blue dye) before entering battle, the Pictish tribes of the North were so named because they continued this custom.

In 43 A.D., when Britain was conquered by Emperor Claudius and became an island province of the Roman Empire, it was found impossible to control the Scottish Highlands. The fierce northern tribes of this mountainous area were free to raid the Roman towns in the North of England and the Scottish Lowlands on a regular basis. At the beginning of the second century, when the Picts even sacked the city of York, defeating a legion of around 5,000 men, the emperor Hadrian visited Britain and in 122 A.D. ordered that a great defensive wall be built across the North of England. When completed, between Newcastle and the Solway Firth, it was over seventy-three miles long, fifteen feet high and some eight feet thick, with sixteen forts along its length, each garrisoned by about a thousand men.

But Hadrian's Wall was not built at the limits of the empire. The Roman area of occupation stretched more than fifty miles further north. Roman forts already existed across this part of Scotland and, from the time of Claudius, they had been considered to be the frontier outposts of the empire. It was along this frontier that Hadrian's successor, Antoninus Pius, constructed another wall, spanning the thirty-six miles between the Clyde and Firth estuaries. Unlike Hadrian's Wall, which was built of stone, the Antonine Wall consisted of a huge linear earthwork surmounted by a wooden stockade and protected by a deep ditch. Around 200 A.D., however, this second wall was abandoned and Hadrian's Wall became the final frontier of the Roman Empire.

Falling as it did between the Antonine and Hadrian's Wall, the kingdom of the Votadini had been part of the empire for well over a century. For this reason, throughout the next two and a half centuries relations between the Votadini and the empire were good. The Romans offered support against the hostile Picts, while in return the Votadini helped police this buffer zone, as did the other two tribes, in what is now southern Scotland, the Selgovae and the Damnonii. However, by the early fifth century, even before the Romans left Britain, the Scotti had settled the South-West of Scotland, overwhelming the Damnonii and threatening the Selgovae.

So shortly after the legions pulled out, the pro-British Votadini were experiencing trouble on three fronts. The Angles were raiding their coastline, the Picts were marauding from the North, and the Scotti were pushing ever closer from the West. The Votadini must certainly have been a formidable people, for they were able to hold out against these combined forces until the early seventh century.

It would not have been difficult for Ambrosius to persuade the Votadini to settle in North-West Wales. In return for their military muscle against the Irish, Votadini warriors and their families would have a new land in which to settle. Indeed, they would have had much in common with the imperialist faction of Gwynedd; no one had greater reason for wishing to see the return of the legions than the people of Gododdin, who were facing annihilation on three fronts.

That Cunedda and the Votadini warriors colonised North-West Wales by the late fifth century can be verified by ceramic evidence. Characteristic Votadini pottery has been discovered in Gwynedd dating from the second half of the fifth century, which not only supports a migration from Gododdin but also places the time of their arrival during the period of Ambrosius. Additionally, the identifying name-affix 'Cun', or in Welsh 'Cyn', of the Cunedda family is found both on tombstones, and in the genealogies of Gwynedd. It occurs in the name of Maglocunus, and in that of his cousin Cuneglasus, whom Gildas also names. Furthermore, the genealogies show that Cunedda's ancestors bear a mixture of Pictish and Roman names.

The Votadìni migration led by Cunedda, referred to in the *Historia Brittonum* and the *Annales Cambriae*, was thus almost certainly an historical event. Its relevance concerns the lineage of Arthur. Was Arthur's father one of the Votadini, perhaps Cunedda himself or one of his sons? The weight of evidence presented in this chapter seems to point in this direction. As it is essential to the unravelling of the mystery of King Arthur, we summarise it here.

1. Gwynedd was undoubtedly the most powerful kingdom by the time of Gildas (around 545). It is not unreasonable to assume that this was a legacy of the Arthurian period.

2. The kingdom from which Ambrosius sprang was almost certainly Gwynedd and, as Arthur appears to have been Ambrosius' successor rather than his deposer, it follows that Arthur was of the same kingdom.

3. The name of Arthur's father in Geoffrey of Monmouth's *Historia* is Uther Pendragon, meaning 'terrible head dragon', a title that would fit the king of Gwynedd in the late fifth century.

4. The Votadini appear to have arrived in Gwynedd at the time of Ambrosius, perhaps accounting for his success in establishing himself over the Vortigern family. If Arthur's father was the king of Gwynedd he would, therefore, almost certainly have been a Votadini.

5. Nennius infers that Arthur was not a British king, perhaps not even a British national. However, he is an equal of the British kings. Such a description would sit with a king of the Votadini who, although not Britons, were a trusted people with a common enemy.

6. After the disastrous policy of the Vortigerns, and the final collapse of the Western Empire, a compromise leader would surely have been essential to assure a unified following. A Votadini was

ideally suited, considering the British leaders' distrust of one another.

7. If Arthur was a Votadini, he would certainly have made an ideal commander-in-chief of the British forces. He came from a hardy warrior race, whose people had much first-hand experience in fighting not only the Anglo-Saxons but also the Scotti and the Picts. More importantly, he would almost certainly have remained isolated from the political and religious wranglings that had divided the people of Britain.

So it would seem that in the Votadini of Gwynedd we have the most plausible candidates for Arthur's people. But is there any corroborative evidence for this theory? The clinching factor comes from the pen of Gildas himself, but before we examine this we should consider what may well be the most ancient of all Arthurian references, an ancient Celtic poem called the *Gododdin*, a work considerably older than the Arthurian poems of Wales which we have looked at earlier. As its title suggests, it comes from the kingdom of the Votadini.

Accredited to a Votadini bard named Aneirin, this epic poem concerns the fate of a group of warriors from the kingdom of Gododdin, who set out to fight the Anglo-Saxons in Yorkshire. In one passage the poet comments on the courage of a particular hero, Gwawrddur, saying that although he fought bravely 'he was no Arthur'. This is tantalising. Why should this isolated Pictish tribe of Scotland choose, on the eve of their demise, to hold up the British warrior, Arthur, as a paragon of military valour? It is difficult to imagine a Votadini poet, who is praising the prowess of his tribe, admitting that one of their great heroes was not comparable with one of the Britons. Unless, that is, Arthur had been a Votadini himself.

The *Gododdin* is set in a period around the end of the sixth century, when the Votadini fought gallantly, but unsuccessfully, against the Anglo-Saxon advance towards their kingdom. The presence of Arthur in the poem has thus led many scholars to conclude that he was from this far northern kingdom. However, it could just as well be taken as evidence that Arthur was from Gwynedd in the North-West of Wales, also a kingdom of the Votadini.

The poem as we know it has survived in two mid-thirteenth-century copies now in the Public Library in Cardiff, but from the style of writing and spelling used, it appears to have been copied from a ninth-century original. Unfortunately, this means that the poem would probably have been recited from memory alone until someone decided to write it down in the 800s. However, it is generally accepted that the *Gododdin* was composed shortly after the end of the sixth century, because the mode of warfare it describes is consistent with that period. What is vitally important to our case is that the mention of Arthur is considered to have survived from the original sixth-century form of the poem. This is due to the rhyme scheme; his name rhymes with the end of the previous line, and is in a dialect that was practised in the sixth century, not around 800. In the British language the lines concerning Arthur read:

> *gochone brein du ar uur*
> *caer ceni bei ef Arthur*

The English translation is:

> 'He glutted black ravens on the wall
> of the fort although he was no Arthur.'

In other words, he fed the ravens with the bodies of the enemy dead.

Given that the writer is lamenting the demise of the Votadini in the face of the Anglo-Saxons, this mention of Arthur seems to hanker after the military heyday of the tribe, a time when there were successes against the Anglo-Saxons, led by a victorious warrior named Arthur.

The *Gododdin* not only tends to confirm that Arthur was of the Votadini, but also attests to the links between Gododdin and Gwynedd. The poem relates that one of the chief warriors, Gorthyn, had come to Gododdin from Gwynedd along with a large company of soldiers. Why should he choose to do so, in a time of great strife, unless powerful ties existed between the two dynasties? It is even tempting to speculate that the poet may be naming Arthur because the warrior chief himself was one of Arthur's descendants.

We now move on to the most intriguing element in the argument that Arthur was a member of the royal house of Gwynedd. Why has nothing been found – not an inscribed stone, a written document or a contemporary record – within three centuries of his time, bearing the name of King Arthur? We could answer 'because he did not exist'.

However, there is another possibility. Arthur might not have been his real name. As with Vortigern and Uther, the name Arthur may have been a by-name or title.

Various scholars have theorised that the name Arthur was a British derivative of the Roman name Artorius, in the same way as Ambrosius became Emrys, Vortigern became Gwrtheyrn, or as Maglocunus became Maelgwn in the later Welsh language. The idea has become current since the poem *Artorius*, by John Heath-Stubbs, was published in 1973, followed by John Gloag's story *Artorius Rex*, published in 1977. Although it has been pointed out that a Roman soldier called Lucius Artorius Castus served as an officer in Britain during the late second century, and another called Artorius Justus was here in the third century, this does not constitute proof that 'Artorius' was the original version of the name Arthur. The fact remains that no-one who bore the name of Artorius, Arthur, or anything like it, could conceivably be linked with an historical warrior who lived around 500 A.D.

The name Arthur does not appear anywhere on record until the end of the sixth century. Around this time, no less than *six* of the various British genealogies include the name of Arthur, which seems to suggest that the royal families of the time were beginning to call their sons after a famous warrior of that time, in the same way that Englishmen began calling their sons Gordon after 1885, commemorating the heroism of General Gordon at Khartoum. By the same token, the fact that the name does not appear earlier than these genealogies suggests that the name had only been concocted shortly before. King Arthur may have been the first person to hold that name, adding weight to the idea that it was originally a title. This seems to have happened with Vortigern, since a number of princes were given this name in the centuries after the original Vortigern had lived.

If Arthur was a form of by-name, what could it mean? The first syllable, *Arth*, from the British language and also preserved in modern Welsh, means 'bear'. If the warrior who led the Britons in the late sixth century was called the Bear, he would not have been the only such warrior to be named after an animal, as this seems to have been a common Celtic practice of the period. Not only are there many examples, from Ireland and Gaul as well as Britain, of various warlords assuming such epithets as the Wolf, the Hound, the Horse *et cetera*, but Gildas himself names a number of British kings and likens them to animals. Apart from Maglocunus, whom he calls the Dragon, there is Aurelius Caninus, the Dog, whose father seems to have been called the Lion (as Gildas also calls him the Lion-Whelp) and Vortipor, the Leopard. It was not only the men who were compared to animals, for Gildas also mentions Boudicca, the famous warrior queen of the Iceni, calling her the Lioness.

As well as rulers, bards and holy men were likened to animals such as the Irish saint Columba (from roughly the same period as Gildas) whose Celtic name is Columcille, meaning 'church dove'. This tradition should not be considered as specifically Celtic. Native American cultures, for instance, use names such as Sitting Bull and Crazy Horse. The name of an animal, in some way typifying the qualities of the individual, was given to many Dark Age kings, in some cases by their enemies or critics as an insult, and in others by their followers as an honorary title. Usually, however, we also know their real name. There may be a particular reason why Arthur's title became far more widely known than his real name. It may have carried special significance.

It should be remembered how important it must have been for the warrior who united the Britons after the time of Ambrosius to have reflected both the nationalist and imperialist viewpoints. The political division in Britain was not only reflected in the two forms of Christianity, it was also a matter of first language, as it still is in many parts of the world today. Britain of the post-Roman era had two main languages: Latin, the Roman language, and Brythonic, which later developed into Welsh. (Of the other languages of the British Isles, English was a later development of the language spoken by the Anglo-Saxons, while Gaelic, spoken by the Scotti who gradually spread throughout Scotland, was the language of the Irish.) The tombstones and other inscriptions from the fifth century provide evidence that the nationalist kingdoms were reverting wholly to Brythonic, while the imperialist kingdoms continued to use Latin. In effect, this is a situation similar to that in Wales today; except now, of course, it is a matter of Welsh versus English.

The leader of the divided Britons of the late fifth century may well have adopted a name which personified both sympathies in order to avoid any implication of favouring one faction more than the other. If his tribal title was the Bear, he may not only have used the Brythonic word *Arth*, but also the Latin word for bear, *Ursus*. His original title may therefore have been *Arthursus*; later being shortened to *Arthur*, as Antonius is shortened to Anthony or Marcus to Marc. If there is any doubt about the symbolic importance of such an act, we need only remind ourselves of the problems facing the traffic authorities, whose task it is to erect road signs, not only in modern Wales but in Belgium, Switzerland and parts of Canada, to name but a few. In

bilingual countries feelings run deep concerning the cultural significance of the first language.

A recent example of a leader adopting a combined name is that of
Albino Luciani, who chose to call himself Pope John Paul I in 1978,
thus introducing the first double name in the history of the Papacy.
Unifying the names John and Paul conveyed a message of deep
significance to the Vatican factions, since the name chosen by a pope
traditionally gives an indication of the direction of his reign.

If Arthur is a by-name, meaning the Bear, it would not be the first
time that a leader had gone down in history under his title. The
emperor Caius Caesar, for example, was better known as Caligula,
meaning 'little boot', a nickname he acquired as a child because he
enjoyed dressing up as a soldier. Another example is the Mongol
warlord Temujin, who is more easily recognised under his title
Genghis Khan, meaning 'universal ruler'.

Bearing this in mind, if we re-examine the *De Excidio* of Gildas, a
new interpretion is possible: it could well be that Gildas does mention
King Arthur after all. Of one of the kings he is attacking, he writes:

'Why have you been rolling in the filth of your past wickedness
ever since your youth, you bear, rider of many and driver of the
chariot of the bear's stronghold, despiser of God and oppressor
of his lot, Cuneglasus?'

Twice he mentions the word bear. First he is calling Cuneglasus 'you
bear', then that he is the charioteer of the 'bear's stronghold'. Here is
something of a mystery. If Cuneglasus is the bear, then how is he also
the charioteer of the bear's stronghold? Gildas seems to be referring to
two bears.

Before we investigate further, we can dismiss Cuneglasus as a
candidate for Arthur. Since Cuneglasus is being addressed personally
by Gildas, he is alive at the time of writing (circa 545). Therefore, if he
was the warrior who led the Britons in the 480s, he would have to be at
least an octogenarian; which is unlikely, since later in the same passage
Gildas implores him to desist from an adulterous affair with his wife's
sister (who, incidentally, appears to have been a nun). Additionally,
the genealogies attached to the *Annales Cambriae* show us that
Cuneglasus (in the Welsh rendering, Cynglas) was not merely a
contemporary of Maglocunus but also his cousin; both men being the
grandchildren of Enniaun Girt, the son of Cunedda.

As Gildas is calling Cuneglasus the 'rider of many and driver of the chariot of the bear's stronghold', surely he is inferring that Cuneglasus is now in control of many people and in command of what had once been the Bear's stronghold. In other words, Cuneglasus has assumed the title of a predecessor who was called the Bear. Whoever he succeeded, Cuneglasus certainly seems to have had some particular military advantage, for Gildas goes on to ask him why he wages war against his fellow countrymen 'with arms special to yourself'.

This particular passage may not only constitute evidence of Arthur's existence, but may also help us discover Arthur's stronghold. If the 'bear's stronghold' was Arthur's capital, and Cuneglasus was in command of it by the time of Gildas, then we must discover over which kingdom Cuneglasus ruled. This is easier said than done, for Gildas neglects to tell us, and no other writer links him with a specific kingdom. We must therefore examine the other four kings named by Gildas and consider which of the five powerful kingdoms can be eliminated – Gwynedd, Dumnonia, Dyfed, Gwent or Powys.

Besides Maglocunus, who we know is from Gwynedd, there are three others. First, there is Constantine, who Gildas tells us is from Damnoniae. Although arguably this could be referring to the region of the Damnonii tribe in South-West Scotland, by Gildas' time this had been conquered by the Irish. It is more likely that he means Dumnonia, the kingdom of the Dumnonii in Devon and Cornwall.

Next is Vortipor, whom he calls the tyrant of the Demetarum. Not only is this almost certainly referring to the Demetae tribe's kingdom of Dyfed, but there is also additional evidence of a contemporary memorial stone inscribed with his name that has been discovered in South-West Wales. (The 'Vort' prefix may indicate that Vortipor was a descendant of Vortigern.)

The final king Gildas calls Aurelius Caninus, 'Aurelius the Dog'. Unfortunately, as with Cuneglasus, Gildas offers no clue to his kingdom. All we can say is that, judging by his name, this man may have been a descendant of Ambrosius Aurelianus.

Having eliminated Gwynedd, Dumnonia and Dyfed, we are left with Gwent or Powys as the kingdom of Cuneglasus.

Since Powys adjoins Maglocunus' (i.e. Cuneglasus' cousin's) kingdom of Gwynedd, it is the most likely candidate. Moreover, there is archaeological evidence that the Cunedda family of Gwynedd had annexed the kingdom of Powys by the end of the fifth century (see Chapter Fourteen).

In addition, the appearance of the 'Cyn' affix in the names of later historical figures, who are known to have been kings of Powys, suggests that these rulers were still members of the Cunedda family. These later kings include Cynan Garwyn (circa 590), who is praised as the king of Powys in the sixth-century Welsh poem *Trawsganu Cynan Garwyn* (in the 'Book of Taliesin'); Cynddylan (circa 650) the son of Cyndrwyn, whose last stand in Powys is the theme of a ninth-century cycle of Welsh poems the *Canu Llywarch Hen* (in the 'Red Book of Hergest'); and Cyngen, whom the *Annales Cambriae* record as dying on a pilgrimage to Rome in 854.

In conclusion, if Powys was Arthur's power base, this would be consistent with its having been the seat of the Vortigerns, who had been subsequently usurped by the forces of Gwynedd under Ambrosius' guidance. Arthur may therefore have been a prince of Gwynedd who, on assuming command of the British forces, made his stronghold in the kingdom of Powys, right in the heart of Britain. Further support for Powys being the kingdom of Arthur comes from the early legend, mentioned by Nennius, concerning the tomb of Arthur's son. He tells us:

'In the district of Ercing, there is a tomb near the well which is called the Eye of Amr; and the name of the man who is buried in the tomb was Amr. He was the son of Arthur the warrior who slew him and buried him there.'

Ercing was the British name for the Roman town of Ariconium, modern Weston-under-Penyard near Ross-on-Wye, and as such this is the earliest recorded legend (circa 830) of Arthur originating in what was then the kingdom of Powys.

So in order to close in on the most elusive character in British history, we must look carefully at the kingdom of Powys as it was in the latter half of the fifth century. In particular we must find out as much as we can about the condition of its capital, the Roman city of Viroconium, for if we are correct, Viroconium would most probably be Arthur's power base.

Summary

We have examined evidence which indicates that Arthur was a Votadini warrior who had assumed the battle name 'the Bear'. Not only is Arthur praised in a Votadini war poem, but Gildas himself mentions a warrior called the Bear. We reason that although Arthur may have originated in Gwynedd, his stronghold by the time of his leadership was in the central kingdom of Powys.

1. Cunedda and his warriors were not native to North Wales, but came from an area around Edinburgh which formed the northern part of the kingdom of the Votadini tribe: a kingdom called Gododdin. This area was abandoned by the Romans in the later years of the empire, which meant that the Votadini were essentially Picts, a Roman term referring to the British tribes that fell outside the limits of the empire. They were British inasmuch as they inhabited the isle of Britain, but they were not Britons, the name for inhabitants of what is now England and Wales.

2. Gododdin had been part of the Roman Empire for well over a century before the legions pulled back behind Hadrian's Wall in 200 A.D. There were therefore good relations between the Votadini and the empire. The Romans offered support against hostile northern tribes, and in return the Votadini helped police this buffer zone between occupied Britain and the unconquered Picts of the Scottish Highlands.

3. Soon after the Romans left Britain, the Votadini began to experience great difficulties. The Angles were raiding their coastline in the East, the Picts were marauding from the North, and the Irish were pushing ever closer from the West. It would therefore have been easy for Ambrosius to persuade the Votadini to settle in North-West Wales. In return for their help, the warriors and their families would have a new home. Additionally, they had much in common with the imperialists of Gwynedd; no-one had greater reason for wanting the return of the legions than the people of Gododdin, who were facing annihilation on three fronts.

4. That the Votadini colonised North-West Wales in the 460s has been verified by archaeology. Characteristic Votadini pottery has been discovered in Gwynedd dating from the second half of the fifth century. This is not only evidence for the arrival of Cunedda, but it also confirms the time of his arrival during the period of Ambrosius. In addition, the identifying family name affix 'Cun' (or in Welsh 'Cyn') is found both on tombstones, and in the genealogies

of Gwynedd – for example, in the name of Maglocunus and his cousin, Cuneglasus, whom Gildas also names.

5. If Arthur was the son of a Votadini king of Gwynedd, he would certainly have made an ideal commander-in-chief of the British forces. He came from a hardy warrior race, whose people had considerable first-hand experience fighting the Anglo-Saxons, the Irish and the Picts. More importantly, he would almost certainly have remained isolated from the political and religious wranglings that divided the Britons.

6. Firm evidence to support that Arthur was one of the Gwynedd Votadini comes from what may be the oldest of all Arthurian references, an ancient poem called the *Gododdin* which was first committed to writing during the ninth century. The *Gododdin* is generally accepted to have been composed shortly after the end of the sixth century, and because the rhyme scheme using Arthur's name is in a sixth-century dialect, the mention of Arthur is considered authentic. As its title suggests, the poem comes from the kingdom of the Votadini and concerns a band of warriors who set out to fight the Anglo-Saxons in the far North. In one passage the poet praises the courage of a hero, saying that although he fought bravely 'he was no Arthur'. The fact that Arthur should be so esteemed in a Votadini war poem suggests that he had been a member of their tribe.

7. The *Gododdin* not only tends to confirm that Arthur was a Votadini, but it also attests to the links between Gododdin and Gwynedd. The poem relates how one of the bands leaders had come to Gododdin from Gwynedd, together with a large company of soldiers. This not only confirms that Votadini warriors had settled in North Wales, but shows that powerful ties existed between the two kingdoms as late as 600 A.D.

8. If Arthur was of the royal house of Gwynedd, why is his name not recorded in the genealogies? As with Vortigern and Uther, the name Arthur may well have been a by-name or title. The first syllable, *Arth*, in the British language, Brythonic, means bear. It was common practice at the time for Celtic warlords to assume the battle-name of an animal. However, Arthur's title may have carried a special significance. Surviving inscriptions of the fifth century

show that the nationalist kingdoms were using Brythonic, whereas the imperialist kingdoms continued to use Latin. For the leader of the divided Britons to personify unity, he may well have adopted a name coined from both languages; using the Brythonic word *Arth*, but also the Latin word for bear, *Ursus*. His original title may therefore have been *Arthursus*, later being shortened to *Arthur*.

9. If Arthur means Bear, then Gildas may mention him after all. During a tirade against Maglocunus' cousin, Cuneglasus, he calls him the charioteer of the 'bear's stronghold'. As Cuneglasus is clearly a king in his own right by the time Gildas was writing (about 545), the passage implies that he was in command of what had once been the stronghold of the Bear. In other words, Cuneglasus' capital seems to have been Arthur's stronghold.

10. During Gildas' time five kingdoms were powerful enough to have been Cuneglasus' kingdom. However, three of these can be dismissed, since Gildas leaves us with no doubt as to who ruled them. As one of these is Gwynedd, it may seem that although Arthur originated here, by the time he became leader of the Britons he had established his power base elsewhere. We are left, therefore, with Gwent or Powys as the kingdom of Cuneglasus. As Powys adjoins Maglocunus' kingdom of Gwynedd, and inscriptions and genealogies from the period show that the Cunedda family were ruling there, it is by far the more feasible of the two. Powys as Arthur's stronghold makes historical sense; it had been the stronghold of the Vortigerns, presumably conquered by the forces of Gwynedd under Ambrosius' leadership.

14
Viroconium

Although it is difficult to determine exactly when the kingdom of Powys came into existence, it must have been soon after the Roman withdrawal. Once the Roman administration had gone from Britain, many of the old tribal areas seem to have made fairly rapid attempts to establish themselves as independent principalities. However, it was not long before a three-fronted threat forced the British chieftains into grudging unity, resulting in the council of leaders referred to by Gildas.

The incursions of Germanic invaders in the East, the Picts in the North and the Irish in the West considerably weakened the border and coastal tribes. The central position of the Cornovii tribe must therefore have afforded them a unique position of strength, providing time and resources to establish an autonomous kingdom long before their neighbours; a kingdom strategically situated to take control of a substantial area of the country. In all probability they discovered that surrounding tribes were all too willing to become satellites of the Cornovii, rather than submit to foreign invasion. In return for the protection of the central kingdom, the British tribal chiefs may have sworn allegiance to a Cornovii king as their 'overlord', Vortigern.

It is impossible to say at what point the kingdom first came to be called Powys, although the Welsh names for the sub-Roman kingdoms do not appear to have been in general usage until the late sixth century. Gildas, for example, refers to them only in tribal terms. However, the name Powys probably came from the Latin word *pagus*, meaning 'country district'. Regardless of its original name, for at least the first century of its existence the capital of Powys was the old Roman city of Viroconium, the capital of the *civitate* that contained the Cornovii.

During the Roman occupation of Britain, the country had been divided into provincial districts known as *civitates*, each founded on existing tribal areas and controlled from an administrative city or capital. For example, the Atrebates of the South were governed from Calleva Atrebatum (modern Silchester), the Cantii of Kent from Durovernum Cantiacorum (Canterbury) and the Dumnonii of the

South-West from Isca Dumnonium (Exeter). Likewise, the Cornovii of Central England and West Wales were subject to the administration of Viroconium Cornoviorum. Now in the county of Shropshire, Viroconium became the fourth largest city in Roman Britain, and was the most important trading centre in the Midlands.

Built on the fertile plain overlooking the River Severn, Viroconium was originally established as a military base to co-ordinate the Roman conquest of Wales. Sometime around 78 A.D. the western command of the island was transferred to the city of Chester, and Viroconium became a thriving civilian town. Although it was to have all the features of other provincial capitals, such as cobbled streets, water supply and drainage system, the Cornovii city was far more elaborate and wealthy than most. Covering a total area of around 180 acres, Viroconium, with its law courts, market-place and other public facilities, became the principal city of Central Britain. Unlike the other main Roman cities – London, Lincoln and York – all that now remains of Viroconium are its ruined walls, standing in quiet farm land outside the tiny village of Wroxeter, to the south-east of Shrewsbury.

Standing as they do in the open countryside, the ruins of Viroconium have provided an excellent opportunity for excavation, and in the last hundred years much archaeological work has been conducted there. Today the dig is open to the public and a small museum stands at the site, where some of the excavated material is on display, although the majority is housed in Rowley's House Museum in Shrewsbury.

Located at an intersection between the old Roman Watling Street and the modern B4380, the visible ruins of Viroconium are the remains of a large bath-house complex erected around 150 A.D., one of the best surviving examples of its kind in Britain. The ancient brick wall that dominates the site, known locally as the 'Old Work', was once the south side of a large aisled basilica that acted as an exercise hall for the baths themselves. It is remarkable that so much of the ruins have survived, as for generations local people used material from the old city to build their houses and, in particular, the parish church of St Andrew.

The public baths became the social centres of Roman towns, and in a damp climate like Britain the basilica served as an all year round recreation hall. Its main entrance overlooked Watling Street (which cut through the heart of the town), while the bath-house itself adjoined the exercise area by way of a large doorway which once stood in the hole that pierces the 'Old Work'. In addition to having surviving walls of the moist and dry saunas, and the cold plunge baths, the baths-complex at Viroconium provides one of the only two visible examples of a Roman swimming-pool in Britain (the other is at Bath). Throughout the site of the bath-house, the reconstructed tile columns called *pilae* can still be seen. These once formed part of the hypocaust or underfloor heating system.

Although the visible ruins represent only a tiny section of the once great city, the rest of which still remains to be excavated beneath the surrounding farm land, they do reveal something of the city centre; not only the leisure complex, but also the administrative centre. On the opposite side of Watling Street from the bath site are a long line of column stumps, which once formed part of the eastern colonnade of the *forum*, where debates were held and municipal decisions made.

All this represents the Viroconium of the Roman era. But what was it like in the early fifth century? Is there any evidence that Viroconium became the principal city of Vortigern's Britain?

Viroconium assumed a new strategic importance during the early fifth century, a time when the cities of the coastal provinces were suffering constant threat of invasion and pillage. London, for instance, the Roman capital of Britain, was easy prey for the Germanic raiders by route of the Thames. It was probably for this reason that Vortigern later installed Hengist and Horsa on the Isle of Thanet, to help protect the Thames estuary. York was continually sacked by the Picts, and Lincoln was constantly under threat from the Angles and their repeated inland incursions from the Wash. Although other major cities such as Cirencester, Exeter or Bath could be considered safe from outside attack, they would not have had the advantage of Viroconium's central position in the heart of Britain.

Vortigern's administration needed to co-ordinate forces on three fronts, and the location of Viroconium made it ideally suited for this purpose. Here Watling Street, arguably the most important Roman road in Britain, makes contact with the River Severn, one of the most significant waterways of the island. Upstream the Severn penetrates deep into the heartland of Wales, while downstream it arcs across the West Midlands, flowing to the sea through the Bristol Channel. Additionally, the Roman road network linked Viroconium with other important fortifications in the area such as Lavrobrinta (Forden Gaer) to the west, Bravonium (Leintwardine) to the south and Deva (Chester) to the north. Much of this network is still preserved in the pattern of modern roads. The A5, for example, which for much of its length almost entirely follows the course of Watling Street, was the great Roman road cutting right through the centre of England.

Not only did Viroconium occupy a site of vital strategic importance, it was also situated in the centre of one of the country's most fertile agricultural areas. Archaeological excavations around the town and along the Severn Valley have revealed a remarkably rich Romano-British farming district, perhaps the most important reason for the apparent size and wealth of the city in Roman times. Whatever location was chosen by Vortigern for his power base, it would certainly need to feed itself in the event of any breakdown in relations with the allied tribes – so again, archaeological evidence supports the candidacy of Viroconium.

If Viroconium was the capital of Vortigern's Britain, we should expect to discover archaeological confirmation of an intensive occupation of the city during the early fifth century. In recent years, archaeologists have indeed provided remarkable evidence that supports this theory, revealing a highly urbanised city which was unique in Dark Age Britain.

Throughout the later Roman period, Viroconium declined in importance and, although it remained occupied, many of its buildings became run down and dilapidated. The recreation basilica, for instance, fell into such a state of disrepair that it collapsed sometime in the mid-fourth century. Within a couple of decades, even before the Romans left, the town was virtually abandoned.

Until only a few years ago, this fragmentary picture was all that was known of Viroconium. However, in the late 1960s, an extensive archaeological excavation was initiated at the site. It was to last for well over a decade, bringing to light a series of new and incredible discoveries. The dig, led by archaeologist Philip Barker, was more thorough than any that had preceded it, and produced a mass of evidence for the period following the collapse of the baths-complex. The results showed that during the final few years of Roman occupation, the whole area was cleared and completely rebuilt; a new city had been constructed on the ruins of Viroconium.

From the excavation of post holes, and other tell-tale signs in the foundations and substructure of the city, the new buildings were found to have been made of timber, not bricks and mortar like the earlier Roman town. When the evidence emerging from the dig was collated, these new buildings were discovered to have been highly sophisticated. From the discovery of the timber remains, it is possible to ascertain that the buildings were large and elaborate constructions of classical design, with colonnades and orderly facades, many being at least two storeys high. It appears, therefore, that in the closing days of the Roman occupation Viroconium assumed a new importance. But the story did not end there. A second stage of rebuilding took place during the early first half of the fifth century, a second phase altogether more grandiose than the first.

The excavation in the vicinity of the baths-complex showed that the area had been entirely rebuilt. Not only were new buildings erected and streets replanned, but the infrastructure of the city was also repaired. A new drainage system and fresh water supply was installed through an elaborate arrangement of aqueducts. Long stretches of the Roman cobbled roads were also dug up and completely relaid. A new kind of town came into existence. Gone was the leisure complex of the imperial occupation, and in its place arose a dynamic trading centre and hive of industry.

The street running across the north of the baths-complex underwent a drastic change, becoming a covered market or shopping arcade, and at its western end, where it joins Watling Street, a large gate-house was erected together with an adjoining guard-room. All the way along the market street were newly-built dwellings and workshops, and towards the eastern end were a number of large storage barns alongside a sequence of sturdy industrial buildings containing hearths and furnaces.

The nerve centre of this new Viroconium appears to have been a massive winged building constructed on the site of the old basilica. It seems to have been a classical mansion, accompanied by a complex of adjoining buildings and out-houses. Could this have been the palace of an important post-Roman chieftain?

The discovery of this new Viroconium created an archaeological enigma, for in no other city of the period had such a transformation been discovered. This remarkable revitalisation of the city would certainly have required considerable wealth and powerful leadership to bring it about. Who had wielded the influence to organise and motivate such an endeavour? According to Philip Barker, it could not have been the work of peasant villagers, nor the Irish or Saxon invaders. It was a city of Roman design, with perhaps the last classical buildings to be erected in Britain for another thousand years. This reconstruction was a major undertaking, and Philip Barker has suggested that the complex of buildings may have been the demesne of a great man.

Could this great man have been Vortigern? The geographical location of Viroconium fits that theory, but does the palace date from the right period? As coinage and other dateable Roman artefacts became scarce in the Dark Ages, the date of the final period of rebuilding was difficult to determine. In the rubble of the buildings that formed the foundations of the new ones, coins were found dating from around 380. The buildings were therefore erected after that time; but how long after?

The dating of archaeological sites is achieved in a number of ways. One widely used procedure is known as radiocarbon dating. Organic matter, in whatever form, animal or vegetable, contains Carbon 14, and once the living organism has died the Carbon 14 gradually decays, until some 60,000 years later it disappears altogether. The amount of Carbon 14 in something organic can be measured by chemical analysis, thus enabling dating. Luckily there was an abundance of organic matter within the deposit strata of the final building phase at Viroconium: bones, for example, were discovered amongst rubble used to form the foundations of the last phase of building. Unfortunately, radiocarbon dating is only accurate to within fifty years, so a number of readings were necessary to gain a more precise date. A mean date around 420 was arrived at by cross-referencing the results of a series of radiocarbon tests on various finds from the dig.

From this evidence, we know that Viroconium began to reassume considerable importance during the last years of imperial rule, and was massively reorganised shortly after the Roman withdrawal. Since the principal British cities of London, Lincoln and York were under constant threat of invasion, and as no excavation of any Roman city has discovered archaeological evidence for any similar large-scale rebuilding during the fifth century, Viroconium could well have become the national capital. The period of the mysterious transformation of the post-Roman city of Viroconium tallies precisely with the time of·Vortigern I himself, and the discoveries at Viroconium seem, at last, to substantiate the writings of Gildas, Bede, Nennius and the *Chronicle*, all of which record a powerful leader of Britain in the post-Roman period: Vortigern.

However, if Viroconium was the capital of Vortigern circa 420, did it remain the administrative capital of the kingdom of Powys during Arthur's time, three quarters of a century later? Again, archaeology can help answer the question. During excavations in 1979, the skeleton of a man was found, buried on the site of one of the buildings that had once overlooked the market street. His grave had been dug in the soil that had come to cover the rubble of the deserted town. From a radiocarbon dating of these remains, and from calculations assessing the time it took for the covering of soil to build up over the buildings, a date around 520 has been obtained for the final abandonment of Viroconium.

However, evidence was also discovered indicating that Viroconium was annexed by the Cunedda family by the late fifth century. At the excavation in 1967, a tombstone was discovered just outside the city ramparts bearing the inscription *Cunorix macus Maquicoline*. The suffix *rix*, derived from the Latin *rex*, means 'king', and *macus* means 'son of', so the inscription reads: 'King Cuno son of Maquicoline'. (The last name is not entirely certain as the stone was damaged.) Once again, we see the name affix 'Cun' so often found in the Cunedda family. As the stone has been dated to about 480, it appears that Viroconium was occupied at the time of Arthur by the Votadini. It has been suggested that the *macus* prefix, which became widely used in Scotland after the Picts were overrun by the Irish (leading to the 'Mac' in many Scottish names), may imply that Cunorix was an Irish chieftain. However, as we have seen, the Irish had almost certainly been expelled from the Shropshire area by the time of Ambrosius. It is therefore more likely that the influence came directly from Scotland (the home of the Votadini), where Irish migrations and inter-cultural exchange had been occurring for decades.

But would Viroconium still have been the capital of Powys? The excavation discovered no indications of flight, fire or hasty evacuation during the final days of occupation. On the contrary, the evidence points to the city being abandoned in an orderly and almost leisurely fashion, buildings being dismantled after their contents had been removed. In short, Viroconium was not overwhelmed by an enemy or sacked by marauding barbarians; it seems it was deliberately taken apart and moved away. The most likely reason is that the size of Viroconium, with its two miles of perimeter walls, would have made the city impossible to defend without large numbers of warriors. As times became more difficult, it appears that Viroconium was abandoned for a site which was more easily defended, probably the Iron Age hill-fort on the Wrekin, a steep hill rising well over a thousand feet, just to the south-east of the city. This suggests that internal feuding between British factions resumed at this time, since Viroconium was far from the Anglo-Saxons and would face no threat from them for decades to come.

For this policy of planned dismantling to have been conceived and executed suggests that Viroconium remained under strong and organised leadership, about a century after Vortigern came to power. Such a continuation of occupation and orderly administration of a sophisticated post-Roman city would have been unique in Dark Age Britain.

Summary

With Anglo-Saxon invaders in the South and East, Pictish invaders in the North, and Irish invaders in the West, the central position of Powys afforded the kingdom a unique position to gain control over a substantial area of free Britain. We have examined the capital city of Powys, Viroconium, to discover evidence that suggests it was the seat of Vortigern, and more importantly, Arthur.

1. During the Roman occupation of Britain the country was divided into provincial districts known as *civitates*, each founded on existing tribal areas and controlled from an administrative city or capital. The Cornovii tribe of the West Midlands and Central Wales was subject to the administration of Viroconium. After London, York and Lincoln, Viroconium became the fourth largest city in Roman Britain, and was without doubt the most important trading centre in the Midlands.

2. By Vortigern's time, Viroconium had become the most important city in Britain. London was easy prey for Saxon raids via the Thames, York was continually sacked by the Picts, and Lincoln was constantly under threat from the Angles. From Viroconium, Vortigern could co-ordinate forces on three fronts. Here Watling Street, the most important road in Britain, made contact with the River Severn, one of the most significant waterways of the island. Additionally, the Roman road network linked Viroconium with other important fortifications in the area. Viroconium is therefore the most plausible site for the seat of Vortigern and British administration at the end of Roman rule.

3. The circumstantial argument is persuasive, but there is further evidence that Vortigern and his successors ruled from Viroconium. In recent years, archaeology has unearthed support for this theory.

In the late 1960s, an extensive archaeological excavation began on the site. The results have shown that during the first half of the fifth century the city was completely rebuilt in a remarkably sophisticated fashion. Nothing like it has been discovered anywhere else in the archaeology of Dark Age Britain.

4. This transformation and revitalisation of the city would have required considerable wealth, and could not have been achieved without powerful leadership. The time and place matches exactly with what we have learned of Vortigern. The discoveries at Viroconium have at last substantiated the writings of Gildas, Bede, Nennius and the *Chronicle*, all of which record a powerful leader of Britain in the post-Roman period; the leader called Vortigern.

5. Evidence that the Votadini ruled Viroconium by the end of the fifth century is supplied by a tombstone, dated at about 480, found at the excavation in 1967. The name on the stone was Cunorix, bearing the name affix 'Cun' of the Cunedda family.

6. The Viroconium excavation revealed that the city was not abandoned for a more defendable site until around 520, and certainly remained the capital of Powys until then. Therefore, it is safe to assume that if Arthur's stronghold had been Powys, then Viroconium would have been his capital.

15

The Final Campaign

The penultimate stage in our search for the real King Arthur involves pinpointing the battle of Camlann, which according to Geoffrey of Monmouth and the subsequent Romancers was Arthur's last battle. From the *Annales Cambriae* we learn that in the ninety-third year there was the 'strife of Camlann in which Arthur and Medraut perished'. We are told nothing else, neither where nor why it occurred, nor even if Arthur and Medraut fought on opposite sides. Unfortunately, other than this entry in the *Annales*, no other Dark Age manuscript mentions Camlann. Before we attempt to locate the battle site, and consider the relationship between Arthur and Medraut, we must first establish a date for the battle.

The ninety-third year of the *Annales* is somewhere around 539, almost certainly too late for the real King Arthur. Since Arthur was fighting when Hengist died in 488, he would have been well over seventy by 539. Although it is not impossible for Arthur to have died in battle in 539, it seems unlikely. Besides, we know from Chapter Seven that the *Annales* is inaccurate when it comes to its dating of the battle of Badon.

A more reasonable date for Arthur's death would be just prior to the abandonment of Viroconium. As we will show in Chapter Sixteen, the evidence of internal feuding and breakdown of central authority suggests the recent death of a powerful, unifying figure, presumably the British leader who had successfully united the country since the time of Badon. As this occurred around 520, the battle of Camlann may have been fought about the year that the *Annales* place Badon, around 518. It is possible that the writer of the *Annales* knew the approximate date of one of Arthur's battles. He may also have known that some two decades separated Badon and Camlann.

Medraut, like the battle of Camlann itself, is not named in any other Dark Age manuscript besides the *Annales Cambriae*. Gildas makes no mention of him; neither does Bede, and even Nennius fails to include him. Nennius however, as we have seen, does not refer to anything connected with Arthur's death. His list of Arthur's battles concerns only Arthur's victories, and since the battle of Camlann appears to have been a disaster, it may not have been included because Nennius' source was a battle poem praising Arthur's successful exploits.

Apart from the cursory mention in the *Annales*, Geoffrey of Monmouth is the earliest writer to provide any details of Medraut and the battle of Camlann. According to Geoffrey, Modred (as he styles him) was Arthur's nephew, who led a rebellion while Arthur was absent from the country. Arthur returns to confront Modred, but although he crushes the rebellion, Arthur is mortally wounded in battle. Although Geoffrey uses the name Modred instead of Medraut, he is clearly referring to the man described in the *Annales*. Welsh literature includes the character of Modred as Arthur's opponent at Camlann, but under the same spelling as the *Annales*, Medraut. The Medraut of the Welsh tales, however, is somewhat different to Geoffrey's Modred. Although he and Arthur are rivals, they are generally depicted as feuding equals or two chieftains involved in a struggle for supremacy.

The battle of Camlann would seem to have been the result of some form of internal struggle between the Britons themselves. Gildas tells us that from the battle of Badon until the time of his writing (circa 545) external warfare had ceased, although the country had been racked by internal feuding. Archaeological evidence, supported by the testimony of the *Anglo-Saxon Chronicle* and Bede, clearly shows that by the mid-sixth century the Britons had been so weakened by internal squabbles that the Saxons were once more able to advance.

There are three main claimants for the site of Camlann. First, those favouring a Somerset Arthur place the battle of Camlann somewhere along the river Camel, not far from the site of Cadbury hill-fort. Second, those who locate King Arthur in the far North (chiefly because of his inclusion in the *Gododdin*) centre their argument around the origin of the name Camlann, which is seen as a derivation of the early Brythonic *Camboglanna*, the name of a Roman fort on Hadrian's Wall. Although the case for either of these two candidates cannot be completely disregarded, they lack the supportive evidence of the third, and more persuasive, argument, which sites the battle of Camlann in Cornwall.

Although in the *Vulgate Cycle*, and later in *Le Morte Darthur*, the battle is fought near Salisbury, according to Geoffrey it took place in Cornwall, where Modred had his power base. It is understandable that he should have included Tintagel as Arthur's birthplace in order to satisfy his patron, but he had no reason to invent a Cornish association with the death of Arthur. It is even less likely that Welsh literature would include Cornwall, unless there was some strong link with the area. We have already seen how Cornish Arthurian folklore existed in the early twelfth century, as demonstrated by the account of Hermann of Tournai.

The spelling 'Medraut' is the Welsh rendering used in Welsh literature; the variant 'Modred', employed by Geoffrey, is a Cornish version of the name (both Welsh and Cornish derive from a common source, Brythonic). Geoffrey's use of the Cornish dialect suggests that this is where the details of his Modred story survived. During the sixth century, however, Cornwall was merely a part of the much larger kingdom of Dumnonia, which also included Devon and part of Dorset.

If the battle of Camlann was fought in Cornwall around 518, it would probably have involved Cunomorus, the king of Dumnonia and father of Drustanus. As we have seen, Cunomorus appears on the sixth-century gravestone of Drustanus near Fowey and his name, in the Welsh spelling Cynfawr, occurs in the genealogies of Dumnonia. The dating of the tombstone of his son Drustanus to about 550 indicates that Cunomorus was likely to have been on the throne of Dumnonia in the first half of the sixth century. This is confirmed by St Paul Aurelian's ninth-century biographer, Wrmonoc, who wrote of the saint being summoned to the court of the Dumnonian king 'Cunomorus, also called Mark', about 540. Moreover, Gregory, bishop of Tours from 573 to 594, who wrote within living memory of the event, tells how Cunomorus died in France in 560. The combined evidence suggests that Cunomorus could well have been alive and of adult age around 518. This dating of Cunomorus' death does not necessarily contradict Gildas when he addresses the Dumnonian leader around 545 as Constantine. The genealogies include a Constantine as one of Cunomorus' sons who many have been left to rule Dumnonia when his father was absent in France. According to Gregory, Cunomorus spent considerable time on his estates in Brittany.

In Chapter Four we examined how King Mark (Arthur's rival in Welsh literature and a number of medieval romances) was almost certainly based on the historical Cunomorus. Tristan (the fictional equivalent of Drustanus) is often portrayed as Mark's son, and Wrmonoc actually calls Cunomorus King Mark. If this is not sufficient evidence to link the historical King Arthur to the historical Cunomorus, in the name Cunomorus we see the element 'Cun' of the

Cunedda family. Could Cunomorus therefore have been a client king – a relative of Arthur's sent to rule in Dumnonia?

In both Geoffrey's account and the medieval Romances, Arthur installs his nephew Modred as regent in Cornwall. King Mark seems to have been based on Cunomorus. Was Modred based on him as well? There is certainly confusion between these two characters in Welsh literature, where sometimes Mark, and sometimes Modred, rules in Cornwall at an unidentified location. Moreover, Arthur's relatives became confused with one another as the legend progressed. By the later Middle Ages, Modred had become both Arthur's nephew *and* his son. A confusion could well have arisen in legend between Mark and Modred. Could this be because they were based on the same historical figure, Cunomorus?

Returning to trying to identify the site of the battle of Camlann, the most popular contender for the Cornish Camlann is a field near Slaughter Bridge, near the village of Camelford. Unfortunately, when the field was excavated, it proved to be the site of a battle between the Cornish and Wessex Saxons around 823. No evidence of a previous battle was discovered. The memory of this battle probably persisted for many years before becoming associated with Arthur in Cornish legend.

But although the battle of Camlann may have been against Cunomorus and Dumnonia, it may not have been fought in Cornwall itself. In Geoffrey's account, Modred is able to lead the rebellion by forming an alliance with the Saxons. Such a scenario is not only possible in the early sixth century; it may be the only solution to an historical enigma, the mystery of Cerdic's invasion of Wessex.

Here we need to recall what we know of Cerdic. According to the *Anglo-Saxon Chronicle*, Cerdic arrived in Britain in 495. Landing first at a location referred to as Cerdicesora, somewhere near modern Southampton, Cerdic and his warriors fought a series of successful battles and established a foothold along the south coast. In 508, they achieved a major victory over the British king Natanleod, and seem to have established control over an area the size of Hampshire.

How did this Saxon army achieve such success so soon after Badon? The answer may be that Cerdic was originally invited into Britain as a mercenary. The dating in the *Chronicle* of his initial landing around the time of Badon may reflect him being invited in to help combat Aelle's forces in Sussex. Since there is also archaeological evidence for the expansion of Dumnonia across Dorset and towards Hampshire around this time, this would place Cunomorus' forces fairly close to Cerdic's. An alliance between Cunomorus and Cerdic to gain control of Dorset may explain the success of both kingdoms, Dumnonia and Wessex.

According to the *Chronicle*, as we discuss in Chapter Nine, in 519 the battle of Certicesford, fought by Cerdic's Saxons, marked the end of their expansion for another three decades. This battle not only falls around the likely time of Camlann, but it is the only recorded battle of the period. Could the battle of Certicesford, therefore, have been fought at a place the British had called Camlann? The *Chronicle*'s name of Certicesford is the Saxon name, as it means, literally, Cerdic's Ford. The *Chronicle*'s very words are that the battle was fought 'at a place that is now called Certicesford'. We have seen how Nennius, for instance, gives both the British and Saxon names for certain battles, often very different from one another. The area can safely be identified as Charford, a few miles south of Salisbury on the River Avon, since the name appears in Norman times under the French spelling as Cerdeford.

If Certicesford was Camlann (which incidentally sites the battle of Camlann near where the *Vulgate Cycle* and *Le Morte Darthur* locate it) we should expect to find evidence for an alliance between Cunomorus and Cerdic. Indeed we do so, in the name of a warrior who fought with Cerdic. The Certicesford entry in the *Anglo-Saxon Chronicle* reads:

'In this year Cerdic and Cynric obtained the kingdom of the West Saxons and the same year they fought against the Britons at a place now called Certicesford. And from that day on the princes of the West Saxons have reigned.'

Cynric is a hybrid name; half British, half Saxon, suggesting he was of mixed blood. Once more we see the distinguishing name affix 'Cyn', as in Cynglas (Cuneglasus) and Cynfawr (Cunomorus). Since 'Cyn' is the Welsh version of the Latin 'Cun', this is further indication that Cynric was a member of the Cunedda family, very possibly a relative of Cunomorus. But who exactly? If we turn to the *Chronicle*, and to an entry for the year 495, we see:

'In this year two princes, Cerdic and Cynric his son came to Britain with five ships.'

So, according to the *Chronicle*, not only did Cynric arrive with Cerdic, but he was also his son. There can be little doubt that he was Cerdic's son, as the *Chronicle* also tells us that he succeeded Cerdic as king of Wessex. But did he actually arrive with him? Since the British part of his name suggests his mother was a Briton, it is more likely that Cynric was not born until after Cerdic's arrival in Britain. Although the *Chronicle* goes on to say that Cynric fought with Cerdic against the British king Natanleod in 508, some doubt can be cast on his being active so early.

The *Chronicle* indicates that Cynric did not die until 560. He was personally involved in fighting the Britons at Salisbury in 552, and at Beranburh (near Swindon) in 556. If he arrived with Cerdic as a young man, one who fought alongside his father in 495, then he must have been at least eighty when he died. This is possible, but he is unlikely to have been sufficiently agile to fight with his men a couple of years earlier. The *Chronicle* may therefore have been wrong about Cynric having arrived with his father.

Regardless of when he was born, Cynric would seem to have been the son of a British woman, additional evidence being that his own son, who succeeded him in 560, is named by the *Chronicle* as Ceawlin, an entirely British name. It appears to have been common practice at the time to seal an alliance between Saxon and Briton families by marriage. Nennius, for instance, relates that Vortigern was remarried to Hengist's daughter to cement the pact between them. If this was the case, then the alliance between Cerdic and Cunomorus could have been sealed by Cerdic's marriage to Cunomorus' daughter, who would thus have been Cynric's mother. Unfortunately we cannot refer to Cunomorus' daughter by name, as the genealogies only recorded the direct line of male descent.

If Cunomorus was the real Modred, who formed an expedient pact with Cerdic, then the battle of Certicesford may have been the result of a counterthrust by Arthur against their combined forces. The battle not only halted the Saxon advance; it immediately preceded the massive refortification of East Dorset. Evidence for the Midlands British having been responsible for this victory comes in the form of characteristic Midlands pottery excavated from Bokerley Dyke, near Cranborne in Dorset. It is unlikely that the Dumnonians themselves refortified Bokerley Dyke, as around 520 they were busy rebuilding fortifications much closer to home. In Devonshire, for example, the refortification of Exeter clearly indicates that Dumnonia had been forced into retreat at this time. Since the Saxons were still entrenched many miles to the east of Exeter, it must have been against rival Britons that the Dumnonians were defending themselves.

A possible explanation for these activities is that the main contingent of Britons in the Midlands pushed southwards and, after the battle of Certicesford, forced a wedge between Cunomorus' Dumnonia and Cerdic's Wessex. If this was Arthur's campaign, then it would tally with what Geoffrey of Monmouth and the subsequent Romancers say about Camlann containing the rebellion. We therefore compare the legend with the historical events.

Legend:

Geoffrey of Monmouth locates Arthur's nephew Modred in Cornwall, where he reigns as regent in Arthur's absence. (In Welsh literature, Modred and King Mark are often confused as the same person.)

History:

Cunomorus was the contemporary of the historical Arthur, as he reigned in Dumnonia – which included Cornwall – during the early sixth century. He also seems to have been of the same family as Arthur. King Mark was almost certainly the historical Cunomorus, as evidenced by the tombstone of his son Drustanus (the Latin version of Tristan), the son of Mark in medieval romance. Also, the ninth-century monk Wrmonoc actually calls Cunomorus King Mark.

Legend:

In Geoffrey of Monmouth's account, Modred leads a revolt by forming an alliance with the Saxons.

History:

Cunomorus seems to have formed an alliance with the Saxon warrior Cerdic, as evidenced by the name of Cerdic's son and the mutual success of their kingdoms in the early 500s. The only recorded battle fought just prior to the abandonment of Viroconium (circa 520) was Cerdic's battle of Certicesford in 519. There is archaeological evidence to suggest that this battle was fought by the Midland British against a Wessex/Dumnonian alliance.

The sequence of events may therefore have been as follows: Arthur installed Cunomorus in Dumnonia. Cunomorus then made a pact with Cerdic while the remainder of the country was consolidating the advantage gained at Badon. Cerdic cemented his alliance with Dumnonia by marrying Cunomorus' daughter, who later bore him a son, Cynric. Eventually, their joint control of the area was broken by Arthur in an all-out counteroffensive aimed at driving a wedge between the rebel forces. Although the thrust was successful, Cunomorus was certainly not killed at Certicesford. (However, as we will further examine in the following chapter, the Modred legend could well have arisen through a confusion of historical characters.) After the battle an uneasy stalemate ensued, during which time the alliance of British kingdoms gradually fragmented, leaving the Saxons free to continue their invasion a few decades later. If this theory is correct, then the Wessex kings who eventually became the Saxon kings of all England were directly descended, via Cunomorus' daughter, from the family that also included Arthur, the greatest hero of their sworn enemies, the Britons.

Summary

The penultimate stage in our search for the real King Arthur comes with the battle of Camlann, which according to Geoffrey of Monmouth was Arthur's last battle. Also, according to the *Annales Cambriae*, it is where Arthur died together with Medraut. We have therefore attempted to locate the elusive Camlann and identify the enigmatic Medraut.

1. According to the *Annales*, in 539 there was the 'strife of Camlann in which Arthur and Medraut perished'. We are told nothing else, neither where nor why it occurred, nor even if Arthur and Medraut fought on opposite sides. Unfortunately, other than this entry no other Dark Age manuscript mentions Camlann or Medraut.

2. Geoffrey of Monmouth is the earliest writer to provide any details of Medraut and the battle of Camlann. According to

Geoffrey, Medraut was Arthur's nephew who tried to take over the kingdom but failed when he died in the battle. The battle of Camlann was probably the result of an internal struggle amongst the Britons themselves, since Gildas tells us that from the battle of Badon until the time of his writing external warfare had ceased, although the country had been racked by internal feuding.

3. Since the *Annales* have proved inaccurate in dating Badon, their dating of Camlann should be treated with caution. It is highly unlikely that Arthur was fighting in 539. It is more probable that the end of Arthur's reign coincided with the abandonment of Viroconium, for at this time internal conflict had broken out amongst the Britons; in which case Camlann occurred somewhere around 520.

4. Medraut, as it appears in the *Annales*, is a Welsh name. The spelling Modred that Geoffrey employs is Cornish. The Welsh and Cornish languages derive from Brythonic. Geoffrey's use of the Cornish dialect implies that this is where the details of his Modred story survived. During the sixth century, however, Cornwall was merely a part of the kingdom of Dumnonia, which also included Devon and part of Dorset.

5. If Modred had Dumnonian connections, and if the battle of Camlann occurred in the second decade of the sixth century, it would certainly have involved Cunomorus, whose name is on the sixth-century Drustanus stone, and who appears to have been ruling in Dumnonia at this time. Since we find the 'Cun' name affix of the Cunedda family in his name, he may have been a Votadini prince despatched to maintain control of the remote province of Dumnonia.

6. As this is consistent with Geoffrey and with the medieval Romances that tell of Arthur installing his nephew Modred in Cornwall, perhaps Cunomorus was Arthur's nephew, the real Modred? We have seen that King Mark seems to have been based on Cunomorus; perhaps Modred was also. There is certainly evidence of confusion between these two people in some works of Welsh literature, which sometimes give Mark and sometimes Modred ruling in Cornwall.

7. In Geoffrey's account, Modred is able to lead the rebellion by

forming an alliance with the Saxons. Such a scenario is certainly possible in the early sixth century. The fact that Cerdic had been able to establish himself in Hampshire so soon after Badon suggests he had help, and since there is archaeological evidence for the expansion of Dumnonia across Dorset at this time, an alliance between Cunomorus and Cerdic may explain the success of both kingdoms, Dumnonia and Wessex.

8. Evidence for an alliance between Cunomorus (called Cynfawr in the genealogies) and Cerdic comes from the *Anglo-Saxon Chronicle*, which tells us that Cerdic's son and successor was called Cynric. This is not only a half British, half Saxon name, suggesting he was of mixed blood, but also contains the Votadini name affix 'Cyn'. As it seems to have been a common practice at the time to seal an alliance between Saxon and Briton dynasties by marriage, the name 'Cynric' is an indication of an alliance between Dumnonia and Wessex.

9. According to the *Chronicle*, in 519 Cerdic's Saxons fought a battle at Certicesford (now Charford, a few miles south of Salisbury), which marked the end of their expansion for another three decades. Since it is the only recorded battle of the period, it is very possible that the battle of Certicesford is the battle of Camlann. (Certicesford was not the original British name for the site as it means, literally, Cerdic's Ford.) If this is the case, then the battle of Certicesford may have been an attempt by Arthur to drive a wedge between the joint forces of Cunomorus and his ally Cerdic.

16

The Real King Arthur

Before we lift the cloak of mystery that has concealed Arthur's true identity, we need to refresh our memories of what we have learned so far.

It is almost certain that the legends of King Arthur were based on a real historical character. Arthur was not the invention of Geoffrey of Monmouth, since he is mentioned in both the *Annales Cambriae* and in Nennius' *Historia Brittonum*. In addition, the usually reliable historian William of Malmesbury, writing around the same time as Geoffrey, makes reference to King Arthur and the legends that had developed concerning him. There is also the evidence of the Modena Archivolt in Italy, indicating that the stories of Arthur had spread throughout Europe by the time of Geoffrey, and the reference by Hermann of Tournai concerning Arthurian folklore in Cornwall perhaps as early as 1113. Although Arthur's name does not appear in any reliable genealogy covering the period in question, this is probably because the name Arthur is a title meaning the Bear.

There are a number of reliable indicators from which to date the period of Arthur's life. There is the battle of Badon, which both the *Annales* and Nennius associate with Arthur, as does William of Malmesbury. There can be no doubt that the battle of Badon was an historical event, for it is attested to by Bede and, more importantly, by Gildas, in whose time it was still a living memory. We can be fairly certain that the battle of Badon occurred around the end of the fifth century. From analysing Gildas' and Bede's reference to Badon having occurred forty-four years after the Saxon advent, we arrive at the year 493. This assumption is supported by the archaeological evidence such as the interruption of Saxon burials, and by the *Anglo-Saxon Chronicle*, both of which indicate a major Saxon withdrawal by the year 500. The most important element of all is the total eclipse of the Saxon kingdom of Sussex by that time. This fact, together with the *Chronicle* including no further advances of the Kentish forces during the closing years of the fifth century, plausibly suggests a major British victory around 493.

From a slightly earlier period we know of Arthur's predecessor Ambrosius, who is named as Arthur's confederate by William of Malmesbury, and as Arthur's forbear by Nennius. There is no doubt that Ambrosius actually existed, for he is named by both Gildas and Bede as the man who successfully reorganised the Britons and turned the tide on the invading Anglo-Saxons. From the events described by Gildas preceding the rise of Ambrosius, his rise to power can be dated to around 460. This date is supported by the evidence relating to Vortigern, who we know preceded Ambrosius. By dating Vortigern's demise, we are able to date Ambrosius. Vortigern (or Vortigern II) certainly remained in power until 455, since the *Chronicle* names him fighting against the brothers Hengist and Horsa in that year, an event also referred to by Nennius. The deposition of Vortigern after this time suggests that Ambrosius was in power by 460.

There is additional evidence for Ambrosius being in power in the 460s. We have seen how Nennius, Bede and Gildas cite Ambrosius as belonging to a high ranking Roman family. This, together with the investigation into the political and religious struggles of the earlier decades, is evidence that Ambrosius stood for the imperialist faction. That some form of imperialist revival occurred in Britain during the 460s is indicated both by the readoption of Roman names at the time, and by a British contingent fighting for Emperor Anthemius in northern France in 470.

From Nennius we can extract an exact date for Arthur which does not contradict what we know of Ambrosius. The *Historia Brittonum* places Arthur's battles directly after the death of Hengist, an event which the *Anglo-Saxon Chronicle* places in 488. In addition, Nennius tells us that Hengist's son Octha withdrew from the North at this time. There is evidence of withdrawal by the Anglo-Saxons from North-East England around the year 490, and archaeological discoveries, such as examples of characteristic Anglo-British pottery dating from this time, that have been found in Germany, suggest a reverse migration to the continent. As Nennius' assertion concerning Octha's withdrawal is supported by archaeology, his dating of Arthur's campaigns after Hengist's death is credible.

Having thus deduced that the date of Arthur's struggle against the Saxons lay a few years either side of 490, we move on to consider his descent. We have seen earlier in Chapter Thirteen that Arthur's dynasty was almost certainly of the northern Votadini tribe. The Votadini's arrival in North Wales to aid in the struggle against the Irish is recorded in both the *Annales* and the *Historia Brittonum*.

There is also the archaeological evidence of Votadini ceramics and mode of burials appearing in North Wales around 460, which is the most likely time of the Votadini arrival according to the material in Nennius and the *Annales*. This date also correlates with archaeological evidence for the expulsion of the Irish from the area in the late fifth century. Most telling of all is the characteristic Cunedda family name affix 'Cun', or 'Cyn' in the Welsh, which often appears on inscriptions and in genealogies of the area during this period.

The Cunedda dynasty was undoubtedly powerful in early sixth-century Britain. Maglocunus was the most powerful British king by Gildas' time, and Cuneglasus was ruling in Powys. Furthermore Cunomorus was ruling in Dumnonia and Cynric in Wessex. For Arthur not to have been of this line seems highly unlikely, especially as the poem *Gododdin* constitutes independent evidence that Arthur was a warrior of the Votadini tribe, originally from the kingdom of Gododdin.

Although Geoffrey of Monmouth may have fallen prey to fantasy and legend concerning Arthur's immediate associates, his predecessors as given by Geoffrey all appear to have been based on historical characters, such as Constantine, Constans, Vortigern and Ambrosius. There is some reason, therefore, to believe that Uther Pendragon, Arthur's father, also actually existed. As we have seen, his name means 'head dragon', a title which was adopted by the kings of Gwynedd. This, together with Gildas' description of Maglocunus as 'the Dragon of Britain', identifies Uther as a King of Gwynedd.

In our search for Arthur's power base, his real 'Camelot', we were drawn to the kingdom of Powys. From the archaeological evidence it is not only clear that Powys wielded considerable influence, but it was very probably the seat of Vortigern. Not only does Nennius associate Vortigern with the kingdom (by saying an ancestor of his founded the city of Gloucester), but the Pillar of Eliseg actually identifies him as a king of Powys. Added to this is the evidence from Viroconium of an unparalleled rebuilding of the Roman city which precisely matches the time when Vortigern I came to power.

There is archaeological evidence not only for the continued importance of Viroconium throughout the fifth century, but also that the Votadini had assumed control of the city. There can be little doubt that the Cunedda family came to rule from Viroconium by the end of the fifth century, as demonstrated by the grave of Cunorix. Moreover, they still ruled the kingdom of Powys in the mid-sixth century, as an analysis of Gildas and his tirade against Cuneglasus reveals.

In conclusion, the warrior who led the British forces during a successful period of warfare against the Anglo-Saxons, culminating with a decisive victory at Badon in 493, must have been a member of the Cunedda family whose seat of government was Viroconium. It is important to remember that we have been using the name Arthur as a convenient label for this warlord. Setting aside the wealth of legend that existed during the Middle Ages, we must now see from the historical evidence whether this warrior – Warrior X – was actually called Arthur.

This is what the historical sources say about someone they name as Arthur:

1. William of Malmesbury, a reliable historian writing about 1125, believed that King Arthur was an historical figure, contemporary with Ambrosius, who defeated the Anglo-Saxons at the battle of Badon.

2. Around 950, the *Annales Cambriae* were compiled, which reference Arthur's victory at Badon and death at Camlann.

3. Around 830, the *Historia Brittonum* was written by Nennius, telling us that Arthur was the leader of the Britons who fought a series of successful battles between the death of Hengist (488 according to the *Anglo-Saxon Chronicle*) and the Saxon defeat at Badon (493 according to the dating derived from Gildas and Bede).

As the other major historical sources, such as Gildas and Bede, fail altogether to name the British leader during the period in which the *Historia Brittonum* locates Arthur, and as no name other than Arthur's has been associated with the British victory at Badon, there seems no reason to doubt that Warrior X was known as Arthur.

If Warrior X *is* Arthur, we should find him in the Cunedda family of Powys around 490. However, as we have demonstrated, the name Arthur derives from the word for bear, and was a title held by a warrior born with a different name. Since the names of the Cunedda family who ruled the West Midlands and North Wales are preserved in the Dark Age genealogies, a process of elimination should enable us to discover the true name of King Arthur.

As both Cuneglasus and Maglocunus were certainly a generation too late to have been the historical Arthur, we must examine their forefathers. According to our line of argument, Arthur was the son of the 'Head Dragon', a king of Gwynedd in the second half of the fifth century. There can be little doubt that Cunedda was succeeded by his son, Enniaun Girt, who in the Dark Age genealogies attached to the *Annales Cambriae* is identified as the *grandfather* of both Maglocunus and Cuneglasus. We know from Gildas that Maglocunus and Cuneglasus were both kings in their own right. Although a king of Gwynedd, like Cunorix in Powys, Enniaun was probably subordinate to Ambrosius, who held the position of overall British leader.

Could Enniaun Girt have been King Arthur? He was certainly the son of a Gwynedd king, and could have succeeded Ambrosius as commander of the British forces. However, as he is recorded by Nennius as a warrior who arrived with his father around 460, he is probably a generation too early to be Arthur. Moreover, the genealogies show that Maglocunus and Cuneglasus both succeeded from Enniaun's *son*, not Enniaun himself. After the death of this son of Enniaun around 520 (the generally accepted date for the accession of both Maglocunus and Cuneglasus), British unity must have fallen apart. These individual successions show that the kingdoms of Powys and Gwynedd must have separated after Enniaun's son's death, and the abandonment of Viroconium at this time is evidence of civil strife between the two kingdoms (see below). This indicates that a strong, unifying figure had just died. It is very likely that Enniaun's son had been that unifying element which was Warrior X; that is, Enniaun's son was Arthur.

The date of Enniaun's death is unknown, although we do know that Cunorix died about 480 so Enniaun's son could not have taken control over Powys before the date. It was, therefore, sometime *after* 480 that Enniaun's son assumed direct control over both Gwynedd and Powys.

So who was Enniaun's son – the most probable candidate for the warrior who assumed the title Arthur? Since from Gildas we discover that Maglocunus was the more powerful of the two kings, perhaps Arthur was his father, who is named in the genealogies as Cadwallon Lawhir.

However, from Gildas we discover that Maglocunus did not succeed from his father, but from his uncle. Gildas accuses Maglocunus of overthrowing his uncle in order to secure the throne for himself. Gildas scolds Maglocunus, saying: 'In the first years of your youth, you crushed the king your uncle and his brave troops with fire and spear and sword.' So was Maglocunus' uncle the warrior who gave rise to the Arthur legend? A similar story of internecine struggle does occur in several later works: Geoffrey of Monmouth and the subsequent Romances portray Modred bringing about the death of *his* uncle, Arthur, in an attempt to seize the throne. What can be made of this?

We have shown earlier how the legend of Modred's rebellion appears to have arisen from the revolt of Cunomorus. Is this how another of the Modred legends arose, namely that Arthur was killed by his nephew? After the battle of Certicesford, did the weakened Arthur return home to his kingdom to be overthrown by Maglocunus? It may well be that Modred, the legendary figure, arose as a fusion of two historical figures, Cunomorus and Maglocunus.

Although Arthur seems to have fought at Certicesford, it may not have been his final battle. The similarity between Certicesford and Geoffrey's battle of Camlann may reflect only half the legend Geoffrey portrays. Just as the roles of Mark and Modred became confused as the Arthurian Romances developed, the circumstances surrounding Arthur's last two battles may have merged into the legend of one battle as the Dark Ages progressed. If King Arthur's nephew was Maglocunus, then his rebellion in Gwynedd may also have been interpolated by Geoffrey into his story of Modred's revolt.

Gildas tells us that Maglocunus overthrew his 'uncle and his brave troops with fire and spear and sword', implying a defeat in battle. Since the genealogies show that Gwynedd and Powys formed a united kingdom prior to the succession of Maglocunus in Gwynedd, the border land between the two kingdoms is the logical site for a battle in which Maglocunus severed his kingdom of Gwynedd from the kingdom of Powys. The *Annales Cambriae* record that Arthur died at the battle of Camlann. A bleak and remote valley about five miles to the east of Dolgellau in the region of Merioneth in Central-West Wales is called Camlan, although it is spelt with a single 'n'. It is surely beyond coincidence that the only location in Great Britain ever known to have been called Camlan is precisely and strategically situated in the border area of the kingdoms of Gwynedd and Powys as they existed in the early sixth century.

But who was Medraut? Medraut is recorded in the *Annales Cambriae* as falling at the battle of Camlann with Arthur, but there is no other record of him in the early sixth century. As the *Annales* simply record that a Medraut fell with Arthur, both his identity and relationship to Arthur seem to have been forgotten by the time Geoffrey came to write the *Historia*. Knowingly or otherwise, Geoffrey may have used the historical Medraut as a convenient character to assume the roles of both Cunomorus and Maglocunus. The real Medraut could well have fought alongside Arthur and perished with him.

Now we need to return to the sixth century. If Maglocunus came to power around 520, he did so during the most likely period of the abandonment of Viroconium. This is further evidence of internal feuding amongst the British, for the city was under no threat from the Anglo-Saxons. The threat could not have been from far away Dumnonia, which, aside from its strategic isolation, was itself in retreat. The only explanation for the abandonment of Viroconium for a more defendable site was a threat from the adjacent kingdom of Gwynedd, the most powerful kingdom by the time of Gildas.

If Maglocunus' uncle had held sway over both the kingdoms of Gwynedd and Powys, the overthrow of this uncle would give Maglocunus power over Gwynedd, but not over Powys, where his cousin Cuneglasus assumed control. In these circumstances, the abandonment of Viroconium could be seen as part of Cuneglasus' strategy to defend himself against a possible attack by Maglocunus.

Although Gildas does not name the uncle from whom Maglocunus succeeded, he must have been Cuneglasus's father: not only were Cuneglasus and Maglocunus cousins (i.e. Cuneglasus' and Maglocunus' fathers were brothers), but the genealogies show that the two kings both succeed from him. Cuneglasus' father is therefore the most credible contender for the warrior who bore the title Arthur.

In the list of genealogies, compiled around 955 from earlier records, attached to the *Annales Cambriae* and contained within manuscript Harley 3859 in the British Library in London, the father of Cuneglasus is identified. He was the son of Enniaun Girt, and his name was *Owain Ddantgwyn*.

All the available evidence indicates that Owain Ddantgwyn was the historical figure who assumed the title 'Arthur'.

- Owain Ddantgwyn was ruling in the last decade of the fifth century, precisely the period in which the *Historia Brittonum* locates 'Arthur'.

- Owain Ddantgwyn was the son of one of the Gwynedd kings,

who were known as the '*head dragons*'. 'Uther Pendragon', meaning 'terrible *head dragon*', was the father of 'Arthur'.

• Owain Ddantgwyn, as king of both Gwynedd and Powys, was the most powerful ruler in Britain at the time of the battle of Badon, where the British were led to victory by 'Arthur'.

• Owain Ddantgwyn was the father of Cuneglasus, whose predecessor was called the 'Bear'. The 'Bear' is almost certainly the origin of the name 'Arthur'.

• Owain Ddantgwyn may have died in battle in the valley of Camlan near Dolgellau. Camlann is where the *Annales Cambriae* record the death of 'Arthur'.

Other than his name, however, nothing is recorded of Owain Ddantgwyn. We know nothing of his appearance, his personality, his beliefs, nor anything of his immediate family. Paradoxically, it could be the very lack of historical information concerning the man who was Arthur that has made him so famous; he was free to become many things to many people. If he had been historically defined he could not later have become the adaptable vehicle for so many different ideas.

Owain Ddantgwyn was not the only warrior of his era to be all but forgotten. In the century following the end of Roman rule, the identities of many British leaders have been lost in the mists of time. Nothing is known of Cunorix, other than his tombstone, and nothing is known of Enniaun Girt other than curt references in genealogies. Even Ambrosius confronts us with almost a complete blank. So how did the name 'Arthur', which was really a title, achieve such legendary status, if the man who bore it has become so hidden to history?

Owain Ddantgwyn, the warrior who ruled from Viroconium around the year 500; the commander of the Britons at the battle of Badon; the warlord who assumed the battle-name the Bear; was the *last* leader of a united Britain. As such, he became the focus of nationalist nostalgia, a historical epicentre from which radiated waves of legend. There is perhaps even greater reason for the rapid growth of the Arthurian legend. The civilisation that survived in the West of Britain during the late fifth and early sixth centuries was to all intents

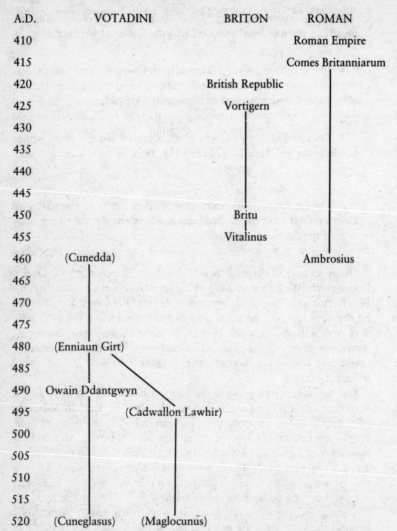

A.D.	VOTADINI	BRITON	ROMAN
410			Roman Empire
415			Comes Britanniarum
420		British Republic	
425		Vortigern	
430			
435			
440			
445			
450		Britu	
455		Vitalinus	
460	(Cunedda)		Ambrosius
465			
470			
475			
480	(Enniaun Girt)		
485			
490	Owain Ddantgwyn		
495		(Cadwallon Lawhir)	
500			
505			
510			
515			
520	(Cuneglasus)	(Maglocunus)	

British Leadership in the Fifth and Early Sixth Centuries.

Members of Owain Ddantgwyn's family bracketed.

and purposes all that remained of the Western Empire, the empire of Rome.

Summary

Having traced the life and times of the real King Arthur, we close in on the historical figure himself, piecing together the evidence to reveal the flesh and blood warrior behind the legend.

1. The most likely date for Arthur's death coincides precisely with the abandonment of Viroconium about 520. This is the generally accepted date for Cuneglasus becoming king of Powys, and Maglocunus becoming king of Gwynedd, a time when the two kingdoms split apart. Since Viroconium was under no threat from the Saxons for decades to come, the only explanation for the abandonment of the city for a more defendable site is a threat from the adjoining kingdom of Gwynedd. In other words, Cuneglasus was preparing to defend himself against the threat from Maglocunus. Internal feuding breaking out at this time is not only evidence for Arthur's demise, but also suggests that Cuneglasus and Maglocunus were his rival successors.

2. Arthur appears to have been the son of the Head Dragon, the leader of the Votadini in the 480s and king of both Gwynedd and Powys. The Head Dragon seems to have been Cunedda's son, Enniaun Girt, who according to the genealogies is the grandfather of Maglocunus and Cuneglasus, both of whom became kings in their own right. If Enniaun Girt was Arthur's father, then Arthur must have been the father of either Maglocunus or Cuneglasus.

3. Since Maglocunus was by far the most powerful of the two kings, then perhaps Arthur was Maglocunus' father, named in the genealogies as Cadwallon Lawhir. However, on reading Gildas we discover that Maglocunus did not succeed from his father, but from his uncle. From the genealogies we discover that this uncle was Cuneglasus' father.

4. The name of this Dark Age warlord survives in a list of genealogies, compiled around 955 from earlier monastic records and now attached to the *Annales Cambriae* in a manuscript indexed

'Harley 3859' in the British Library. The genealogy reveals that Cuneglasus' father was called Owain Ddantgwyn.

5. All the available evidence indicates that Owain Ddantgwyn was the historical figure who assumed the title 'Arthur'. He ruled in the same place and at the same time as our research has located King Arthur. He ruled Gwynedd and Powys simultaneously, and was thus the most powerful ruler in Britain at the time of the battle of Badon, in which Arthur led the British to their most important victory of the era. Arthur almost certainly means the Bear and Owain Ddantgwyn was the father of Cuneglasus, whom Gildas refers to as the 'charioteer of the Bear's stronghold'.

6. According to Geoffrey of Monmouth, Arthur was mortally wounded at the battle of Camlann while attempting to quash a revolt led by his nephew. Although this nephew is called Modred, the legend may have sprung from the real-life Maglocunus who, according to Gildas, acquired his kingdom by overthrowing his uncle. Since Gwynedd and Powys formed a united kingdom prior to the succession of Maglocunus in Gwynedd, the border land between the two kingdoms is the logical site for a battle in which Maglocunus severed his kingdom of Gwynedd from the kingdom of Powys.

7. A bleak and remote valley about five miles to the east of Dolgellau in Central-West Wales is actually called Camlan, although it is spelt with a single 'n'. It is surely beyond coincidence that the only location in Great Britain ever known to have been called Camlan is precisely and strategically situated in the border area of the kingdoms of Gwynedd and Powys as they existed in the early sixth century. Not only is Camlann the name given to Arthur's last battle by Geoffrey of Monmouth, but the *Annales Cambriae* also record Arthur's death at the battle of Camlann.

17

The Arthurian Dynasty

There is one question left to answer: What became of Arthurian Britain and the dynasty of Owain Ddantgwyn?

Although Welsh tradition names Owain's brother, Cadwallon Lawhir, as the man who finally expelled the Irish from Anglesey, all that is known of the life and deeds of Owain himself seems to have been preserved under the name of Arthur, as we have already shown. After Owain's death, Britain moved progressively into a period of recorded history. The *Annales Cambriae* no longer rely on Irish annals; the records which later formed the *Anglo-Saxon Chronicle* were compiled, and the gradual conversion of the Anglo-Saxons to Christianity from the end of the sixth century led to the founding of monasteries and the spread of writing skills. The decline of Powys is therefore easier to trace than its ascendancy.

In the mid-sixth century, Gildas implored the British kings to cease their internecine strife for fear they would lose everything to the real enemy, the Anglo-Saxons. Within a few years his fears were realised. According to the *Anglo-Saxon Chronicle*, in 552 Cynric (Cerdic's son) moved north, defeating the British near Salisbury, and in 556 he again fought the British at Beranburh, near Swindon. The *Chronicle* does not record a victory for Cynric at Beranburh, and it appears that his campaign was halted for a time.

Some fifteen years later, the Britains were presented with a new threat to the East. According to the *Anglo-Saxon Chronicle*, in 571 the Saxon king Cuthwulf (of the Eslingas of South-West Cambridgeshire) routed the Midlands British in Bedfordshire. Immediately afterwards, he marched on Abingdon. Although his forces were victorious, Cuthwulf himself appears to have been killed. His successor, Cuthwine, seems to have formed an alliance with Ceawlin of Wessex (Cynric's son). The alliance marched west and in 577 defeated the British at the battle of Dyrham, seven miles north of Bath. With the cities of Gloucester, Cirencester and Bath now under Saxon control, the Saxons had succeeded where they had failed at Badon over eighty years earlier, effectively severing Dumnonia from the rest of Celtic Britain. The heartland of Powys was now under direct threat from the Saxon alliance.

The Powys king responsible for the loss of Gloucester is unknown, but it was probably Cuneglasus' successor, Brochfael Ysgithrog. No record of Brochfael's campaigns survive, although his son, Cynan Garwyn, seems to have halted the Saxon advance in the South. The 'Book of Taliesin' contains a poem, *Trawsganu Cynan Garwyn*, believed to have been composed at the time by Taliesin himself, which praises the prowess of Cynan in battle against the English.

With stalemate in the South the theatre of war shifted north, where two Anglian kingdoms of the North-East joined forces against the British for the decisive battle of Catraeth (Catterick in Yorkshire) about 598. There, King Aethelfrid of Bernicia (in modern Northumberland) and King Aelle of Deira (in modern Yorkshire) defeated the British. This humiliation is the theme of the *Gododdin*, in which the Votadini fought with warriors from Gwynedd. Since the *Gododdin* names the warrior Cynan, this may imply that Powys was also involved in the battle of Catraeth, as Cynan Garwyn seems to have been king of Powys at the time.

In the *Gododdin*, the battle of Catraeth marked both a decisive defeat for the Britons and the beginning of the end of the British kingdom of Rheged in the North of England. Before securing the North, the Anglo-Saxons were involved in a final battle. In 603, according to Bede, the Irish king Aedan (who ruled in South-West Scotland) marched against the Anglo-Saxons, but lost. The following year, Aethelfrid moved against Aelle himself and occupied the Deira capital at York, thus creating the huge Anglian kingdom of Northumbria, covering much of northern England.

After a decade of consolidation, about the year 613 (according to the *Annales Cambriae*) Aethelfrid attacked North Wales and defeated a joint Gwynedd/Powys army at Chester, where Cynan's son, Selyf, was killed. Northumbria thus drove a wedge between the British forces of North and Central Britain.

Within a couple of years the Angles again began to fight amongst themselves. Aelle's exiled son, Edwin, marched with the army of King Redwald of East Anglia against Aethelfrid and defeated him. The *Annales* record the death of Aethelfrid around the year 617, after which Edwin became king of Northumbria and Aethelfrid's sons were exiled to Ireland. Edwin appears to have continued with the expansionist policy of his predecessor and invaded Gwynedd during the

620s. However, the internal wranglings of the enemy seem to have given the British a breathing space. After being besieged in 629 on an island the *Annales* call Glannauc (probably off the coast of Anglesey) Cadwallon, the king of Gwynedd, fought back.

In 633, in alliance with the Anglian prince Penda (who had broken away his East Midland kingdom of Mercia from Edwin's influence), Cadwallon defeated Edwin, who died in battle. Any hope of a British revival was dashed two years later when Aethelfrid's son, Oswald, returned from exile in Ireland and defeated Cadwallon with (according to Bede) a much smaller army. Gwynedd then seems to have been overrun by the Northumbrians, as independant Irish records mention the burning of Bangor in 634, while in the North, Gododdin was conquered four years later.

With the power of Gwynedd broken, in 644 a Mercia/Powys alliance finally defeated Oswald at a place recorded in the *Annales* as Cogwy (probably modern Oswestry). Within a few years only Powys remained as the last bastion of British power, the *Annales* recording the 'hammering of Dyfed' in 645 and the 'slaughter of Gwent' in 649, perhaps by the Irish and West Saxons respectively.

Penda of Mercia and Aethelhere of East Anglia, the last remaining allies of Powys, were defeated by Oswald's brother, Oswy, at a battle which Bede describes as being near the River Vinwed, probably in the area of Leeds, about the year 655. Having defeated Penda and Aethelhere, Oswy installed Penda's son, Peada, and Aethelhere's brother, Anna, as puppet kings in Mercia and East Anglia. Powys now stood alone against Oswy.

The final days of greater Powys are recorded in a collection of early Welsh poems, the *Canu Llywarch Hen* (the 'Song of Llywarch the Old'). Now preserved in the 'Red Book of Hergest' at Oxford's Bodleian Library, the cycle of poems have been dated to the mid-ninth century. (The dating was based not only on linguistic grounds, but also on the similarity of the cycle to the *Juvencus Englynion*, three verses of ninth-century saga poetry preserved at Cambridge University.) Although the *Canu Llywarch Hen* appears to have been committed to writing around 850, its record of names, locations and events from the mid-seventh century indicates that it formed part of a saga composed much nearer this time. Details in the *Canu Llywarch Hen* can be cross-referenced in Bede, the *Annales Cambriae* and the *Tribal Hidage*. The *Canu Llywarch Hen* is thus considered to be an accurate portrayal of events in seventh-century Powys.

The *Canu Llywarch Hen* concerns the ruling family of Powys and the failing struggle of their king, Cynddylan, against the invading Anglo-Saxons. The first of Cynddylan's battles referred to in the poems is the battle of Maes Cogwy (Cogwy Field). The *Annales Cambriae* also record this battle, in which Penda defeated Oswald in 644. In the *Canu Llywarch Hen*, the poet relates:

> I saw the field of Maes Cogwy
> Armies, and the cry of men hard pressed
> Cynddylan brought them aid

This suggestion of Cynddylan's close ties with Penda is also echoed in the writings of Bede, where he names the queen of the Mercians as Cynwise, and Penda's daughter as Cyneberga, inferring that an inter-family marriage had taken place between the kingdoms of Cynddylan and Penda.

The *Canu Llywarch Hen* also refers to what may well have been the last of Cynddylan's victories, at Caer Luitcoet (Wall, near Lichfield). This must have been fought after Penda's death around 655, as the Anglo-Saxon army is described as being accompanied by Christian priests. According to Bede, Penda died a pagan, although Peada converted to Christianity under Oswy's guidance.

It is with reference to this battle that the poet of the *Canu Llywarch Hen* includes a line describing the kings of Powys as actually being descended from King Arthur himself. Cynddylan and his family are described as 'heirs of great Arthur'. The dating of 850 means that, other than the *Gododdin* and the *Historia Brittonum*, the *Canu Llywarch Hen* may contain the oldest reference to Arthur in existence. Since the poem also describes Cynddylan as 'vested in purple', it would seem that around the year 850, when the *Canu Llywarch Hen* was written down, the kings of Powys were still considered to be the direct descendants of Arthur and the last of the Roman emperors.

Unlike later Welsh poems, such as 'Culhwch and Olwen' and the 'Spoils of Annwn', which portray Arthur in a clearly mythical context, the *Canu Llywarch Hen* and the *Gododdin* are sombre, Dark Age war poems, unfettered by myth or elaboration. In both works the references to Arthur are set against a background of known historical events.

The only other reference to Arthur as early as the ninth century is in the *Historia Brittonum* which, as we have seen, refers to Arthurian folklore in the region of Ercing in Powys. If the reference to Camlann in the *Annales Cambriae* does refer to Camlan in Central Wales, then

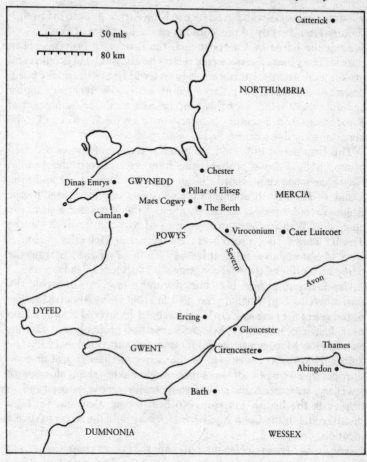

Catterick •

50 mls

80 km

NORTHUMBRIA

• Chester

Dinas Emrys •   GWYNEDD

• Pillar of Eliseg

Maes Cogwy •   • The Berth

MERCIA

Camlan •

POWYS

• Viroconium   • Caer Luitcoet

Severn

Avon

DYFED

Ercing •

• Gloucester

GWENT   Cirencester•

Thames

Abingdon •

Bath •

DUMNONIA   WESSEX

West Britain in the Mid-Seventh Century

all surviving works which reference to King Arthur prior to the twelfth century refer directly to the Votadini or the kingdom of Powys.

After the battle of Caer Luitcoet, the Britons of Powys were in retreat. The *Canu Llywarch Hen* relates how Cynddylan is killed and his kingdom sacked. During an elegy on Cynddylan's death, the poem describes Cynddylan's pillaged court at *Dinlle Wrecon*, almost certainly the Wrekin, probably reoccupied after the abandonment of Viroconium over a century before. Now even the Wrekin had to be abandoned and the British fled beyond the Severn.

This final defeat of Cynddylan and the sacking of Powys occurred around 658, and was probably the event referred to in the *Annales Cambriae* when they record that in that year 'Oswy came and took plunder'. The British of Shropshire were certainly conquered by the Anglo-Saxons by 661, as the peoples of the Wroxeter district are entered as *Wrocensaetna* in the census of Mercian territories in the *Tribal Hidage*. Also, a ford over the Severn near Melverley, ten miles west of Shrewsbury, is recorded as 'Wulfhere's Ford', bearing the name of Wulfhere, the Mercian king who succeeded Peada in 658.

Cynddylan must have been buried within a few years of his old ally Aethelhere of East Anglia, who died fighting Oswy about 655. The burial site of the East Anglian kings has been discovered at Sutton Hoo near Ipswich; indeed Aethelhere himself is probably the famous Sutton Hoo Man, whose burial mound was excavated in 1939. The Sutton Hoo dig revealed one of the richest archaeological finds in Europe: the remains of an entire Anglo-Saxon ship, along with jewellery, armaments and other family treasures, now restored and on display in the British Museum. No British equivalent has yet been discovered, but the *Canu Llywarch Hen* may hold the secret to such a location.

The *Canu Llywarch Hen* not only calls the Powys kings 'the heirs of Arthur', but it also names the burial site of Cynddylan and the ruling dynasty of Powys. It may, therefore, reveal the most elusive secret of all, the burial site of Owain Ddantgwyn: King Arthur himself.

In one of the monologue poems of the *Canu Llywarch Hen*, the *Canu Heledd* (the 'Song of Heledd'), the death of Cynddylan is mourned by his sister Heledd. She relates how, after a final battle, the body of Cynddylan is taken to be buried at *Eglwyseu Bassa*, the 'Churches of Bassa'. It is clear from the poem that *Eglwyseu Bassa* has long been a sacred burial site, for Heledd also refers to 'the gravemound of Gorwynnion' and other 'green graves'. In fact, in a second elegy on Cynddylan's death within the *Canu Llywarch Hen* cycle, one of Cynddylan's family, Llywarch (after whom the cycle is named), says that he will 'grieve for the death of Cynddylan' until he too 'rests beneath the mound'.

Historians believe that the Churches of Bassa is almost certainly the village today called Baschurch, situated some nine miles to the north-west of Shrewsbury. In secluded countryside on the edge of the village is the Berth, an ancient fortified hillock surrounded by marshland and linked to the mainland by a gravel causeway. The hill is completely encompassed by Iron Age earth and stone ramparts, and joined to a low lying oval enclosure by a second causeway some 150 yards to the north-east.

The Berth, its name deriving from the Saxon word *Burh*, meaning castle or fort, was certainly in use during the sixth century, since archaeological excavations in 1962–63, by Peter Gelling of Birmingham University, uncovered fragments of pottery dating from the period. If the hero of the poem, Cynddylan, was buried at the Berth, then one of the grassy mounds lying within the ramparts may have been his tomb. A legend that the Berth was an ancient burial site was recounted by archaeologist Lilly Chitty in 1925, who had been told by a village school teacher that a prince was buried beneath a mound on the south slope after a great battle and that his men were buried in a longer, narrower mound nearby.

Since the hero of *Canu Heledd* was specifically taken for burial to the Churches of Bassa, it appears that Bassa was a place of sanctuary, a holy site. It is currently impossible to gauge the degree of sacred associations the Berth may have had, since the modern archaeological work has been limited to that of Peter Gelling. However, according to the *Transcript of the Shropshire Archaeological & Historical Society* (Vol XLIX 1937–38) the use of the plural, the *Churches* of Bassa, suggests a 'Celtic group of little churches'. Such a group of churches, of a kind more commonly found in Ireland, implies that at some time the Berth supported a monastic or religious community, which lends credence to the Berth being the genuine burial site of the kings of Powys. Since Owain Ddantgwyn was of the same ruling dynasty as Cynddylan, it is quite possible that the Berth was also his burial site.

The 1962–63 excavations were severely limited due to lack of funding. To this day, most of the Berth, including the mounds, has not been excavated. It is possible, therefore, that one of the mounds may still contain the remains of Owain Ddantgwyn.

In Chapter Six we considered the list of Arthur's twelve battles given by Nennius in the *Historia Brittonum*. Having established that the legendary 'Arthur' was the historical Owain Ddantgwyn, we are able to speculate on Nennius' list in a fresh light. Do any of the battle sites relate to the Gododdin/Votadini/Powys findings?

The first five battles in the list seemed to refer to 'Arthur' fighting the Angles in Lincolnshire, and Badon was identified as a battle at Little Solsbury hill-fort near Bath. Four of the remaining six sites are named as: Bassas, Cat Coit Celidon, the City of the Legion and Agned.

The City of the Legion is considered to be either Caerleon or Chester. The *Annales Cambriae* actually refer to Chester as the 'City of the Legion', which, coupled with the fact that Chester may well have fallen within the borders of northern Powys as they existed in the early sixth century, makes it an interesting contender.

Cat Coit Celidon, the battle of the Caledonian forest, is believed to refer to the wooded country north of Hadrian's Wall, which sits geographically with Owain Ddantgwyn fighting in the region of his family homeland of Gododdin. The battle at Mount Agned has been linked by philologists with Bremenium, the Roman fort at High Rochester in the Cheviots, which if correct would locate this battle on the borders of Gododdin.

One battle site has hitherto remained unidentified, the battle fought 'upon the river which is called *Bassas*'. Given the linguistic similarity between *Bassa* ('the Churches of') and *Bassas* ('the river which is called'), could *Bassa* and *Bassas* be referring to the same location? The *Canu Heledd* tells us that *Bassa* was the early British name for the area today identified as Baschurch. Perhaps a nearby river was named after the area, making it the river of *Bassas*. This battle could therefore have been fought in central Powys, actually in the area of the possible burial site of the Powys kings themselves. This would also imply that Owain Ddantgwyn/'Arthur' fought a battle in the vicinity of the site in which he was ultimately buried.

This reconsideration of Nennius is certainly illuminating. Apart from the six battles that Arthur fought against the Saxons (five in East Anglia and one in Bath) of the six remaining, the City of the Legion could have been Chester in northern Powys; Agned and Cat Coit Celidon · were probably fought in the Votadini homeland of Gododdin; but perhaps most intriguing of all is that the battle of Bassas could be linguistically and geographically associated with the burial site of Owain Ddantgwyn at the Berth, in central Powys.

Nennius' list is generally agreed to have been taken from a Welsh battle poem. It is therefore tempting to speculate that Nennius, who seems to have lived in Bangor in the Votadini kingdom of Gwynedd, took his list from a *Votadini* battle poem.

The *Canu Llywarch Hen* names Votadini warriors, Votadini battles and the burial site of the Votadini Powys kings as the *Churches of Bassa*. If Nennius was drawing on a Votadini poem, perhaps it took a similar form, naming the Votadini warrior 'Arthur', listing Votadini battles fought by 'Arthur', and including a battle fought on the river of *Bassas*. The locations are consistent with campaigns that could well have been fought by Owain Ddantgwyn: battles against the Angles and the Saxons, plus battles in his family homeland of Gododdin and in his kingdom of Powys. The speculation that the poem used by Nennius could have been a Votadini battle poem seems to be further strengthened by the almost direct linguistic link – *Bassa* and *Bassas* – between the Votadini *Canu Heledd* and Nennius' list.

We have already established that prior to the twelfth century all four surviving works which reference 'Arthur' (Arthurian folklore in the region of Ercing in the *Historia Brittonum*; the battle of *Camlan* in the *Annales Cambriae*; the references to Arthur in the *Canu Llywarch Hen* and the *Gododdin*) all refer directly to the Votadini or the kingdom of Powys. If the battle site speculations are correct, Nennius' list in the *Historia Brittonum* also refers to the Votadini and the kingdom of Powys, in addition to battles fought in Owain Ddantgwyn's family homeland of Gododdin.

In concluding that the legendary 'King Arthur' was Owain Ddantgwyn, we have not employed Nennius' battle 'upon the river which is called Bassas' as part of our argument. But when considering the name of Owain Ddantgwyn's possible burial site, it is intriguing to note that it almost directly correlates with the name of one of King 'Arthur's' battles as given by Nennius.

An isolated site, silent and eerie, the Berth could hardly be a more appropriate last resting place of the man who was Arthur. In the past, before the area was drained for farming purposes, the marsh surrounding the hill would have become a shallow mere after heavy rain. Centuries ago, the Berth could have appeared almost as an island rising above the waterlogged terrain. In this evocative location, one of the few Arthurian legends with an historical origin may have arisen; the legend of Excalibur. We have seen how the return of Excalibur to the Lady of the Lake seems to be based on the authenticated Celtic tradition of votive offerings. The making of votive offerings also appears to have been included in funeral rites, as such artifacts have often been discovered in lakes close to Celtic burial sites. If this ritual was followed in the case of 'Arthur's' death, it may have been into

	POWYS	MERCIA	NORTHUMBRIA
480			
490	Owain Ddantgwyn (c488–c520)		
500			
510			
520	Cuneglasus (c520–c550)		
530			
540			
550	Brochfael Ysgithrog (c550–c580)		
560			
570			
580	Cynan Garwyn (c580–c598)		
590			
600	Selyf (c598–c613)		Aethelfrid (604–617)
610	Cyndrwyn (c613–c630)		Edwin (617–633)
620			
630	Cynddylan (c630–c656)	Penda (633–655)	Oswald (635–644)
640			
			Oswy (644–670)
650		Peada (655–658)	
660		Wulfhere (658–675)	
670			

The Struggle for the Midlands: 480–670.
British and Anglian leaders.

Berth Pool below the hillside that the sword of Owain Ddantgwyn was ultimately cast.

There is already evidence that Berth Pool did receive votive offerings. In 1906, a workman cutting turf at the edge of the stream draining from the pool discovered a bronze cauldron, some eighteen inches high and twelve inches wide. It was presented to the British Museum where it was dated from the early first century. The cauldron was buried where the stream cuts through the southern causeway, about a hundred yards from the pool, and it is thought to have been carried there from Berth Pool itself, leading to conjecture that the cauldron was originally cast into the pool as a votive offering. Was Owain Ddantgwyn's sword also thrown into Berth Pool, perhaps during or after his burial? Only further archaeological investigation of the area can help answer that question.

With the invasion of Shropshire in the late 650s, nearly all of what is now England was lost to the Anglo-Saxons. The descendants of Owain Ddantgwyn, however, continued to rule the smaller Welsh kingdom of Powys until about 854, when the *Annales* record the death of King Cyngen while on a pilgrimage to Rome. After his death the king of Gwynedd, Rhodri Mawr, became the king of Powys. Intriguingly, it was Cyngen who erected the Pillar of Eliseg, celebrating his descent from Vortigern. This could well imply that, at some point over the previous three centuries, there had been a dynastic marriage between the Vortigern family of Dyfed (the descendants of Vortipor) and the royal family of Powys. It is unfortunate that many names on the pillar were obliterated by the time that Edward Lhuyd copied the inscription in 1696, for the Pillar of Eliseg may have told us more about Owain Ddantgwyn himself.

We began our investigation with an outline of the Arthurian legend. We now conclude, therefore, with a summary of what we believe to be the events surrounding the life of the historical 'King Arthur', Owain Ddantgwyn.

Around 460, while eastern Britain was being overrun by the Anglo-Saxons, the Britons themselves were engaged in civil war. Ambrosius Aurelianus, from his seat of power high in the mountains of Gwynedd, marched on the central kingdom of Powys and defeated the last of the Vortigern kings. With the support of his army of Votadini warriors, Ambrosius occupied the capital city Viroconium and assumed command of the British forces. From this stronghold Ambrosius set about the arduous task of reorganising the Britons to resist the foreign invasion.

It is most likely around this time that Owain Ddantgwyn was born. Owain was the son of the Votadini king Enniaun Girt, who ruled the kingdom of Gwynedd while Ambrosius continued his struggle against the Anglo-Saxons. As he grew the war dragged on, the sides evenly matched for more than twenty years. Eventually, Owain fought alongside Ambrosius, where he proved himself to be an exceptional warrior and strategist. Before long, Owain was given command of the British forces in the East of England, where he defeated the Angles in a series of decisive battles in Lincolnshire and around the Wash.

With the Angles in retreat, their ally, the Saxon king Hengist, despatched his son Octha to the far North to make an alliance with the Picts. It was here, to the north of Hadrian's Wall, that Owain may have fought his fiercest campaign. In 488, Hengist died and Octha returned south to become king of Kent. With the Pictish threat eliminated, Owain also returned south, where Ambrosius was no longer in command. However, Owain's succession as leader of the Britons does not appear to have occurred without a fight. He seems to have been drawn into conflict in South Wales, perhaps against the Vortigern family who may have attempted to regain authority from their remaining power base in Dyfed. Owain's eventual triumph made him undisputed leader of the British alliance of kings, and to demonstrate his resolve to unify the nation he adopted, or was given, the battle name the Bear – Arthur.

With civil conflict having weakened their position, the British in the South suffered a massive defeat in 491 when the fort of Anderida was overrun by the Saxon warrior Aelle. Having established control over the whole of Sussex, Aelle joined forces with Octha and the Saxons began their push into western Britain. By 493, with the Saxons advancing on the city of Bath, and threatening to cut the entire British nation in two, Arthur gathered his forces for a decisive stand on Little Solsbury Hill (Badon). Here, at the refortified hill-fort, the Britons were besieged by superior forces for three days, until a counterattack led by Arthur ultimately defeated the Saxons. With the enemy forces routed, the British reoccupied Sussex and drove the remaining Saxons back to the South-East.

With the majority of Britain free from invasion, Arthur left his relative Cunomorus to rule in far away Dumnonia, possibly to protect the southern coast from further incursions. Cunomorus, however, soon chose to ally himself with a new Saxon leader, Cerdic, who gained control of Hampshire in 508 when he defeated the British king Natanleod. For ten years, both Cerdic and Cunomorus continued to extend their influence around the south coast. Then, after ruling from Viroconium for over twenty years, Arthur was eventually compelled to march against the Wessex/Dumnonian alliance, which by this time posed a considerable threat.

Although the aging Arthur led a successful campaign, defeating Cunomorus and driving a wedge between the enemy forces, he was weakened after the battle of Certicesford. Soon after, perhaps on returning north, he was killed by his own nephew, Maglocunus, at the battle of Camlan in West-Central Wales. Arthur's son, Cuneglasus, assumed control in Powys, while Maglocunus seized the throne of Gwynedd and all-out civil war threatened the land.

With Arthur dead and British unity doomed, Cuneglasus was forced to abandon Viroconium, the last urban city in Britain. The Dark Ages were now truly upon the country and the final hope for a Celtic Britain was dashed.

The turbulent years of the early sixth century saw the end of Owain Ddantgwyn, the man, but marked only the beginning of the most famous legend in British history. The legend will doubtless continue to flourish, indeed the romantic fiction of the Middle Ages and the medieval folklore are fascinating areas of study in their own right. We have concerned ourselves solely with charting the development of the legends inasmuch as they could inform our investigation, endeavouring to reconcile them with information supplied by history and archaeology in the quest for the true story. It seems the ultimate irony that a man whose real name history had all but forgotten should have been the unwitting inspiration for the most famous legend of them all.

After further archaeological excavations at Viroconium and the Berth, the world may come to know more about the historical 'King Arthur': more about his lifestyle, his beliefs and his compatriots, perhaps even elevating Owain Ddantgwyn onto the rostrum of history alongside his now legendary persona.

Summary

Having examined the fate of Owain Ddantgwyn's descendants, we consider evidence for the burial site of the kings of Powys, and the final resting place of the historical 'King Arthur'.

1. About 577, with the British defeat at the battle of Dyrham, the cities of Gloucester, Cirencester and Bath were occupied by the Saxons. Although the *Anglo-Saxon Chronicle* fails to record the British leader, it was probably Brochfael Ysgithrog who was ruling in Powys about that time.

2. Brochfael's son, Cynan Garwyn, although containing the Saxon advance in the South, appears to have been defeated at Catterick about 598. After the battle (the theme of the *Gododdin* poem) most of northern England was lost to the Angle king, Aethelfrid, who established the kingdom of Northumbria.

3. According to the *Annales Cambriae*, around 613 Aethelfrid attacked North Wales and defeated a joint Gwynedd/Powys army at Chester, where Cynan's son Selyf was killed. The Anglo-Saxons thus drove a wedge between the British forces of North and Central Britain.

4. With the power of Gwynedd broken, in 644 an alliance between Cynddylan and the Angle kingdom of Mercia finally defeated the Northumbrians at Maes Cogwy in Oswestry. However, within a few years only Powys remained as the last bastion of British power, as the *Annales* record the 'hammering of Dyfed' in 645 and the 'slaughter of Gwent' in 649, perhaps by the Irish and West Saxons respectively.

5. The final days of greater Powys are outlined in a collection of ninth century Welsh poems called the *Canu Llywarch Hen* (the 'Song of Llywarch the Old'), now preserved in the 'Red Book of Hergest' in Oxford's Bodleian Library. In the poems, Cynddylan and the kings of Powys are said to have been descended from King Arthur himself.

6. The final defeat of Cynddylan and the sacking of Powys probably occurred around 658. The British of Shropshire were certainly conquered by the Anglo-Saxons by 661, as the people of the Wroxeter district are entered as *Wrocensaetna* in the census of Mercian territories in the *Tribal Hidage*. Also, a ford over the

Severn near Melverley, ten miles west of Shrewsbury, is recorded as 'Wulfhere's Ford', bearing the name of Wulfhere, the Mercian king from 658.

7. One poem of the *Canu Llywarch Hen* cycle, composed about 850, gives the burial site of the kings of Powys in the seventh century. Called the *Canu Heledd* (the 'Song of Heledd'), it identifies the burial site as *Eglwyseu Bassa*, the 'Churches of Bassa'. *Eglwyseu Bassa* is almost certainly the Shropshire village of Baschurch, and just outside the village is the Berth, an ancient fortified hillock. Archaeological excavations have shown that the Berth was in use in the early sixth century, but as yet the mounds themselves have not been excavated. One of them may still contain the remains of the historical King Arthur, Owain Ddantgwyn.

8. Since the Celtic tradition of votive offerings (from which the legend of Excalibur and the Lady of the Lake may derive) also appear to have been included in funeral rites, it could have been into Berth Pool, the lake below the Berth, that the sword of Owain Ddantgwyn was ultimately cast. There is evidence that Berth Pool received votive offerings. In 1906, a workman cutting turf at the edge of a stream which drains from Berth Pool, discovered a bronze cauldron dating from the first century. Since it was buried where the stream cuts through the southern causeway, about a hundred yards from the pool, it is considered to have been carried there from Berth Pool itself, leading to archaeological conjecture that the cauldron was originally cast into the pool as a votive offering. If Owain Ddantgwyn's sword was thrown into Berth Pool during his burial, it may still be preserved and awaiting discovery.

Research Update

Bath – The Battle of Badon

1993 marks the 1500th anniversary of the battle of Badon, when Arthur finally defeated the Saxons in 493, according to the evidence of Gildas and Bede. The theory expounded in Chapter Nine, that the battle took place in the vicinity of Bath, is the conclusion reached independently by Tim and Annette Burkitt and published in the 'Proceedings of the Somerset Archaeological and Natural History Society' Volume 134, 1990.

Firstly, the Burkitts provide evidence supporting the theory that Bath was once called Bathon, the original pronunciation of the name Badon. Examining a spelling of Bath as Baðan in the 'Burghal Hidage' (originally compiled in the tenth century), and a charter of the Mercian king Ecgfrith in 796 calling the city Baðun, they point out that in both instances the ð (called the 'thorn') of the Old English alphabet is employed, a symbol that was pronounced 'th'. Furthermore, they show that the 'Domesday Book' (compiled for William the Conqueror in 1086) includes Bath as Bathoniensis. The Burkitt research further reveals that the 'Burghal Hidage' and the 'Domesday Book' also give names for Bath such as Badaran and Bada, demonstrating the interchangeable 'Bad' and 'Bath' prefixes used in the city's name throughout the medieval period.

They also present a convincing theory for the origin of the name Bath itself, demonstrating that not only was it so called before the Saxon era, but that the Britons did indeed call the city Baddon. The original Latin name was *Aquae Sulis* – the 'Waters of Sul' – after the naturally-heated springs that fed the Roman baths complex. The Burkitts suggest that the *Sulis* was dropped from the name by the Romans after their conversion to Christianity, as Sul had been the name of a pagan god. Therefore in the later days of the empire the town had simply been called *Aquae* – 'Waters'. The Burkitts propound that the name Bath may have evolved from this name.

> 'The indigenous population would probably have continued to use their own Welsh name for a bath, which, if it was the same as in modern Welsh, would have been *baddon*, pronounced bathon.'

Finally they provide further evidence that the 'baths of Badon' were in the city of Bath, as suggested in Chapter Nine examining the *Historia Brittonum's* reference to the 'hot lake, where the baths of Badon are, in the country of the Hwicce'. The Burkitts point out that Osric, a king of the Hwicce, granted lands to Bath Abbey in 675, further evidence that Bath fell within the country of the Hwicce by the time that Nennius compiled his *Historia Brittonum* around the year 830. The Burkitts conclude:

> 'Bath, of course, was in the land of the Hwicce and it has the hot baths. Nennius is here undoubtedly describing Bath, so that one may seriously consider that his Badon of the hot spring and the battle of Badon which he mentions when talking of the campaigns of Arthur are one and the same place.'

Warwick Castle – The Bear and Ragged Staff

The emblem of the bear, still incorporated in the crest of the earls of Warwick, could be the surviving relic of Owain Ddantgwyn's battle-name Arthur – the Bear. Furthermore, Warwick Castle may well have been considered the site of the legendary Camelot before Winchester Castle.

Although construction of the present Warwick Castle did not begin until the eleventh or twelfth century, the original fortification of the site seems to have commenced in 914 A.D. According to the *Anglo-Saxon Chronicle*, in that year Alfred the Great's daughter, Ethelfleda, fortified Warwick against the invading Danes. The mound on which this earliest fort is thought to have stood is known locally as Ethelfleda's Mound and still lies within the grounds of Warwick Castle. Ethelfleda, one of the few warrior queens in British History, was the wife of Ethelred, the ealdorman of Mercia. As we saw in Chapter Seventeen, Bede provides evidence of an inter-dynastic marriage between the British kings of Powys and the Saxon kings of Mercia. Further evidence of this appears in the various Saxon genealogies which shown the 'Cyn' affix in the names of Mercian rulers, for example Cynreow and Cynewald. By the tenth century, however, Mercia had been annexed by the Wessex Saxons and its kings were now given the less regal title of 'ealdorman'. Therefore, the earliest warlords of Warwick seem to have been descended from the family of Owain Ddantgwyn, the historical Arthur.

With this in mind, it is intriguing that the crest employed by the medieval earls of Warwick (and still used today as the county emblem of Warwickshire) included the device of a bear – a bear holding a large ragged staff. Its origins are obscure, but the bear is generally thought to have been the symbol of the Saxon Mercians. Could it therefore have been a legacy of the Arthurian era? Just as the Welsh dragon is a legacy of the tribal emblem of the kings of Gwynedd, who eventually extended their influence throughout Wales, the emblem of the bear could have been adopted by the Mercian kings who came to rule what had once been Arthur's kingdom of Powys, Mercia being the Anglo-Saxon name for what had been the greater area of Powys. Indeed, the earliest surviving reference to the origin of the Warwick crest suggests just this.

According to John Rous, a fifteenth-century Warwick priest educated at Oxford, the bear device was first adopted by an earl of Warwick who had been a knight of King Arthur's Round Table. Although clearly legend, Rous's account may contain an element of truth that confirms the Warwick bear's link with the historical Arthur.

In his book the 'Rous Rol' (now in the British Library), written around 1480, Rous suggests that the bear was originally the emblem of one Arthgallus, an early lord of Warwick and 'a knight of the Round Table in Arthur's day, a lord of royal blood and witty in all his deeds'. Rous goes on to explain that *arth* is Welsh for 'bear', and hence the reason for the crest. Rous fails to point out that in Welsh *gallus* means 'mighty'. In other words, Rous seems to have discovered that the Warwick crest developed from someone called the 'Mighty Bear', who was of royal blood and closely connected to Arthur. Although, as Rous points out, Arthgallus is mentioned in passing by Geoffrey of Monmouth, and in a list of Arthur's knights in the chronicle of John Hardyng (1378–1465), there is no contemporary historical evidence relating to Arthgallus.

Geoffrey, however, does provide a clue to Arthgallus's identity. Although Geoffrey seems uncertain as to exactly where and when he reigned, he includes Arthgallus as a king in his own right who seems to have ruled jointly with his brother Owain. As we have seen with other historical characters in Geoffrey's *Historia*, it is very possible that Owain, the 'Mighty Bear', has been confused as two separate characters who reigned at the same time. They could well be one and the same person – the historical Arthur. Bear was the origin of the name Arthur and, as we have argued, Owain Ddantgwyn was indeed the mighty Bear.

It is possible, therefore, that the 'Mighty Bear' referred to Arthur himself, the title Arthgallus being confused as a separate character in later legend. Rous may have read of the Warwick crest originally being the emblem of the 'Mighty Bear', and like Geoffrey and Hardyng assumed that the Welsh rendering *Arth Gallus* was the warrior's personal name.

It would support the Arthur/Warwick bear theory if Rous simply wrote that the crest originated with a character called Arthgallus, but his association of Arthgallus with King Arthur renders the argument all the more compelling. Moreover, Rous's source material further supports the case, for he refers to a Welsh chronicle from the land of Powys, the kingdom of the historical King Arthur. Although Rous fails to identify the manuscript, there seems no reason to doubt its existence, as the other two sources he names – Geoffrey and Hardyng – not only exist but also include Arthgallus as he claimed. It would therefore seem that Rous learned of both Arthgallus's association with Warwick and the origin of the bear crest in the Welsh chronicle from Powys.

Rous also relates other Arthurian legends concerning Warwick that he appears to have discovered in the Powys manuscript. Not only does he say that the ragged staff, held by the bear in the Warwick crest, was the emblem of Arthur's cousin Gwayr (who is included in both the early Welsh literature and the Romances), but that Warwick itself was the site of Caerleon – the city of the legion – where Arthur holds court in Geoffrey of Monmouth's account.

This provides us with yet another intriguing association with Warwick Castle. In describing the city as the site of Arthur's court, Rous is implying that the castle was Camelot itself. Rous's work was written around the same time that Malory's *Le Morte Darthur* established Winchester as Camelot. From its content we know that the 'Rous Rol' was written between the death of the Duke of Clarence in 1477 and the death of Richard III in 1485, while Malory's *Le Morte Darthur* was composed between the ninth year of Edward IV's reign (an event Malory mentions) – March 1469 to March 1470 – and its printing by William Caxton in 1485. Could Warwick Castle, therefore, have been the traditional site of the legendary (although not the historical) Camelot before it was accepted as Winchester? As Thomas Malory came from Newbold Revel, just a few miles from Warwick, and was alive at the same time as Rous, he may well have been familiar with these Arthurian legends of Warwick.

It is tempting to speculate that Thomas Malory may have initially based his Camelot on Warwick Castle, the Winchester connection being a subsequent attempt to cash in on the popularity of Winchester's famous 'Round Table'. In fact, Malory's publisher, William Caxton, in his preface to *Le Morte Darthur* actually mentions the 'Round Table,' adding that in his opinion Winchester was not the site of Camelot. To this day it has remained a mystery why Caxton should have voiced this curious rejection of Winchester. Perhaps he had clashed with Malory over substituting Winchester for Warwick.

The extent of the Arthurian legends that existed around Warwick Castle during the fifteenth century may never be known. However, the possibility that the earliest lords of Warwick prided themselves as being Arthurian heirs may well explain the survival of the bear motif and the notion that the Castle had been the seat of Arthur himself. Furthermore, the uncovering of additional Arthurian legends in and around Warwick Castle may well provide a greater insight into the historical Arthur, just as the legend of the bear emblem seems to have been founded on historical fact.

The 'Dream of Rhonabwy' – The True Story of King Arthur?

In light of our discoveries, an examination of the medieval Welsh tale the 'Dream of Rhonabwy', may reveal evidence of a Dark Age war poem telling the true story of the historical King Arthur, Owain Ddantgwyn.

The 'Dream of Rhonabwy' (from the 'Red Book of Hergest') is generally considered to have been composed in Powys around 1150 to address Madog ap Maredudd, an historical figure who ruled the kingdom in the mid-twelfth century. In 1149, Madog recaptured part of Shropshire from the English, but while his army was away, Owain ap Gruffudd, the king of Gwynedd, seized the opportunity to invade northern Powys. The 'Dream of Rhonabwy' seems to have been written between that date and Madog's death around 1159, as a cautionary tale likening his rash campaigning with King Arthur's ill-fated demise at the battle of Camlann centuries before.

In outline, this is the 'Dream of Rhonabwy':

While on a mission for Madog ap Maredudd, the warrior Rhonabwy falls asleep and finds himself transported back to the time of Arthur. There he is met by a mysterious guide called Iddawg, who claims to have been a royal messenger at Arthur's final battle of Camlann.

Iddawg takes Rhonabwy to Arthur's encampment in the Severn Valley, where 'on every side of the road, there were tents and pavilions and the gathering of a great host'. A mile from the road at a place named as *Rhyd y Groes* – the 'Ford of the Cross' – they find Arthur consulting with his two advisors: Bishop Bidwini to one side, Gwarthegwydd to the other.

Before long, Arthur's cousin, Caradawg Strong Arm, urges Arthur to prepare himself for the battle of Badon, where he must defeat the warrior Osla Big Knife.

When soldiers from all over Britain come to join the army, Cadwr of Cornwall arrives bearing Arthur's sword, which is described as having 'a design of two serpents on the golden hilt'. A servant appears with a white cloak, which he spreads on the ground and places a huge golden throne upon. For the remainder of the story Arthur sits on the throne, playing a game of *gwyddbwyll* (probably an early board game similar to chess) with a fellow chieftain called Owain ap Urien. Although Arthur is described as emperor, both men appear to be of equal status and Arthur is able to read Owain's thoughts.

During the *gwyddbwyll* match, various characters arrive with news. Firstly a warrior, identified as Selyf of Powys, emerges from a tent decorated with a serpent, to inform Owain that Arthur's men are harassing Owain's ravens. Although Owain asks Arthur to call off his men, Arthur ignores the request and continues with the game.

A second warrior, Gwgawn Red Sword, emerges from a tent decorated with a lion, telling Owain that Arthur's men are now killing his ravens. Once more, Owain implores Arthur to put a stop to the slaughter, but again Arthur merely continues with the game.

Finally, a warrior identified as Gwres of Rheged emerges from a tent decorated with an eagle, and angrily tells Owain that his noblest ravens are now dead. Owain's protests are met with Arthur's curt reply 'if you please, play on'. Owain takes matters into his own hands and orders Gwres to raise a standard where the fighting is fiercest. Gwres obeys and the ravens fight back with a new-found resolve to defeat their opponents.

Back at the *gwyddbwyll* match, a rider approaches wearing the crest of a leopard on his helmet. This warrior, Blathaon ap Mwrheth, informs Arthur that Owain's ravens are now killing Arthur's men. It is Arthur's turn to tell Owain to call off his ravens, but Owain answers simply 'your move'.

A second rider, Rhuvawn the Radiant, with the crest of a lion on his helmet, approaches and tells Arthur that his nobles are now being killed. 'Owain, call off your ravens,' orders Arthur. 'Your move,' replies Owain.

The final rider, Heveydd One Cloak, with a griffin crest on his helmet, arrives to tell Arthur that Owain's ravens have massacred Arthur's nobles. This is too much for Arthur and he responds by crushing the game pieces to dust. Owain orders Gwres to lower the banner, whereupon there is 'peace on both sides'. At this point, Osla's men arrive to request a truce.

Arthur ultimately seeks advice from Rhun, the son of Maelgwn of Gwynedd, and, acting upon it, leads his men to Cornwall. The dream ends abruptly and 'with the great turmoil that followed Rhonabwy awoke'.

On closer inspection, it seems possible that the dream sequence is a direct adaptation of a Dark Age war poem allegorising the true story of Arthur's reign. Now we have identified Arthur as Owain Ddantgwyn, a fifth-century king of Powys, it is possible for the first time to offer a plausible interpretation of the mysterious symbolism in Rhonabwy's dream.

Significantly, the site of Arthur's encampment is a real geographical location, in the district of Forden, along the Roman road some 15 miles to the south-west of Viroconium. Here, the river crossing (at O.S. reference 248006) is still called *Rhyd-y-Groes*, just as the 'Dream of Rhonabwy' relates. The 'Dream of Rhonabwy' is also geographically precise in saying that *Rhyd-y-Groes* is a mile from the road; *Rhyd-y-Groes* is indeed a mile from the Roman road running beside Offa's Dyke to the west. In the fifth century this road linked Viroconium with Central Wales. Moreover, it is feasible that an army could have been encamped at Forden, as it is the location of Lavrobrinta, an important Roman fort on what is now the Welsh border (see Chapter Fourteen). Moreover, Arthur's encampment at a fortification guarding the approach to Viroconium is exactly where we might expect to find the historical Owain Ddantgwyn, right in the heart of Powys, only 15 miles from his capital city.

As Rhonabwy's guide Iddawg is a messenger at Camlann, it would appear that the encamped army is preparing to fight that very battle. And as Arthur is later advised to prepare for Badon, a battle that occurred well before Camlann, it would seem that what follows is an allegory of the events that led up to Camlann. In other words, the story of Arthur's reign.

A comparison of the dream with the suggested reign of Owain Ddantgwyn (in Chapter Sixteen) reveals remarkable similarities.

When Arthur is first seen two advisors are seated either side of him, Bishop Bidwini and Gwarthegwydd. These might represent the two British factions that Owain, the historical Arthur, was seeking to unite (see Chapter Thirteen); the bishop representing the Catholic imperialist faction, Gwarthegwydd representing the Pelagian nationalists. Indeed, as the Welsh name Gwarthegwydd could mean 'disgraced teachings' (*gwarth* – disgrace, *egwyddori* – to teach) the interpretation is all the more persuasive, since Pelagianism was considered a disgraced philosophy.

The first event, Caradawg urging Arthur to prepare for the battle of Badon, might refer to the subsequent narrative being the process of unification necessary before the Saxons could be defeated. Interestingly, Arthur's opponent at Badon is named as Osla, very possibly a British rendering of the name of Arthur's most likely Saxon opponent at the historical Badon, Octha (see Chapter Nine).

Arthur then receives his sword, the tribal symbol of authority over an alliance of kingdoms (see Chapter Five). Arthur next being seated on a throne could therefore represent his accession to kingship and commencing his reign as the British leader of battles.

The game of *gwyddbwyll* may symbolise Arthur's strategy of unifying the Britons, while his opponent appears to have been a late sixth-century warrior wrongly interpolated into the tale. As Owain ap Urien seems to have been an historical chieftain of Rheged almost a century after the Arthurian period, Arthur's opponent in the earliest rendering of the tale may have represented Arthur's own alter-ego; possibly his persona split by conflicting loyalties towards the opposing factions. Not only is the opponent of equal status, but Arthur can read his thoughts. The opponent may originally have been called simply Owain (Arthur's true name, Owain Ddantgwyn) but was eventually replaced by a warlord of a later era who bore the same forename.

The fighting between Arthur's men and Owain's ravens appears to represent the squabbling British kingdoms. Not only are two of them named (Rheged and Powys), but each of the messengers is coupled with a tribal emblem; indeed the lion and the leopard are actually mentioned by Gildas (see Chapter Thirteen). It is only after the two sides are brought together that Osla's men arrive to sue for peace, surely symbolising that following tribal unity the battle of Badon was fought and won.

The last scene could well represent Arthur's final campaign. The turmoil before Rhonabwy awakes appears to be the battle of Camlann. Not only is it preceded by Arthur marching on Cornwall, perhaps against Cunomorus and his Dumnonian rebellion as suggested in Chapter Fifteen, but Arthur is actually advised to do so by the son of Maelgwn of Gwynedd – the historical Maglocunus, Owain Ddantgwyn's treacherous nephew. As surmised in Chapter Sixteen, Maglocunus overthrew Owain Ddantgwyn at Camlann after he was weakened by the Dumnonian Campaign. Remarkably, the final lines of the 'Dream of Rhonabwy' actually name the very person coupled with the overthrow of Owain Ddantgwyn.

This may therefore reflect the real events which prompted Arthur to make an unwise decision to recapture the South. He might have been advised to do so by the family of Maglocunus, who then used the opportunity to overthrow Arthur during his absence. Indeed this is precisely the same mistake made by Madog up Maredudd in 1149, when the king of Gwynedd took advantage of Madog's absence to seize control of northern Powys. This is seemingly the moral of the 'Dream of Rhonabwy', the parallel between the historical incursions into Powys by warlords of Gwynedd in both the sixth and twelfth centuries.

If the conjecture concerning Owain Ddantgwyn's demise is corrent, then Arthur's camp at Forden is both strategically and historically feasible. Owain may have been mustering his army on the Severn Plain in preparation for the march on Gwynedd and ultimate defeat at Camlann near Dolgellau. However, the 'Dream of Rhonabwy' may offer an alternative location for Camlann. It may not have been fought in Central Wales, but at Forden itself. The river beside Rhyd-y-Groes is called the Camlad, perhaps originally the Camlann? If Camlann was fought here, it would suggest that in Owain Ddantgwyn's absence Maglocunus had seized power in Viroconium itself, as Arthur is encamped in the ideal location to prepare to recapture the capital.

If the 'Dream of Rhonabwy' was written before the Romances, around 1150, it would be contemporary with Geoffrey of Monmouth, the earliest detailed account of Arthur's supposed life. However, unlike Geoffrey's anachronistic locations, such as the twelfth-century castle at Tintagel, Forden is historically feasible as a military site in the authentic Arthurian period of the late fifth and early sixth centuries. Furthermore, the 'Dream of Rhonabwy' not only names a historical figure who was both contemporary and related to Owain Ddantgwyn, Maglocunus, but it also names the leader at Badon as Osla, a close rendering of the Saxon Octha. It accurately allegorises fifth century Britain and outlines the events of the historical life of Arthur in the correct chronological order.

In conclusion, the tale offers an authentic geographical location, names real historical figures and allegorises true historical events. Furthermore, the tale was both composed and set in the kingdom of Powys, the very kingdom of Owain Ddantgwyn. The 'Dream of Rhonabwy', therefore, not only evidences the existence of an early war poem but, considered in isolation, may well constitute confirmatory evidence that Owain Ddantgwyn was Arthur.

Excalibur – The Wilkinson Sword

Having discovered the historical Arthur, it is at last possible to make an informed speculation on the appearance of an historical 'Excalibur'.

As detailed in Chapter One, the sword of a fifth-century British warrior would have been of the Roman *spatha* type – a Roman style cavalry sword, some two and a half feet long with a stunted cross guard – not the huge broadsword of the Middle Ages.

A description of the ornamentation on Arthur's sword is contained in the 'Dream of Rhonabwy', in which it bears 'a design of two serpents on the golden hilt'. Since Geoffrey of Monmouth fails to describe Caliburn (his name for Arthur's sword) and the 'Dream of Rhonabwy' may have been written as early as 1150 (before the first of the Romances) it is probably the earliest description of Arthur's sword still in existence.

In the *Notitia Dignitatum*, a late Roman document of the Western administration containing military insignia (circa 420), a shield bears the insignia of two crossed serpents. The design is the insignia of the *Segontienses Auxilium Palatinum* unit, believed to be the former garrison of Segontium (Caernarvon, the principle Roman garrison of North-West Wales) in Gwynedd, the homeland of the historical Arthur.

If Arthur inherited a sword of office from his predecessors, the pro-

Roman leaders of Gwynedd (Enniaun Girt, Cunedda, and Ambrosius) it is historically feasible that such a sword would have born the motif of the double serpents, the insignia of the former Roman administration of the area. Gwynedd was not only the heartland of the imperialist faction in late fifty-century Britain (see Chapter Eleven), but the dragon, or serpent, was its tribal emblem (see Chapter Twelve) and twin dragons are associated with Ambrosius in Nennius's *Historia Brittonum* (see Chapter Eleven).

This evidence, alongside the apparent accuracy of detail in the 'Dream of Rhonabwy', makes it very possible that Arthur's sword would indeed have had 'a design of two serpents' on its hilt.

To commemorate the 1500th anniversary of the battle of Badon in 1993, and to raise public awareness and interest in the discovery of the historical King Arthur, Wilkinson Sword – sword cutlers to Her Majesty the Queen – are producing replicas of Excalibur in association with the authors.

The sword can be ordered in full size or miniature, with accompanying literature. For further information please contact Wilkinson Sword, 11–13 Brunel Road, Acton, London W3 7UH, marking correspondence 'Excalibur – The Wilkinson Sword'.

Illustration Appendix

The illustrations on the following pages have been prepared by Dan Shadrake of Britannia, an Arthurian re-enactment society based in Essex. The illustrations are based on his research into the weaponry, clothing and modes of warfare of the authentic Arthurian period.

1. British officer c. 493 A.D. The Roman style still persists. Often, well maintained, inherited weapons supplied the warrior elite.

2. Everyday life in fifth-century Viroconium.

3. Unhorsed British cavalry officer, wearing lamellar body armour, attacked by Pict.

4. British warlord outside a fortified settlement.

5. Saxon attack on a fortified British settlement.

6. Octha faces defeat at Badon.

Chronology of Key Events

A.D.

43–47   Britain is conquered by Emperor Claudius and becomes an island province of the Roman Empire.

78   Western command of Britain is transferred to the city of Chester and Viroconium becomes a thriving civilian town.

122   Emperor Hadrian orders the building of Hadrian's Wall between Newcastle and the Solway Firth.

200   The Antonine Wall is abandoned and Hadrian's Wall becomes the empire's northern frontier.

380   Pelagius leaves Britain for Rome and comes into conflict with the Church.

383   Magnus Maximus is proclaimed emperor by the British legions, invades Gaul and Italy and is defeated by Theodosius I.

401   Alaric, king of the Visigoths, invades northern Italy.

407   Constantine III is proclaimed emperor by the British legions and invades Gaul.

408   Alaric lays siege to Rome and Emperor Honorius is forced to withdraw troops from Britain.

409   Picts and Irish tribes invade North-West Britain and West Wales.

410   Alaric sacks Rome. Honorius is unable to respond to the British plea for reinforcements. The last of the Roman legions leave Britain.

411   Constantine III is defeated at Arles and is later executed by Honorius.

412   Honorius sends the *Comes Britanniarum* to Britain, together with an auxiliary field force.

416   The Roman Church proclaims that the teachings of Pelagius constitute a heresy.

418	The *Comes Britanniarum* is withdrawn from Britain, together with any military presence that remains.
420	The kingdom of Powys is founded. A major rebuilding of Viroconium takes place.
425	Vortigern assumes control of central and southern Britain.
429	Germanus, bishop of Auxerre, visits Britain as an envoy of the Catholic Church.
445	A plague epidemic reaches Britain, severely weakening Vortigern's control.
446	Pictish raids recommence in northern Britain. Further Irish invasions of West Wales take place.
447	Germanus visits Britain for a second time. Vortigern dies and is succeeded by his son, Vortigern II (probably Britu).
448	The British make an unsuccessful request for military aid to the Roman consul, Aetius, in Gaul.
449	Vortigern II invites Anglo-Saxon mercenaries into Britain to fight the Picts and Irish.
451	Attila the Hun is defeated at Châlons-sur-Marne.
455	A Saxon revolt is led by Hengist and Horsa. The battle of Egelesprep (Aylesford) takes place, in which Horsa and Cateyrn die. Hengist establishes the kingdom of Kent. British forces are defeated.
455–60	The Anglo-Saxons take control of eastern Britain. Vortigern II is deposed.
459	The battle of Guoloph is fought, at which Ambrosius fights Vitalinus (probably for control of Powys).
460	Ambrosius becomes leader of the British forces. British defences are reorganised. Cunedda and the Votadini are invited into North Wales to expel the Irish. There is an Imperialist revival in Britain.
470	A British contingent fights for Emperor Anthemius in northern France.
476	Odovacer defeats Emperor Romulus Augustulus and proclaims himself king of Italy. The final collapse of the Western Roman Empire occurs.
477	The Saxon leader Aelle lands in Sussex.
480	There is a military stalemate between the Britons and the Saxons in the South of England. The Angles suffer defeat in the North. Cunorix is buried in Viroconium.
485	Aelle defeats the British at Mearcredesburna.

485–8	Arthur fights for Ambrosius against the Angles.
488	Hengist dies and is succeeded by Octha. Arthur succeeds Ambrosius.
488–93	The Arthurian campaigns.
491	Aelle besieges the fort at Anderida (Pevensey) and establishes the kingdom of Sussex.
493	Arthur defeats Aelle and Octha at the battle of Badon. The Anglo-Saxons retreat into South-East England.
495	Cerdic lands in Hampshire, possibly as a mercenary.
508	Cerdic achieves victory over a British king named Natanleod, and establishes control over an area roughly the size of modern Hampshire. An alliance is made between Cerdic and Cunomorus.
512	Oisc is king of Kent.
519	The battle of Certicesford. The battle of Camlan. **The death of Arthur.** Maglocunus becomes king of Gwynedd. Cuneglasus becomes king of Powys.
520	Viroconium is abandoned.
522	Oisc dies.
530	The Byzantine emperor, Justinian I, fails to recapture the Western Empire.
534	Cynric becomes king of Wessex.
540–5	Gildas writes the *De Excidio Conquestu Britanniae*.
549	Maglocunus dies.
550	The Drustanus stone is erected.
552	Cynric defeats the Britons at Old Sarum.
555	Buckinghamshire is overwhelmed by the Saxons.
556	The battle of Beranburh (near Swindon).
560	The death of Cynric.
571	Cuthwulf routs the Midland British in Bedfordshire.
575	The battle of Arfderydd, after which Myrddin goes insane (according to the *Annales Cambriae*).
577	The British are defeated at the battle of Dyrham; Bath, Cirencester and Gloucester are lost to the Saxons.
598	The Angle kings Aethelfrid and Aelle defeat the British at Catraeth (Catterick in Yorkshire).
603	The Irish king Aedan is defeated by Aethelfrid in northern England.
604	Aethelfrid moves against Aelle, occupies York and founds the kingdom of Northumbria.
610	The poem *Gododdin* is composed.

613	Aethelfrid defeats a joint Gwynedd/Powys army at Chester, where the Powys king Selyf is killed.
614	Wessex Saxons move into Devon.
617	The death of Aethelfrid. Edwin becomes king of Northumbria.
626	Penda breaks with Northumbria and establishes the kingdom of Mercia in the East Midlands.
629	Cadwallon of Gwynedd is besieged by Edwin in North Wales.
633	Edwin is defeated by Cadwallon and Penda.
634	The *Irish Annales* record the burning of Bangor.
635	Cadwallon is defeated by Oswald of Northumbria.
638	Gododdin is overrun by the Angles.
644	Penda of Mercia, in alliance with Cynddylan of Powys, defeats Oswald of Northumbria at the battle of Maes Cogwy (Oswestry).
645	The 'hammering of Dyfed' (perhaps by the Irish) took place, according to the *Annales Cambriae*.
649	The 'slaughter of Gwent' (perhaps by the Saxons) takes place according to *Annales Cambriae*.
655	Penda, together with Aethelhere of East Anglia, is defeated by Oswy. Peada is king of Mercia. Anna is king of East Anglia. Mercia and East Anglia become subservient to Northumbria.
656	Cynddylan defeats the Mercians at Caer Luitcoet (near Lichfield).
658	Oswy sacks Powys. The death of Cynddylan. The British lose Staffordshire and Shropshire. Mercians occupy western Powys. Wulfhere is king of Mercia.
661	The 'Tribal Hidage' is compiled.
682	The Wessex Saxons consolidate their hold on the entire South-West peninsular, apart from Cornwall.
731	Bede writes the *Historia Ecclesiastica Gentis Anglorum*.
800	The pope crowns Charlemagne of the Franks as Holy Roman Emperor.
830	Nennius writes the *Historia Brittonum*.
850	The *Gododdin* is committed to writing. *Canu Llywarch Hen* and *Canu Heledd* are composed. Cyngen, king of Powys, erects the Pillar of Eliseg.
854	Cyngen dies while on a pilgrimage to Rome. Rhodri

	Mawr of Gwynedd becomes king of Powys.
871–99	The *Anglo-Saxon Chronicle* is compiled from early monastic records under the supervision of Alfred the Great.
926	Cornwall is conceded to the English.
927	Athelstan effectively unites the Anglo-Saxon people and becomes first king of all England.
955	The *Annales Cambriae* are compiled.
990	'Culhwch and Olwen' is composed.
1100-	Lifris writes the 'Life of St Cadoc', in which Arthur is briefly mentioned.
1110	The Chronicle of Mont Saint Michel is compiled, in which Arthur is mentioned as king of Britain.
1120	A surviving manuscript containing the *Historia Brittonum* and the *Annales Cambriae* is compiled.
1125	William of Malmesbury writes the *Gesta Regum Anglorum*, in which he refers to King Arthur.
1120–40	The Modena Archivolt, on the north portal of Modena Cathedral, is decorated with an Arthurian scene.
1130	William of Malmesbury writes *De Antiquitate Glastoniensis Ecclesiae*.
1130	Geoffrey of Monmouth composes the *Prophetiae Merlini* while working on the *Historia*.
1135	The *Historia Regum Britanniae* is completed by Geoffrey of Monmouth.
1135	Henry of Huntingdon writes the *Historia Anglorum*, in which he includes Nennius' list of Arthur's battles.
1130–40	Hermann of Tournai records the visit of the Laon Cathedral officials to England, when they were told of Arthurian legends in Cornwall.
1140	Caradoc of Llancarfan, in his 'Life of Gildas', includes Arthur in the life of the monk.
1150	Geoffrey of Monmouth's *Vita Merlini* is composed.
1155	Wace completes his poem, *Roman de Brut*, based on Geoffrey's work, and introduces the Round Table to the Arthurian story.
1160	The 'Dream of Rhonabwy' is composed.
1160–80	Chrétien de Troyes writes his five Arthurian poems, which are chiefly responsible for establishing King Arthur as a fashionable subject of romantic literature.

He introduces many of Arthur's knights and the name Camelot.

1190 The monks of Glastonbury Abbey claim to have discovered the grave of King Arthur and Guinevere.

1195–1200 Robert de Boron composes a trilogy of Arthurian verses. He introduces the notion of the Holy Grail as the vessel used at the Last Supper by Christ, along with the sword and stone motif.

1200 The English priest Layamon is the first to relate the Arthurian saga in native English. His work, *Brut*, is an adaptation of Wace's *Roman de Brut*.

1200 The Arthurian story enters Germany in the form of two poems, *Erec* and *Iwein*, by the poet Hartmann von Aue.

1205 Wolfram von Eschenbach writes his epic Arthurian story *Parzival*, in which he depicts the Grail as a magical stone.

1215–35 A large number of rambling Arthurian stories, known collectively as the *Vulgate Cycle*, are compiled. Anonymously composed, this Cycle is chiefly responsible for many of the story's embellishments.

1247 Glastonbury Abbey produces a revised edition of William of Malmesbury's *De Antiquitate Glastoniensis Ecclesiae*.

1250 The 'Black Book of Carmarthen', the oldest surviving manuscript to contain Welsh poems that include Arthur, is compiled.

1265 The 'Book of Aneirin', containing the surviving copy of the *Gododdin*, is compiled.

1275 The 'Book of Taliesin', containing the 'Spoils of Annwn', is compiled.

1325 The 'White Book of Rhydderch', containing the earliest section from 'Culhwch and Olwen', is compiled.

1400 *Sir Gawain and the Green Knight* is composed by an anonymous writer from the North-West Midlands.

1400 The 'Red Book of Hergest' is compiled. It contains the 'Dream of Rhonabwy', the tale of 'Culhwch and Olwen', and the surviving copy of *Canu Heledd* and the *Canu Llywarch Hen*.

1470 Sir Thomas Malory completes *Le Morte Darthur*, the most famous of all Arthurian Romances.

Bibliography

Source Material, in the
Original and in Translation

The *Anglo-Saxon Chronicle*: *The Anglo-Saxon Chronicle*: trans G. N. Garmonsway. Everyman's Library, London 1967.

Annales Cambriae: *The Welsh Annals*: Latin and trans John Morris, in *History from the Sources Vol 8*: Phillimore, Chichester 1980.

Bede: *The Ecclesiastical History of the English Nation*: trans J. A. Giles. Everyman's Library, London 1970.

Chrétien de Troyes: *Chrétien de Troyes: A Study of the Arthurian Romances*: L. T. Topsfield. Cambridge University Press, Cambridge 1981.

Geoffrey of Monmouth: *History of the Kings of Britain*: trans Lewis Thorpe. Penguin, London 1966.

Gildas: *De Excidio Britanniae*: Latin and trans Michael Winterbottom, in *History from the Sources Vol 7*. Phillimore, Chichester 1978.

The *Gododdin*: *The Gododdin*: Edinburgh University Press, Edinburgh 1969.

Layamon: *Arthurian Chronicles*: trans Eugene Mason. Dent, London 1912.

Sir Thomas Malory: *Le Morte Darthur*: (2 Vols): Thomas Malory. Dent, London 1972.

Nennius: *Historia Brittonum*: Latin and trans John Morris, in *History from the Sources Vol 8*: Phillimore, Chichester 1980.

The *Vulgate Cycle*: *Arthurian Fictions: Re-reading the Vulgate Cycle*: Jane E. Burns. Ohio State University Press, Columbus 1985.

Wace: *Arthurian Chronicles*: trans Eugene Mason. Dent, London 1912.

William of Malmesbury: *Chronicle of the Kings of England*: William of Malmesbury. Bell and Daldy, London 1866.

Wolfram von Eschenbach: *An Introduction to Wolfram's 'Parzival'*: Hugh D. Sacker. Cambridge University Press, Cambridge 1963.

Welsh Literature

Canu Llywarch Hen: ed. Ifor Williams. University of Wales Press, Cardiff 1935.

The Earliest Welsh Poetry: Joseph Clancy. Macmillan, London 1970.

A Guide to Welsh Literature: ed A.O.H. Jarman and Gwilym Rees Hughes. Christopher Davies, Swansea 1976.

A History of Welsh Literature: Thomas Parry. Trans H. Idris Bell. Oxford University Press, Oxford 1955.

The Mabinogi and Other Medieval Welsh Tales: Patrick K. Ford. University of California Press, Los Angeles 1977.

The Oxford Companion to the Literature of Wales: ed Meic Stephens. Oxford University Press, Oxford 1987.

The Penguin Book of Welsh Verse: Anthony Conran. Penguin, Harmondsworth 1967.

Selected Bibliography of Secondary Sources

Alcock, Leslie. *Arthur's Britain: History and Archaeology A.D. 376–634*. Penguin, London 1971.

Ashe, Geoffrey. *The Quest for Arthur's Britain*. Pall Mall Press, London 1968.

Ashe, Geoffrey. *Camelot and the Vision of Albion*. Heinemann, London 1971.

Ashe, Geoffrey. *A Guidebook to Arthurian Britain*. Aquarian, Wellingborough 1983.

Ashe, Geoffrey. *Avalonian Quest*. Fontana, London 1984.

Ashe, Geoffrey. *The Discovery of King Arthur*. Debrett's Peerage, London 1985.

Barber, Richard. *King Arthur in Legend and History*. Cardinal Books, London 1973.

Cavendish, Richard. *King Arthur and the Grail*. Weidenfeld and Nicolson, London 1978.

Copley, Gordon K. *The Conquest of Wessex in the Sixth Century*. Phoenix House, London 1954.

Chadwick, Nora K. *Celtic Britain*. Praeger, New York 1963.

Chadwick, Nora K. *The Age of the Saints in the Early Celtic Church*. Oxford University Press, London 1981.

Chadwick, Nora K. *The Celts*. Penguin, Harmondsworth 1970.

Clancy, Joseph. *Pendragon: Arthur and his Britain*. Macmillan, London 1971.

Comfort, W. W. *Arthurian Romances*. Dutton, New York 1914.

Crossley-Holland, Kevin. *British Folk Tales*. Orchard Books, London 1987.

Davidson, H. E. *Gods and Myths in Northern Europe*. Penguin, Harmondsworth 1964.

Delaney, Frank. *Legends of the Celts*. Hodder & Stoughton, London 1989.

Dillon, Myles and Chadwick, Nora K. *The Celtic Realms*. New American Library, New York 1967.

Dunning, Robert. *Arthur – King in the West*. Alan Sutton, Gloucester 1988.

Fife, Graham. *Arthur the King*. BBC Enterprises, London 1990.

Frere, S. *Britannia*. Routledge and Kegan Paul, London 1967.

Goetinck, Glenys. *Peredur: A Study of Welsh Tradition in the Grail Legends*. University of Wales Press, Cardiff 1975.

Goodrich, Norma. *Merlin*. Franklin Watts, New York 1987.

Goodrich, Norma. *Arthur*. Franklin Watts, New York 1989.

Green, Miranda. *The Gods of the Celts*. Alan Sutton, Gloucester 1986.

Gurney, Robert. *Celtic Heritage*. Chatto and Windus, London 1969.

Hodgkin, R. H. *A History of the Anglo-Saxons: Vol 1* Oxford University Press, Oxford 1952.

Hodgkin, R. H. *A History of the Anglo-Saxons: Vol 2* Oxford University Press, Oxford 1952

Jarman, A. O. H. *The Legend of Merlin*. University of Wales Press, Cardiff 1960.

Jarman, A. O. H. and Hughes, Gwilym Rees. *A Guide to Welsh Literature*. Davis, Swansea 1976.

Jones, A. M. H. *The Decline of the Ancient World*. Longman, London 1966.

Lacy, Norris (Ed). *The Arthurian Encyclopedia*. Boydell, London 1988.

Loomis, Roger Sherman (Ed). *Arthurian Literature in the Middle Ages*. Clarendon Press, Oxford 1959.

Loomis, Roger Sherman. *Celtic Myth and the Arthurian Romance*. Columbia University Press 1927.

Loomis, Roger Sherman. *Wales and the Arthurian Legend*. University of Wales Press, Cardiff 1966.

Markale, Jean. *King Arthur: King of Kings*. Gordon and Cremonesi, London 1977.

Morris, John (Ed). *The Age of Arthur: Vol 1*. Phillimore, Chichester 1977.

Morris, John (Ed). *The Age of Arthur: Vol 2*. Phillimore, Chichester 1977.

Morris, John (Ed). *The Age of Arthur: Vol 3*. Phillimore, Chichester 1977.

Owen, D. D. R. *The Evolution of the Grail Legend*. Oliver and Boyd, London 1968.

Pollard, Alfred. *The Romance of King Arthur*. Macmillan, London 1979.

Salway, Peter. *The Frontier People of Roman Britain*. Cambridge University Press, Cambridge 1965.

Stephens, Meic (Ed). *The Oxford Companion to the Literature of Wales*. Oxford University Press, Oxford 1986.

Thomas, Charles. *Britain and Ireland in Early Christian Times*. Thames and Hudson, London 1971.

Thomson, E. A. *A History of Attila and the Huns*. Clarendon Press, Oxford 1948.

Treharne, R. F. *The Glastonbury Legends*. Cresset, London 1967.

Williams, A. H. *An Introduction to the History of Wales*. University of Wales Press, Cardiff 1962.

Westwood, Jennifer. *Albion: A Guide to Legendary Britain*. Paladin, London 1987.

Whitelock, Dorothy (Ed). *English Historical Documents: 500–1042*. Eyre and Spottiswoode, London 1955.

Index

OTHER TITLES AVAILABLE IN ARROW